THE TENNESSEE HISTORICAL SOCIETY — SINCE 1849

# *Emancipation*
## AND THE FIGHT FOR FREEDOM
### TENNESSEE AFRICAN AMERICANS, 1860–1900

Crystal A. deGregory, Editor

Tennessee in the Civil War:
The Best of the *Tennessee Historical Quarterly*
Carroll Van West, Series Editor
Volume 6

The Tennessee Historical Society
Nashville

Copyright © 2013 by
The Tennessee Historical Society
ISBN: 978-0-9615966-8-2

All Rights Reserved.

First Edition

All chapters previously published
in the *Tennessee Historical Quarterly*
a publication of The Tennessee Historical Society

This book is printed on acid-free paper.

Library of Congress Control Number: 2012949832

The Tennessee Historical Society
Telephone: 615-741-8934
Email: info@tennesseehistory.org
Website: www.tennesseehistory.org

*Tennessee in the Civil War* is made possible in part by a publication series partnership with the Tennessee Civil War National Heritage Area and a publication sponsorship by the Tennessee Civil War Sesquicentennial Commission.

# CONTENTS

vii    Introduction:
       **EMANCIPATION AND THE FIGHT FOR FREEDOM**
       *By Crystal A. deGregory*

1    **DAVID G. COOKE JOINS**
         **THE UNITED STATES COLORED TROOPS**
      *By James S. McRae*

8    **FORT PILLOW, FORREST,**
         **AND THE UNITED STATES COLORED TROOPS IN 1864**
      *By Kenneth Bancroft Moore*

24    **MEMPHIS RIOTS:**
      White Reaction to Blacks in Memphis, May 1865–July 1866
      *By Bobby Lovett*

46    **STAND BY THE FLAG:**
      Nationalism and African-American Celebrations of the
         Fourth of July in Memphis, 1866–1887
      *By Brian D. Page*

66    **BLACK RECONSTRUCTIONISTS IN TENNESSEE**
      *By Walter J. Fraser, Jr.*

94     STATE COLORED CONVENTIONS OF TENNESSEE, 1865–1866
*By Judy Bussel Leforge*

121     BEFORE BLACK ATHENS:
Black Education in Antebellum Nashville
*By Crystal A. deGregory*

142     FISK UNIVERSITY: THE FIRST CRITICAL YEARS
*By Joe M. Richardson*

158     E.O. TADE, FREEDMEN'S EDUCATION, AND THE FAILURE OF RECONSTRUCTION IN TENNESSEE
*By C. Stuart McGehee*

172     THE NASHVILLE INSTITUTE AND ROGER WILLIAMS UNIVERSITY:
Benevolence, Paternalism, and Black Consciousness, 1867–1910
*By Eugene TeSelle*

192     CONTRIBUTORS

194     INDEX

# Introduction:
# EMANCIPATION AND THE FIGHT FOR FREEDOM

## Crystal A. deGregory

This volume, *Emancipation and the Fight for Freedom*, explores the African American experience in both slavery and freedom amid and following the turmoil of the Civil War. Paying special interest to the efforts of blacks to secure educational opportunities, it explores the continued centrality of the concept of black self-determination in the *Tennessee Historical Quarterly*'s black historiography.

Examining historiographical themes of the Civil War, Reconstruction, and pre- and post-war education chronologically, the volume begins with an unexpected selection, James S. McRae's Fall 2005 article on the experiences of white Union Army volunteer David G. Cooke. Appearing in a special 1864 Nashville Campaign issue, it utilizes the correspondence between Cooke, who became a first lieutenant in the Twelfth United States Colored Troops (USCT) in 1863, and his wife between 1863 and 1864 to offer a candid look at the complex motivations for white service in the USCT. While Cooke and many of his counterparts may have felt sympathy for the black cause of freedom, the opportunities the USCT gave for advancement to white soldiers, who were often previously denied promotions in white regiments, served as the principal motivating factor.

But even the tragedy of Cooke's execution at the hands of the Confederate army as a result of his capture during USCT service in 1864 pales in comparison to the carnage suffered by black USCT troops at Fort Pillow the same year. Kenneth Bancroft Moore's Summer 1995 article is a hedged examination of the divergent views of this seminal battle in Tennessee's Civil War history. While Confederate General Nathan Bedford Forrest's insistence on defending the actions of his troops at Fort Pillow stigmatized him, the events at Fort Pillow also served as motivation for the USCT's increased efforts to demonstrate their military value through gallant service.

The Fort Pillow massacre should have been a distant memory by the time Tennessee blacks secured their freedom, but the often violent reaction of whites to fledgling black freedoms kept blacks in a perpetual state of unease. Nowhere was this feeling more appropriate than in the city of Memphis where Tennessee State University scholar Bobby L. Lovett asserted that blacks endured "the bloodiest reaction to black freedom and the quest for racial equality." Published in Spring 1979, the article chronicles how and why the Memphis Riot of May 1866 took place. Threatened by the role of the Freedmen's Bureau, resentful of the city's occupation by USCT troops, and angry over the intrepid attitudes of urban blacks, a white mob instigated a riot that resulted in the arrest (and likely beating) of 2,000 blacks and the death of forty-six others. But as Brian D. Page's Winter 1999 article demonstrates, black Memphians were not deterred from their efforts to celebrate their freedoms, including their patriotic spirit. The same year as the riots, parades, and festivities celebrating the Fourth of July became a rite for black locals who used annual celebrations to reinforce their racial and nationalistic identities throughout Reconstruction.

It is hard to imagine that Walter J. Fraser, Jr.'s, 1975 article on black reconstructionists in Tennessee was written amid the revisionists' vanguard that revised interpretations of the Redeemers and their sympathizers who characterized Reconstruction as an era of Negro rule and corruption. As the first state readmitted to the Union, the study of Tennessee in general, and its western region, which had a cotton-based economy, is of special interest. By exploring the connectedness between Negro voters and the Republican Party and the inner workings of the interracial but white-led Lewis-Eaton machine in particular, the fragility of their limited cooperation is revealed. Black loyalty to the interracial alliance, once secured in exchange for low-level political appointments, faltered under the weight of black leaders' increased demands for political power.

Dissatisfied blacks such as Edward Shaw, who left the Lewis-Eaton machine to make his own bid for office in 1870 against a white Republican candidate, leveraged their influence with the State Convention of Colored Men to advance the causes of concern to the African American community. Published in 2006, Union University professor Judy Bussell Leforge's essay on the 1865 and 1866 state colored conventions helped to resurrect interest in this forgotten part of Reconstruction history. By demonstrating the long standing commitment of blacks to securing political liberty and equality through self-determination, Leforge succeeds in her efforts to place the conventions at the foundation of the struggle for civil rights that followed almost a century later in its wake as the modern Civil Rights Movement. Despite enjoying only limited success, the colored conventions and the demands of its delegates serve as compelling testaments of black Tennesseans' early commitment for educational, political, and economic equality.

My own Summer 2010 article traces the educational efforts of black Nashvillians to the pre-Civil War period. In spite of the constant threat of white terror and vigilantism, blacks independently owned and operated native schools for three decades before the coming of the Civil War. From classrooms of black teachers emerged a generation of civic-minded black children who not only assumed influential positions in black Nashville, but who also assumed the mantle of civil rights through the creation of additional educational opportunities as well as economic and political empowerment for blacks across the South.

Now-Florida State University Professor Emeritus Joe M. Richardson offers a groundbreaking narrative history of American Missionary Association (AMA) flagship school, Fisk University, in his Spring 1970 essay. By exploring the interrelationship of white missionary zeal and black enthusiasm for educational opportunities at Fisk, Richardson reveals important and still-neglected dimensions of black educational efforts, namely the importance of black self-determination and the limits of paternalistic white support for it. The school's Northern white faculty often suffered ostracism from southern whites yet their sacrifices paled in comparison to the violence and indignities black students suffered. The narrative culminates with the gallant fundraising efforts of the Fisk Jubilee Singers, a student singing troupe, who saved the school from closure.

West Virginia historian C. Stuart McGehee also explored many of these themes in his Winter 1984 article on the pioneering work of Chattanooga black educational leader E.O. Tade who arrived in Chattanooga in 1866, and assumed the mammoth task of a tripartite strategy of black religious, economic, and educational institution building. It was the latter, however, that offered Tade and black Chattanoogans the most success. Not only did Tade found Howard School, the city's first public educational institution, he soon after emerged as community leader. In addition to being an active minister, Tade organized a local branch of the National Freedmen's Savings and Trust Bank and was Hamilton County's first superintendent of education. As Tade's notoriety grew, so too did his personal wealth, which, combined with his penchant for isolating potential allies, helped to put into motion a series of events that led to his downfall.

Unlike Fisk and the Howard School, Nashville's now-defunct Nashville Institute and Roger Williams College was virtually forgotten in black educational historiography until Eugene TeSelle's Winter 1982 essay. Although knowledge of the school was once primarily limited to a handful of history enthusiasts, the institution's relatively short but nevertheless fascinating history unfolds against a backdrop of missionary work led by white Baptist minister Daniel W. Phillips. Opened in 1867 and eventually supported by the American Baptist Home Society (ABHS) for more than three decades, the school incorporated as Roger Williams in 1883. Although it survived a student protest during the winter of 1886–87, the school could not survive two mysterious fires in the spring of 1905 and was closed the same year.

As these articles all too often demonstrate, despite gallant efforts at black self-determination, the efforts of black Tennesseans to secure and enjoy American freedoms often fell short of their ideals. Even so, together, the experiences of black Tennesseans in slavery and freedom serve as important and necessary threads in the rich fabric of Tennessee's Civil War history. It is my hope that we never forget that the issue of slavery was the epicenter of the Civil War, making it impossible to discuss the war, even a moment, without including the sufferings as well as strivings of African Americans during the Civil War era.

Crystal A. deGregory
Assistant Professor
Tennessee State University

# DAVID G. COOKE JOINS THE UNITED STATES COLORED TROOPS

## James S. McRae

On December 15–16, 1864, a decisive battle was fought around the defenses of Nashville. Confederate General John Bell Hood attempted to surround the city with his exhausted and undermanned army in a desperate gamble. Union Major General George H. Thomas launched a two day offensive that shattered Hood's command. Thomas's plan included a flanking attack around the Confederate left, preceded by a feint at the Confederate right. This feint drew Hood's attention from the main attack and caused him to shift his forces away from the main Union effort. A group of untested regiments of the United States Colored Troops, who suffered heavy casualties in frontal assaults, bore the burden of the feint. The USCT regiments proved their courage to many observers, including General Thomas who said, "Gentlemen, the question is settled; negroes will fight."[1]

In the aftermath of the Union victory, Confederate cavalrymen captured and executed First Lieutenant and Quartermaster David Grant Cooke of the Twelfth USCT. The story of Lieutenant Cooke's capture comes from a survivor of the incident, First Lieutenant George W. Fitch of the same regiment. Confederate cavalry scouts, from the command of Nathan Bedford Forrest captured Fitch and Cooke, along with an officer from the Forty-Fourth USCT on December 20 about ten miles from Murfreesboro. The officers had become separated from their units during the pursuit of Hood's rapidly disintegrating army. Their guards marched them for nearly two days toward what they were told was General Forrest's headquarters. Abruptly on December 22, the guards led them off the road into a nearby ravine where they were "shot down like so many dogs."[2] All three men sustained head wounds at point blank range. Fitch survived with a pistol ball lodged behind the ear and pretended to be dead in order to escape.[3]

Lieutenant Cooke was not so lucky. He died leaving behind a wife and young son. Through a collection of letters Cooke wrote to his family, we may examine the lieutenant's motivations for seeking a commission in the United States Colored Troops. Cooke was a schoolteacher and ordained minister before the Civil War. He was married to Elizabeth "Lizzie" Lockey in October 1860 and the couple had two sons, born in 1861 and in January, 1863.

In the fall of 1862, he volunteered for service in the Ninety-Second Illinois Volunteer Regiment. The unit served in Kentucky and Tennessee and eventually received Spencer rifles and horses. Cooke saw his first action in the spring of 1863 with the Ninety-Second in the Tullahoma Campaign. After a brief illness, Cooke began seeking a commission in the USCT in August 1863. He sat for a review board at General Rosecrans's headquarters and received his commission by the end of August. Cooke participated in the mustering of the Twelfth USCT Regiment and served with the regiment until his death in December 1864.[4]

Joseph T. Glatthaar explains in *Forged in Battle* several reasons why white Union soldiers volunteered for service in black regiments. These motivations included sympathy for the black race, dedication to the Union war effort, financial reward from higher pay, and the prestige of a commission.[5] All these motivations weighed into Lieutenant Cooke's decision to pursue a commission in the USCT.

Serving in the USCT was especially hazardous duty. Officers expected to be tried for inciting a slave insurrection if caught leading black troops into battle, a crime punishable by death in Southern courts.[6] Officers had a keen awareness of this risk. After the war one officer in the Twelfth USCT commented, "The officers of colored regiments at this time had every incentive to do the utmost within their power to make their men good soldiers. Their own personal safety was dependent on the fighting qualities of their men, more than in white regiments."[7] Lieutenant Cooke must have been aware of this risk when he applied for a commission in August 1863.[8] Yet his reasons for joining ultimately outweighed this risk and he proceeded with his application.

As Glatthaar suggests, many USCT officers "felt sympathy for the black race and wanted to help elevate them through military service."[9] Some officers were active abolitionists before the war and joining the USCT was a logical evolution of these beliefs. Officer selection favored those who were willing to do service with blacks, but this was not necessarily a measurable factor.

Lieutenant Cooke's view on blacks is hard to ascertain from his letters. He seems to support the destruction of slavery. Following the initial Emancipation Proclamation, Cooke wrote, "The Proclamation just sent out shows that the day of grace has passed and that the destruction of slavery inevitable."[10] A diary entry reveals even stronger anti-slavery feelings. When the men of the Ninety-Second Illinois confronted a southern slave-catcher in one incident in the fall of 1862, they refused to turn over a runaway slave who had sought refuge with the Union troops. Cooke validated this action by stating, "It is not necessary that Illinois soldiers should become bloodhounds to prove their loyalty. Their valor has been proven on too many bloody fields."[11]

Upon entering the USCT, Lieutenant Cooke showed his feelings toward the soldiering ability of black troops. The soldiers of the Twelfth, he wrote, "are in uniform and look first rate, the[y] like soldiering very well and will be good ones."[12] Cooke initially seemed to appreciate the ability and professionalism of the black soldiers in his command. After a few weeks in the USCT, Lieutenant Cooke revealed a different view. He was assigned to the adjutant general's office and heard cases brought against enlisted men. The black troops that came before him were in his opinion "very childish and it would amuse you to see me sitting in judgment, healing differences, deciding questions, and smoothing difficulties the best way I can."[13] Cooke saw the black troops as many mid-nineteenth century whites did, as childlike and in need of white supervision.

One of Lieutenant Cooke's most curious statements comes from a letter in September 1863. He says, "There is one drawback to my position." Cooke sees a drawback in the requirement of a servant for every officer. Perhaps the drawback existed because "we are charged by the government for their services." The use of servants was so convenient for him that he states, possibly jokingly, "They are very useful indeed and I begin to see why the idea of giving up their domestic servants is so repugnant to the feelings of the south. They save me a good many steps and when you find an intelligent and trusty one he is a great convenience indeed."[14]

Lieutenant Cooke's view of blacks seems to coincide with that of many white Northerners of his time. Most likely he felt that men in the Twelfth USCT were capable soldiers but needed guidance from whites. His letters rarely mention black soldiers by name and he seems to associate primarily with other white officers. It is hard to characterize Cooke as joining the USCT out of sympathy toward blacks or being imperviousness to their condition. Abolitionist ideals were not at the core of his decision.

Glatthaar discusses the financial motives of many of those who sought USCT commissions. There is strong indication that this was the case with David G. Cooke. As he admits to his wife, "Lizzie it is quite a step to go from a private position to that of Second Lieutenant, from $13 per month to $100. What do you think of that?"[15] Cooke thinks very highly of this pay increase, given that prewar debts were a major concern for him and he sent large amounts of money home to his wife. He worried, "Will it be any satisfaction to me to know that my wife saved money enough to pay my debts while I was in the Army and killed herself in the attempt?"[16]

The nearly ten-fold increase in pay must have been a major motivation for many officers, especially ones like Cooke who had a young family. His family was always at the forefront of his thoughts. He revealed his reason for seeking a promotion as, "All this advancement… simply because I can make my little family more comfortable than I could in the ranks."[17] He even entertained thoughts of a career in the Army past the war:

> We are in the Regular Army and I can remain in the service as long as I wish, and as soon as the war closes I can have my wife and boy to live with me for we will be guarding some post, that is something of a consideration for a situation in the regular army is a prize seeing as it will pay me $1100 per year.[18]

Not only would the commission have been useful during the war period, but also Cooke predicted that the army could be a decent career for a family-oriented man.

Another adjustment that Lieutenant Cooke explains is the deferential treatment he now received from the enlisted ranks. He told his wife, "Not a man from 1st Sergeant to the humblest private will dare come into our tent without removing his hat or think of sitting in our august presence without any order or an invitation."[19] This respect carried over into the civilian world. After Cooke had been promoted, he instructed his wife "if any of your admiring friends inquire what position I hold, you can tell them that I am 1st Lieutenant and regiment Quarter Master 12th USCT."[20] Cooke's assertion that his wife should be proud of the position tells a lot about his feelings toward the USCT. Serving as an officer in a black regiment must also have been looked highly upon by his social circle.

The USCT provided a welcome opportunity to those denied promotion in white regiments and this seems to be the case with Cooke. "I wonder what John Hitchcock thinks of this change," wrote Cooke, "through his influence and false representation I was reduced to the ranks. Now I am a commissioned officer while he is only

3rd sergeant. Surely he [Hitchcock] is punished for his sins against me."²¹ Although the background of the situation is not clear, Cooke seems to have harbored a grudge against Hitchcock after being denied promotion within the Ninety-Second Illinois. For Cooke, being able to outrank and advance rapidly in rank seems to have been a compelling motivation for serving in the USCT.

Lieutenant Cooke, like the vast majority of USCT officers, had seen action with his former all-white unit. A high number of USCT officers had been wounded prior to joining the USCT.²² Cooke was a veteran of one previous engagement in Tennessee while serving with the Ninety-Second Illinois and seems to have accounted for himself well. Cooke's action on the first day of the Battle of Nashville reveals that he was a man not complacent with staying in the rear. He wrote his wife,

> I did not go out with the Regiment this morning when they started, as a Quartermaster I was in charge of the train but in an hour of fear I became so uneasy I could not contain myself to remain in the rear. So I loaded up a wagon with ammunition and started for the front.²³

Cooke could have sent an orderly to resupply the regiment rather than go himself. At the front, he found Confederate shells being fired into his vicinity. The regiment was in a trench built for the defense of Nashville. Ironically these fortifications had been built earlier by many of the same men who were now enlisted in the regiment.²⁴

Cooke describes to his wife the exchange of sharpshooter and artillery fire between the two sides. Then, "Before long however the Rebs who had been considerably annoyed by our sharpshooters and battery which was just to our rear opened up upon us with six guns and more than a hundred shells were fired on us."²⁵ The Confederates "soon got the range, they burst fully fifty shells within a circle of a hundred yards from where we were lying."²⁶ The barrage made an impression on Cooke and he admitted, "I don't want to be in a hotter place than what was for about two hours and I never expect to be."²⁷ Cooke's voluntary exposure to fire reveals his bravery.

The last letter Cooke wrote to his wife is dated December 16 and 17, 1864. He admits not having heard from the regiment during these two days and that his quartermaster teams were out of his reach.²⁸ The events leading up to his capture on December 20 are not entirely clear. The Twelfth USCT advanced toward Murfreesboro on December 18 in pursuit of Hood's routed army. The regiment pursued the fleeing Confederates out of Tennessee and reached Decatur, Alabama, by December 27.²⁹ Cooke seems to have been separated from the regiment, possibly bringing up the supply wagons in the rear. His capture is fairly ironic, since the Confederate army had been completely routed and his seizure described as accidental.[30]

The execution of prisoners was not condoned by the Confederate government. It became common practice, however, on many battlefields to execute black Union troops and their officers. The most famous incident happened following the capture Fort Pillow in April 1864, when Forrest's Confederates allegedly massacred dozens of black soldiers in the act of surrendering.[31] Perhaps some of the same Confederates who participated in the Fort Pillow Massacre were in Middle Tennessee during the Battle of Nashville. An attitude undoubtedly prevailed in portions of the Confederate army that blacks and their officers did not deserve humane treatment. The murder of David G. Cooke cannot be justified by any means and can be characterized as a war crime.

Cooke's motivations to seek a commission in the USCT are complex. His love of Union and family held a great sway over his decision making. His sympathy for the cause of blacks and antagonistic feelings toward slavery surely played a major part in his willingness to command black soldiers. The most important motivating factors for Cooke can be summed up in the gain of prestige and increase in pay that came with promotion. Cooke felt that he was not getting the respect due a man of his abilities while serving in the Ninety-Second Illinois. The Ninety-Second did not offer the opportunity for promotion and increased pay that was available in the USCT. Cooke was struggling to support a wife and young child back home in Illinois. His prewar debt was taking a great toll on his means to provide for his family. Promotion provided the chance to regain a sound financial footing and begin to remove financial burdens.

Cooke represents many of the reasons that attracted whites to the USCT. Other officers held more fervor for the cause of blacks and Union, but some displayed more selfish motives toward financial gain and exploitation of the system. Cooke's correspondence also shows the complexity of human decision making.

*This article first appeared in the Fall 2005 issue of the* Tennessee Historical Quarterly.

1. Quoted in James M. McPherson, *The Negro's Civil War: How American Negroes Felt and Acted during the War for the Union* (New York, 1965), 233. Wiley Sword, *Embrace an Angry Wind: The Confederacy's Last Hurray: Spring Hill, Franklin, and Nashville* (New York, 1992) offers the best description of the Battle of Nashville and Thomas's strategy.

2. Henry V. Freeman "A Colored Brigade in the Campaign and Battle of Nashville," *Military Essays and Recollections: Papers Read Before the Commandary of the State of Illinois, Military Order of the Loyal Legion of the United States* (Chicago, 1894), 403.

3. Fitch's account is in *The War of the Rebellion: A Compilation of the Official Records of the Union and Confederate Armies* (Washington, D.C., 1881–1901), series 2, vol. 8, 19–20. Hereafter referred to as OR.

4. D.G. Cooke Collection, from a private collection, Atlanta, Ga.

5. Joseph T. Glatthaar *Forged in Battle: The Civil War Alliance of Black Soldiers and White Officers* (New York, 1991), 38–41.

6. Glathaar, *Forged in Battle*, 201.

7. Freeman, *A Colored Brigade*, 401.

8. David G. Cooke to Lizzie Cooke, 10 August 1863.

9. Glatthaar, *Forged in Battle*, 39.

10. Cooke to Lizzie, 28 September 1862, Cooke Collection

11. D.G. Cooke Diary, 2 November 2 1862, Cooke Collection.

12. Cooke to Lizzie, 29 August 1863, Cooke Collection.

13. Cooke to Lizzie, 6 September 1863, Cooke Collection.

14. Ibid.

15. Cooke to Lizzie, 29 August 1863, Cooke Collection.

16. Cooke to Lizzie, 29 July 1863, Cooke Collection.

17. Cooke to Lizzie, 29 August 1863, Cooke Collection.

18. Ibid. The Cooke's first child seems to have died as an infant in 1861.

19. Cooke to Lizzie, 6 September 1863, Cooke Collection.

20. Cooke to Lizzie, 22 November 1864, Cooke Collection.

21. Cooke to Lizzie, 29 August 1863, Cooke Collection.

22. Glatthaar, *Forged in Battle*, 268–269.

23. Cooke to Lizzie, 15 December 1864, Cooke Collection.

24. OR III, 4, 763.

25. Cooke to Lizzie, 15 December 1864, Cooke Collection.

26. Ibid.

27. Ibid.

28. Cooke to Lizzie, 16–17 December 16–17 1864, Cooke Collection

29. "12th U.S. Colored Infantry Regiment" *Tennesseans in the Civil War: A Military History of the Confederate and Union Units with Available Rosters of Personnel, Part 1* (Nashville, 1964), 397–398.

30. Freeman, *Military Essays and Recollections*, 403.

31. McPherson, *The Negro's Civil War*, 216–217.

# FORT PILLOW, FORREST, AND THE UNITED STATES COLORED TROOPS IN 1864

## Kenneth Bancroft Moore

On April 12, 1864, General Nathan Bedford Forrest's force of about 1,500 Confederates attacked and surrounded Fort Pillow in Tennessee, a stronghold on the Mississippi River fifty miles above Memphis.[1] By 3:00 p.m. the Confederates had gained advantageous positions outside the fort. Forrest asked for a surrender, but Major William F. Bradford, commander of the 557 black and white Union troops, refused in spite of the Southerners' overwhelming numbers and strong positions.[2] After unsuccessful negotiations with Bradford, Forrest did not hesitate to attack.

The bugler sounded the charge, and with a yell the Confederates vaulted in unison over the eight-foot parapets and fired into the Union ranks from all sides. Outnumbered almost three to one, the blue line wavered and broke under the tremendous weight of the volley. A wave of Confederates charged into the fort as the Union men retreated toward the river in confusion, some firing back, others only running. Rebel sharp-shooters on surrounding hills opened fire on the white and black troops as they neared the banks of the Mississippi River, thus adding to the turmoil and carnage. As their sharpshooters continued a withering fire, the charging gray invaders closed in from three sides while the river prevented escape. Many Union soldiers tried to swim for freedom but were shot in the water or drowned. According to several reports, Union troops threw down their arms in surrender but were shot nonetheless. The battle was over within twenty minutes. The black regiments suffered over 60 per cent casualties, and the North labeled it the "Fort Pillow Massacre."³

The Northern press and government popularized this event and stigmatized Forrest by labeling himm a butcher. This reputation quickly spread through the Union army, especially to the regiments of the United States Colored Troops (U.S.C.T.) stationed at Memphis. If captured in battle, black troops already knew they would be returned to slavery or sentenced to manual labor. They were also aware that in every theater of the war Confederates sometimes shot down black troops instead of taking them prisoner. The soldiers of the U.S.C.T. had good reason to fear the next encounter with Forrest.

The U.S.C.T.'s feelings of apprehension and anger were first apparent at the Battle of Brice's Crossroads on June 10, 1864. They sought to avenge the Fort Pillow massacre but soon found themselves in the midst of a chaotic Union disaster. However, from the Battle of Tupelo in July to the Battle of Nashville in December 1864, the U.S.C.T. improved as professional soldiers. As they gained experience, they performed coolly under fire despite the menial status accorded them by their adversary. Nevertheless, Forrest's brutal reputation prompted black troops to realize they may meet a more horrible fate. Rumors, the press's focus on Fort Pillow, and indeed the caution exhibited by Union commanders at Memphis, all seemed to intensify the fear that Forrest would repeat the butchery committed on April 12, 1864.

This notoriety adversely affected Forrest's command. Perhaps most clear is that Forrest was brought into the limelight. It intensified the Union army's focus on the Confederate raider just when he needed to be invisible—as General William T. Sherman split the Deep South. Forrest's various battles in Mississippi gave valuable experience to the previously untested black troops. Perhaps most important, the fighting of the spring and summer of 1864 in Northern Mississippi, Northern Alabama, and West Tennessee proved to Union commanders that black troops would indeed fight, and fight hard, prompting their increased use in the Union army. Ultimately, the "success" of Fort Pillow became a weight on Forrest's back that contributed to his army's eventual demise in the war and, furthermore, its notoriety created a stigma that dogged him until death.

Maximum publicity was given to Fort Pillow and Forrest throughout the North in the spring of 1864. On April 16, the *New York Times* headlined the event with a detailed description of the atrocities. The story described the rebels as "devils incarnate" and as "fiends." Men were said to be buried alive but were dug up before they suffocated. Descriptions informed Northerners that men were shot, bayoneted, and burned after an attempted surrender. The *Times* headlined the event for three days and reported further details through the April 20.[4]

Other newspapers also devoted great attention to the battle in Tennessee. It remained a front-page story for four days in the *New York Herald* and the *New York Tribune*.[5] The *Herald* reported that President Abraham Lincoln, while speaking in Maryland, promised quick and decisive retribution if the accounts proved to be true. The president, unlike many, questioned the validity of the reports.[6] Horace Greeley's *Tribune* certainly did not doubt the story's validity. Its entire front page of April 23 was devoted to Fort Pillow.[7]

In Memphis, headquarters of the black troops in the Western theater, the *Bulletin* of April 23 described the battle as "barbarous, savage, and unworthy of savages." The *Chicago Tribune* recounted Forrest's past as a slave trader and said, "Let no quarter be shown to these dastardly butchers of Forrest's command while the war lasts." The *Daily National Intelligencer* of Washington also covered the story extensively.[8] By the end of April, the name of Nathan Bedford Forrest in the North was synonymous with the murder of black troops.

The Fort Pillow massacre also gained the attention of the United States Congress. The Joint Committee on the Conduct of the War quickly dispatched Senator Benjamin F. Wade and Representative Daniel W. Gooch to Cairo, Illinois, to question survivors of the battle. Gooch, an Ivy League graduate from Massachusetts, was a noted Republican congressman who had studied law and had been a member of the Massachusetts bar since 1846.[9] Benjamin F. Wade, also an accomplished lawyer, was a senator from Ohio who studied medicine at one time and was judge of the 3rd Judicial Courtt of Ohio from 1847 to 1851.[10] Significantly, Wade was a Radical Republican and abolitionist, and his son, Henry, was a commander of black troops.[11]

Gooch and Wade reported that Forrest, indeed, had committed atrocities. They wrote that the garrison was "indiscriminately slaughtered" and the rebels murdered, "sparing neither age nor sex, white or black, soldier or civilian." Men were reportedly shot down in lines execution-style, and civilians and soldiers alike were hacked with sabers amidst cries of "no quarter, no quarter, kill the damned niggers; shoot them down!" The congressmen elaborated that Forrest ordered the carnage to continue into the night and the following day. Men were shot, burned, and buried alive. Union survivors testified that their dead were nailed to doors of the dwellings in the fort and were left as horrible effigies to the plight of the black troops.[12]

Wade and Gooch exaggerated the fight and its aftermath at Fort Pillow. The interviews were not conducted objectively. Unsubstantiated stories were accepted if they served the Republicans' purposes. One black survivor, for example, claimed he witnessed Forrest directing the massacre. He described the Confederate general as "a little bit of a man."[13] Forrest, in fact, was six feet tall, a very large man in those times.

The congressmen framed their questions to elicit certain responses. W.P. Walker, a sergeant in the Thirteenth Tennessee Cavalry (Union), reported to them that during the battle he was shot in the arm, shoulder, neck, and eye. Gooch asked Walker who shot him and why. Walker stated that a rebel private not only wounded him with a pistol, but also told the bloodied Yankee that a Confederate general had ordered him to do so.[14] Such a conversation in the midst of battle seems unlikely, but Gooch's line of questioning masterfully extracted the anticipated answer: a Confederate general was responsible for the massacre. The report had other shortcomings as well.

It neglected to include relevant evidence that cast a dim light on the congressmen's interpretation of the battle. Washington's *Daily National Intelligencer* printed a revealing account that posited that Fort Pillow was as much the fault of the garrison as it was that of the Southerners. The *Intelligencer*'s correspondent reported that an "intelligent Irishman" witnessed the event. Blacks, the Irishman reported, "immediately ran away" in contrast to their white comrades who "surrendered as soon as the rebels entered the fort." The black soldiers, "not understanding matters" due to their inexperience and "being afraid of falling into the hands of the rebels," hurriedly "ran away with their arms and occasionally fired on their pursuers."[15] Thus, surrendering Union men were killed because a number of their comrades continued to fight with guns in hand. Whether or not the views of this source are to be lent much credence is certainly questionable. But this contemporary account shows another perspective that the joint committee clearly ignored. Their report was, at least partly, a manifestation of the investigators' own bias. They wrote down what they expected and, indeed, wanted to hear. Referring to this report, Secretary of the Navy Gideon Welles succinctly stated, "I distrust Congressional committees. They exaggerate."[16] Nonetheless, the exaggerated report on Fort Pillow convinced many and was a useful propaganda tool for the North.

While Gooch and Wade investigated the battle, the Union army quickly retaliated. On April 17, 1864, five days after the battle, General Ulysses S. Grant announced he would no longer exchange prisoners as a result of Fort Pillow.[17] In Washington, meanwhile, United States government officials debated several avenues of action. Secretary of War Edwin M. Stanton endeavored not only to disallow prisoner exchanges, but also wanted to indict Forrest and General James R. Chalmers, Forrest's subordinate who led the initial attack at Fort Pillow, for war crimes.[18] Stanton also urged holding Confederate prisoners hostage for insurance in case any more atrocities were committed against Union soldiers. Secretary of State William H. Seward also advocated holding Confederates until their government guaranteed no more hostilities toward black troops.[19]

Gideon Welles recorded in his diary that the cabinet discussed wholesale retaliation—"killing man-for-man."[20] Welles, Secretary of the Interior John Palmer Usher, and Attorney General Edward Bates opposed such a policy.[21] Welles justifiably questioned how the rebel commanders could be punished if they could not be captured. Would the United States government consult General Robert E. Lee or the Confederate government if at all? He admitted that the entire affair was "beset with difficulties." The cabinet concluded that President Lincoln should declare the responsible Confederates "massacre outlaws" and further stipulated that any federal officers who captured the accused should detain them for a trial. This was the most they could do, for their options were extremely limited within the confines of the continuing war.[22]

Following the battle, Forrest retired into Mississippi and soon issued statements defending his actions at Fort Pillow. He denied any massacre took place but his sentiments were clear in his report of the battle. He admitted that the Union loss was heavy, "upward of 500 were killed," and that "the river was dyed with the blood of the slaughtered for 200 yards." He boldly asserted, "It is hoped that these facts will demonstrate to the Northern people that negro soldiers cannot cope with Southerners."[23] General Chalmers also displayed a harsh prejudicial attitude in his report of April 20. He claimed that his brigades "taught the mongrel garrison of blacks and renegades a lesson long to be remembered."[24] These statements exhibit the very prejudices that angered black Union troops and worried Union commanders. By summer 1864, they would get an opportunity to vent their frustration.

In early June, Union General Samuel D. Sturgis was preparing his new army in Memphis for an invasion of Mississippi intended to destroy Forrest and to prevent him from hindering Sherman's invasion of Georgia. The Fifty-Fifth and Fifty-Ninth U.S. Colored Infantries and Company F of the U.S. Colored Artillery were ready for a fight. They took an oath on their knees to show the Confederates no mercy, or "no quarter," as they termed it, and wore black badges that read "Remember Fort Pillow."[25]

The black brigade, commanded by Colonel Edward Bouton, marched with vengeful determination through Mississippi. The Reverend Samuel A. Agnew, a white resident of the area, found the soldiers "especially insolent" in their attitude. They endeavored to to "show Forrest they were his rulers." Agnew confirmed that the black troops wore badges reading "Remember Fort Pillow" and that they carried a black flag which signified their unwillingness to take prisoners. William Witherspoon, a Confederate private, recalled that the black soldiers boasted they were going to whip Forrest and bring him to justice.[26]

Their opportunity arrived on June 10, 1864, when Forrest attacked Sturgis's army on the Ripley Guntown Road, near an intersection called Brice's Crossroads. The battle raged through most of the hot, humid day and soon turned into a Union disaster. After a spirited fight, Sturgis's heat-exhausted troopers could no longer bear the weight of Forrest's attacks and began to retreat. The black brigade, which initially guarded the wagon train in the rear, covered the retreat that soon became a panic-stricken melee of Union soldiers running back to Memphis. The Fifty-Fifth and Fifty-Ninth regiments were hastily thrown into the chaotic battle as the rest of the army was breaking up. They fought stubbornly despite constant flanking movements by Forrest's men. Bouton's brigade suffered heavy losses: eight hundred casualties out of 1,350 men, although many of these were listed as missing, and 312 were characterized as "slightly wounded."[27]

Colonel Bouton reported on June 17 that during the battle he "was left entirely cut off" and was "surrounded by several hundred" of the flanking Confederates. The black troops massed around their colonel and "fought with terrible desperation." Some, Bouton reported, "Having broken up their guns in hand-to-hand conflict, unyielding, died at my feet, without a thing in their hands for defense." The black brigade managed to break out and started a splintered retreat. As ammunition ran low, they gathered caps and balls thrown away earlier by the retreating white regiments ahead of them. They fought their way back to Memphis over the next two days.[28]

Brice's Crossroads was a victory in the field for Forrest and a humiliation for Sturgis, but it demonstrated the potential of the black troops. Their stubbornness in the fight helped prevent the destruction of the entire army. On the morning of June 11, for example, the Confederates attacked at Ripley, Mississippi, to cut off the Union retreat to Memphis. Formed up and fighting with no more than ten rounds of ammunition per man, troopers from the Fifty-Fifth and Fifty-Ninth regiments led two spirited charges that drove the rebels back two hundred yards and allowed the rest of the Union army to continue up the road. In fact, the black soldiers held off Forrest's cavalry for sixty miles before reaching Collierville, Tennessee, where the command was reformed to protect the rear as the army moved into Memphis.[29]

Union commanders had nothing but praise for the performance of the black brigade. Colonel Bouton reported that his men were "deserving of great credit for the bravery with which they fought in the main engagement." General Sturgis praised them when he wrote,

"The colored troops deserve great credit for the manner in which they stood to their work."[30] From another perspective, however, the black brigade did not deserve such praise.

Confederate veterans had their own view of the blacks' performance in the battle. Henry Ewell Hord, a private in Forrest's command, recalled that the blacks had "sworn before they left Memphis never to take any of Forrest's men prisoners," but conversely, he wrote that "they did not put up much of a fight—seemed more intent on getting rid of their equipment and plunder."

Another rebel veteran recalled that the blacks threw down their guns without firing a shot and "bounded off with the fleetness of a deer."[31]

The black troops were inexperienced in contrast to their adversaries who were seasoned veterans. The Fifty-Ninth Regiment, for example, had been training for a year and was considered disciplined and certainly ready for a fight. But they had not yet seen a large scale engagement, and certainly not one with Forrest.[32] The Battle of Brice's Crossroads, significantly, was lost by the time the black brigade was put into action. The Union army was, in fact, running away, a panicked mob. Witherspoon and Hord certainly witnessed black troops running, as was the entire Union army. The black brigade regained some semblance of order, however, which was evident at the skirmish at Ripley.

Brice's Crossroads also demonstrated that fears were rampant within the black soldiers' ranks and among their white commanders. Agnew recalled that many blacks were frantic after the battle. They reportedly asked, "Would Mr. Forrest kill them?"[33] William Witherspoon wrote that his unit encountered surrendered federal soldiers, black and white, who were fighting amongst themselves. The whites were "endeavoring to force the negroes away and the negroes equally determined on staying with the [white] Yanks. The Yank afraid to be caught with the negro and the negro afraid to be caught without the Yank."[34]

Union Colonel Arthur T. Reeve, commander of the Fifty-Fifth Colored Infantry, recalled that his troops did not intend to take prisoners. And he, himself, "fully expected to be killed if captured." Forrest's reputation "made the Federals afraid to surrender" and, in turn, this "greatly exasperated" the Confederates. A Southern artilleryman recalled Brice's Crossroads to have been "more like a hunt for wild game than a battle between civilized men."[35]

The desperation displayed by the black troops incited the rebels to a fever-pitch, causing more chaos. Private Witherspoon related that when he and his comrades were exhausted from the heat and from the chase of the Union army someone cried out, "Here are the d[amne]d negroes!" Black Union troops were forming a line of battle in the rebels' front when immediately "new life, energy and action coursed through our bodies." The Southerners charged in a "maddening rush" and drove the federal troops back, with the spirited fighting costing heavy black casualties.[36]

The intensity of the battle and the black troops' state of mind drew an adamant protest from General Forrest. After the battle, he wrote to Union General Cadwallader C. Washburn, commander of the troops in Memphis. Northern commanders in Memphis, Forrest argued, were aware of the vengeful oath taken but ignored it, thereby putting Forrest's soldiers in jeopardy, as well as the black troops. Forrest confessed to Washburn that Brice's Crossroads "was far more bloody than it would otherwise have been but for the fact that your men evidently expected to be slaughtered when captured," and related that neither yanks nor rebels "felt safe in surrendering, even when further resistance was useless." Union prisoners captured by the Confederates admitted that they "expected no quarter." Forrest inquired as to how Washburn was going to treat Confederate prisoners taken at Brice's Crossroads and admitted that he wished to continue the prisoner exchange as before.[37]

Washburn replied to General Stephen D. Lee, Forrest's superior, and claimed that, despite the absence of evidence, another massacre of black troops occurred at Brice's Crossroads, much like the one at Fort Pillow. He warned Lee that such actions would "lead to consequences hereafter fearful to contemplate." The Union general also wrote: "If it is intended to raise the black flag against that unfortunate race, they will cheerfully accept the issue."[38]

The Union army was extremely suspicious of Forrest's methods. In Washburn's letter to Lee, he admitted that he worried about the fate of the black regiments in Sturgis's command until he learned that Lee, not Forrest, was in command of the Confederate forces. Then he was satisfied atrocities would not occur.[39]

General Washburn demanded that Forrest and Lee unequivocally state their policy in regard to captured black soldiers. If they were to be treated as prisoners, Washburn was satisfied. On the other hand, if they were to be returned to slavery or slaughtered, he had no choice but to let their oath of no quarter stand. He further cautioned that if Confederate policy was not specifically outlined, he would leave the black troops in his command to their own devices. In other words, he would overlook any atrocities they might commit in the future.[40]

General Forrest responded citing the generic Confederate policy: "I regard captured negroes as captured property and not as captured soldiers." He went on to say that it was not his place to decide Confederate policy; that responsibility belonged to the Confederate government. He would wholeheartedly obey any directive it issued. He elaborated, "It is not the policy nor the interest of the South to destroy the negro—on the contrary, to preserve and protect him."[41] In conclusion, Forrest delivered his own warning to Washburn of dire consequences if the Union army continued to leave the treatment of Confederate prisoners to the discretion of vengeful black troops.

The Confederates were concerned not only about the treatment of their soldiers, but also about the desperate fighting which had been occurring. Referring to the oath taken by black troops before Brice's Crossroads, Forrest stated, "Had I and my men known it... the Battle of Tishomingo Creek would have been noted as the bloodiest battle of the war." Forrest even threatened to hold Union prisoners hostage to insure the fair treatment of Confederate prisoners and demanded that Washburn forbid the black flag to prevent his troops from taking more oaths of "no quarter."[42]

The Confederate government reaffirmed Forrest's policy toward black prisoners, although it had been relaxed over the previous year. When news reached Richmond in 1863 that black troops were being raised in the North, the Confederate Congress proclaimed that white officers in command of black troops could be put to death and that the black rank and file would be dealt with according to the laws of the state in which they captured.[43] This policy was later rescinded, however, when President Lincoln retaliated by promising the same treatment for Confederate prisoners.[44]

Black prisoners were typically used for manual labor if not returned to slavery. In a letter dated April 22, 1864, C.S.A. President Jefferson Davis ordered Lieutenant General Leonidas Polk, who was in Alabama, to hold black prisoners who were escaped slaves until they could be recovered by their owners. Black prisoners from Fort Pillow were shipped to Mobile to work on fortifications. And black troops captured in Alabama in September 1864 were forced to work on railroads.[45] This was not the Union's idea of how prisoners of war should be treated. To compound the problem, the prisoner exchange was discontinued. This alienated the black troops and heightened tensions between the Northern and Southern armies because without the exchange prisoners were, in effect, abandoned. This increased the likelihood of mistreatment, especially for blacks. Forrest's admissions, the rumors of his barbarity, and Grant's policy gave black troops few options.

The war of words soon ended in July, nearly one month after Brice's Crossroads, when the U.S.C.T. encountered the Confederate raider on a hot and dusty day near Tupelo, Mississippi. Union General Andrew Jackson Smith was ordered to dispose of the relentless Forrest with another foray into Mississippi, and Colonel Bouton's black brigade was again called on to fight. It consisted of the Fifty-Ninth, Sixty-First, and Sixty-eighth U.S. Colored Infantries and Battery I of the Second U.S. Colored Light Artillery—a "total aggregate exclusive of brigade staff' of 1,899 men.[46]

They initially guarded the wagon trains in the rear of the column, but when Smith ordered a forced march to Tupelo, this inactive role changed. Forrest attacked the rear of the moving column, hoping to cause confusion within the Union ranks. Despite constant harassment from Forrest's troops, the black soldiers maintained their order as General Smith moved his 14,000-man army east toward Tupelo. For the first time, a Union army did not disintegrate as a result of Forrest's move-and-hit tactics. Forrest defeated three armies under Samuel D. Sturgis, William Sooy Smith, and Abel D. Streight by using the same style of warfare. The black troops, however, did not panic and protected Smith's rear well by "moving in close order."[47] Edwin C. Bearss, a historian of the Brice's Crossroads and Tupelo campaign, concluded that the black brigade "acquitted itself with honor" by holding Forrest's men in check.[48]

Bouton reported on July 25 that his men "opposed [the rebels] with a will and determination highly commendable." He further conveyed that the battle "was a severe test of the soldierly qualities and power of endurance of my men." He elaborated that his command "was under fire over half the time and was in line of battle an average of over ten times." They withstood an artillery barrage from their rear and flanks for a "full three hours." But the black brigade managed to remain calm and marched in column "with men closed in ranks without wavering."

Bouton's men proved a point. They fought Forrest's troopers in heated engagements, including hand-to-hand combat a number of times.[49] General Smith reported on July 25 that the black brigade "fought excellently well" and wrote that their effectiveness eliminated his "prejudice of twenty years standing."[50] The U.S.C.T. had certainly improved on the performance at Brice's Crossroads. Most importantly, Smith's army had once more pinned Forrest in Mississippi.

Forrest would again encounter the U.S.C.T. In September, he attacked a well-defended fort in Athens, Alabama, which was garrisoned by the 106th, 110th, and 111th Colored Infantries, as well as the white Third Tennessee Cavalry and Ninth Indiana Cavalry.[51] Colonel Wallace Campbell commanded a garrison of 571 Union soldiers, close to the size of the army at Fort Pillow months before. After a two-hour artillery barrage, Forrest sent a message to Campbell demanding "an immediate and unconditional surrender." He warned that he had a "sufficient force" to take the fort. He also informed Campbell of the consequences and related that "white soldiers shall be treated as prisoners of war and the negroes returned to their masters." This was the standard manner in which Forrest asked for surrender, and Campbell was clearly intimidated by it. He believed that the rebel army contained upwards of ten thousand men because of its deceptive movements. Campbell was convinced that his garrison would be massacred if he did not accept Forrest's terms.[52]

The black troops and several of the officers did not want to surrender, especially to Forrest. But Campbell lost his nerve and surrendered the fort. A Union officer recalled that the men nearly revolted and were only brought into line by gunpoint. The black troops "would prefer to die than to be transferred to the tender mercies of

General Forrest and his men," the officer asserted.⁵³

Later controversy surrounded the affair at Athens. While in captivity in Mississippi, the surrendered officers wrote a report critical of Campbell's decision. They pointed out that Campbell did not fully consult his officers before he capitulated. They maintained that the fort was well defended and the soldiers were in good spirits and thus could have fought on. Each officer who surrendered against his will signed the report to clear his name.⁵⁴ This report was important to the blacks who were trying to gain respect as soldiers in what had been a white man's war.

Three days after Athens, Forrest attacked the Fourteenth U.S. Colored Infantry that defended a ridge near Pulaski, Tennessee. The commander of the Fourteenth, Colonel Thomas J. Morgan, reported that "the massacre of colored troops at Fort Pillow was well known to us, and had been fully discussed by our men." He and his troops heard rumors that General Forrest "had offered a thousand dollars for the head of any commander of a 'nigger regiment.'" Despite this, the black troops exclaimed, "Colonel, dey can't whip us, dey nebber get de ole 14th out of heah, nebber. Nebber drives us away widout a mighty lot of dead men [sic]."⁵⁵ The Fourteenth repulsed Forrest, and he retreated east to Murfreesboro. The U.S.C.T. had finally defeated the man they considered responsible for Fort Pillow.

The Fort Pillow massacre was a motivating factor for the U.S.C.T. They fought with spirit, and high casualties were apparent due to each side's reluctance to surrender. Historian Bobby Lee Lovett estimates that the black troops were partly responsible for 2,234 casualties inflicted on Forrest's command from February to December 1864. These were men the South could not replace, whereas the 2,242 lost from the black brigades were replaced by the Union without much difficulty. In fact, the casualties in the string of battles from April to December 1864 prevented Forrest from engaging in offensive operations.⁵⁶ These battles, moreover, achieved no strategic victory for the South. They only served to waste men who could have been better used elsewhere.

The black troops also played an important role in keeping Forrest away from Sherman's invasion of Georgia. Sherman was well aware of Forrest's ability and kept track of him at all times. He mentioned Forrest in almost every dispatch during the Atlanta campaign and called him "the very devil." Not long after the Battle of Brice's Crossroads, Sherman exclaimed that Forrest must be stopped, "if it costs 10,000 lives and breaks the Treasury. Tennessee will never have peace until Forrest is dead."⁵⁷ Sherman, as it turned out, was overly cautious of Forrest because the invasions from Memphis served their purpose. Whether or not the Confederate cavalry commander could have actually affected Sherman's invasion can only be left to speculation. The fact remains that the invasions into Mississippi prevented Forrest's active role in Georgia or East Tennessee.

Nathan Bedford Forrest was himself deeply affected by the Fort Pillow massacre. It stigmatized him until his death. His obituary in the *New York Times* read, "Forrest would be remembered only as a daring and successful guerilla [sic] cavalry leader were it not for the one great and indelible [sic] stain upon his name." It further pointed out that he spent the rest of his life defending his war record. He reportedly almost fought a duel with U.S. Cavalry General Judson Kilpatrick because he apparently called Forrest a murderer.[58]

The effects of the Fort Pillow massacre can easily be exaggerated. Although capturing the interest of the nation, how much influence did it actually have? Mistreatment of black soldiers was certainly not limited to this theater of the war or to Nathan Bedford Forrest. It was pervasive from Virginia to Arkansas. Moreover, even though the Northern newspapers extensively reported the event, what did Northerners really think about the massacre? After all, they were not without their share of racism and prejudice. We have to ask if the war in this theater would have turned out differently if there had not been a Fort Pillow. Of course, speculation is a dangerous endeavor, but this question shows that Fort Pillow's full and exact impact is clearly immeasurable.

It did make its mark, however. The attention Forrest received was detrimental because stealth was his livelihood. It created a focus on him that could not have been comfortable. It further incited and motivated the black troops which, in turn, increasingly angered the Confederates. Casualties were heavy as a result. Indeed, John Hubbard, who was in Forrest's cavalry, admitted after the Memphis raid in August that their lines were "becoming shorter."[59]

It also affected the recruitment of black troops. In Missouri, for instance, General William A. Pile reported on May 21, 1864, that enlistment of blacks had "nearly ceased" with only two hundred men reporting in the previous month. He explained that potential black soldiers were looking forward to the farming season and were deterred by the affair at Fort Pillow in April.[60]

The U.S.C.T. emerged from the spring and summer of 1864 as professional, seasoned fighters. They gained fighting experience at Brice's Crossroads and Tupelo and, as at Fort Wagner, South Carolina, these battles proved that black men were indeed able combatants. Soldiers of the U.S.C.T. further confirmed this at the Battle of Nashville where they helped drive John Bell Hood's army from Overton Hill on December 16, 1864. They comprised 15.9 per cent of the front line attackers at Nashville and played a vital role in the victory.[61] Indicative of the Union's increasing confidence in black men, the U.S.C.T. regiments fought on the front lines with their white comrades at the Battle of Nashville; months earlier, at Brice's Crossroads and Tupelo, they had guarded supply trains. Confirming the U.S.C.T.'s resolve, Union General George H. Thomas, the "Rock of Chickamauga," confidently declared, "Gentlemen, negroes will fight."[62]

From the summer of 1864 to the end of the war, the United States Colored Troops compiled a courageous and distinguished record of combat in their battles in Mississippi, Alabama, and Tennessee.

*This article first appeared in the Summer 1995 issue of the* Tennessee Historical Quarterly.

1. This summary of the battle follows those presented in several different accounts. See Charles W. Anderson, "The True Story of Fort Pillow," *Confederate Veteran* 3 (January 1895): 322–326; Robert Selph Henry, *First With the Most: Forrest* (New York, 1991), 248–262; Albert Castel, "Fort Pillow: A Fresh Examination of the Evidence," *Civil War History* 4 (1958): 37–50; John Allan Wyeth, *That Devil Forrest: The Life of General Nathan Bedford Forrest* (New York, 1959), 299–341. For further information on Fort Pillow, consult Lonnie E. Maness, "The Fort Pillow Massacre: Fact or Fiction?" *Tennessee Historical Quarterly* 45 (Spring 1986): 287–315; Charles Robinson, "The Fort Pillow 'Massacre': Observations of a Minnesotan," *Minnesota History*; 43 (Spring 1973): 186–190; John Cimprich and Robert C. Mainfort, "The Fort Pillow Massacre: A Statistical Note," *Journal of American History* 76 (December 1989): 830–837; Ibid., "Fort Pillow Revisited: New Evidence about an Old Controversy," *Civil War History* 28 (December 1982): 293–306; John L. Jordan, "Was There a Massacre at Fort Pillow?" *Tennessee Historical Quarterly* 6 (1947): 99–133.

2. Bradford assumed command after the original commander, Major L.F. Booth, was killed in the initial attack. It should be noted that this was not the Confederates' first encounter with black troops. In the Battle of Moscow, Tennessee, on 3–4 December 1863, Confederate cavalry had a sharp skirmish with the Sixty-First Colored Regiment and the Second West Tennessee Memphis Light Artillery of African Descent. The black troops fought well despite their inexperience. See Bobby Lee Lovett, "West Tennessee Colored Troops in Civil War Combat," West Tennessee Historical Society *Papers* 34 (October 1980): 53–70; L.D. Bejach, "Documents and Brief Notes: The Battle of Moscow, Tennessee," West Tennessee Historical Society *Papers* 27 (1973): 108–112.

3. Joseph T. Glatthaar, *Forged in Battle: The Civil War Alliance of Black Soldiers and White Officers* (New York, 1990), 156.

4. *New York Times*, 17–20 April 1864.

5. They printed the same descriptions given in the *Times*; *New York Herald*, 16–23 April 1864; *New York Tribune*, 16–20 April 1864.

6. *New York Herald*, 17 April 1864.

7. *New York Tribune*, 23 April 1864.

8. Bobby Lee Lovett, "The Negro in Tennessee, 1861–1866: A Socio-Military History of the Civil War Era" (PhD diss., University of Arkansas, 1978), 64; Jack Hurst, *Nathan Bedford Forrest: A Biography* (New York, 1993), 178–179; (Washington) *Daily National Intelligencer*, 18–23 April 1864.

9. United States Congress, *Biographical Directory of the United States Congress: 1774–1989* (Washington, 1989), 1071.

10. Ibid., 1989.

11. H.. L. Trefousse, *Benjamin Franklin Wade: Radical Republican from Ohio* (New York,. 1963), 214–217, 316.

12. Congress, Senate, Joint Committee on the Conduct of the War, *Fort Pillow Massacre* (Washington, 1864), 1–27.

13. Ibid., Testimony of Jacob Thompson, 30. For a more extensive critique of the Joint Committee's report, consult Robert Selph Henry, *First With the Most: Forrest*, 259–268.

14. Joint Committee, *Fort Pillow*, 32.

15. *Daily National Intelligencer*, 23 April 1864. This account, it should be pointed out, was given by the *Intelligencer* after it had already printed descriptions of the battle that laid the blame with Forrest.

16. Gideon Welles, *The Diary of Gideon Welles: Secretary of the Navy under Lincoln and Johnson*, with an introduction by John T. Morse, Jr., Vol. 2 (New York, 1911), 23.

17. Hudson Strode, *Jefferson Davis: Tragic Hero, The Last Twenty-Five Years: 1864–1889* (New York, 1964), 29.

18. Edwin M. Stanton to President Lincoln, 5 May 1864, War Department, *War of the Rebellion: A Compilation of the Official Records of the Union and Confederate Armies* (Washington, 1890–1901) 7, ser. 2, 113. Hereafter cited as OR.

19. Joe H. Mays, *Black Americans and Their Contributions Toward Union Victory in the American Civil War, 1861–1865* (Lanham, Md., 1984), 34.

20. *Diary of Gideon Welles*, 24.

21. Dudley Taylor Cornish, *The Sable Arm: Negro Troops in the Union Army, 1861–1865* (New York, 1956), 176..

22. *Diary of Gideon Welles*, 24–25.

23. OR, Report of Nathan Bedford Forrest on Fort Pillow, 15 April 1864, 32, ser. 1, pt. 1, 609–611.

24. OR, Report of Gen. James R. Chalmers on Fort Pillow, 20 April1864, 32, ser. 1, pt. 1, 623 .

25. In correspondence after the Battle of Brice's Crossroads, or Tishomingo Creek, General Cadwallader C. Washburn, the commander of the Union army in Memphis, admitted that such an oath was taken although not in the presence of the Union commander. See OR, Washburn to Forrest, 19 June 1864, 32, ser. 1, pt. 1, 588–589; Ibid., Forrest to Washburn, 14 June 1864, 586.

26. Reverend Samuel A. Agnew, "Battle of Tishomingo Creek," *Confederate Veteran* 8 (1900): 402; Robert Selph Henry, ed., *As They Saw Forrest: Some Recollections and Comments of Contemporaries* (Jackson, Tenn., 1956), 134.

27. Edwin C. Bearss, *Forrest at Brice's Crossroads and in Northern Mississippi in 1864* (Dayton, 1979), 143; Glatthaar, *Forged in Battle*, 165; Report of Colonel Edward Bouton, 17 June 1864, OR, ser. 1, pt. 1, 127.

28. OR, Report of Colonel Edward Bouton, 17 June 1864, 39, ser.l, pt.l, 127.

29. Joseph T. Wilson, *The Black Phalanx* (New York, 1968), 362–364.

30. OR, Report of Colonel Edward Bouton, 17 June 1864, 39, ser. 1, pt. 1, 127; Wilson, *Black Phalanx*, 365.

31. Henry Ewell Hord, "Brice's Crossroads from a Private's View," *Confederate Veteran* 12 (1904): 529; Henry, ed., *As They Saw Forrest*, 124.

32. Robert Cowden, *A Brief Sketch of the Organization and Services of the Fifty-Ninth Regiment of the United States Colored Infantry, and Biographical Sketches* (Dayton, 1883; reprint, Freeport, N.Y., 1971), 47; The Fifty-Fifth and Fifty-Ninth regiments had seen some action at the Wolf River and on Big Hill, Tennessee. See Lovett, "The West Tennessee Colored Troops," 61–62. 33Agnew, "Tishomingo Creek," 402.

33. Agnew, "Tishomingo Creek," 402.

34. Henry, *As They Saw Forrest*, 134.

35. Wilson, *Black Phalanx*, 348–349.

36. Henry, *As They Saw Forrest*, 124.

37. OR, Forrest to Washburn, 14 June 1964, 32, ser.l, pt.l, 586–587.

38. OR, Washburn to General Stephen D. Lee, l7 June 1864,32, ser.l, pt.1, 587–588.

39. Ibid., 587.

40. Ibid., 586–589.

41. OR, Forrest to Washburn, 25 June 1864, 32, ser.l, pt.l, 590.

42. OR, Forrest to Washburn, 23 June 1864, 32, ser.l, pt.1, 591–593.

43. Morris J. Macgregor and Bernard C. Nalty, eds., *Blacks in the United States Armed Forces: Basic Documents*, Vol. 2, in *Civil War and Emancipation* (Wilmington, Del., 1977), 196–197

44. Mays, *Black Americans*, 32.

45. Dunbar Rowland, ed., *Jefferson Davis: Constitutionalist: His Letters, Papers, and Speeches*, 6 (Jackson, Miss., 1923), Davis to General Leonidas Polk, 22 April1864, 233; OR, General Dabney H. Maury to General Cooper [regarding Fort Pillow prisoners], 20 May 1864, 7, ser.3, 155; Lovett, "Negro in Tennessee," 89.

46. OR, Report of Colonel Edward Bouton, 25 July 1864, 39, pt.l, ser.l, 300.

47. Recollection of John Milton Hubbard in Henry, *As They Saw Forrest*, 175.

48. Bearss, *Forrest at Brice's Crossroads*, 185–189.

49. OR, Report of Colonel Edward Bouton on the Tupelo Campaign, 25 July 1864, 39, ser.l, pt.l, 301–303.

50. OR, Report of Andrew J. Smith on the Tupelo Campaign, 5 August 1864, 39, ser.l, pt.l, 253.

51. The U.S.C.T. also saw some action on 21 August 1864, when Forrest raided Memphis. After the initial shock of the dawn attack wore off, the black soldiers, like those in the Sixty-First U.S.C.T., aided their white comrades in driving the Confederates from the city. This attack forced General A.J. Smith to return from his foray into northern Mississippi, but ended as another example of Forrest's audacity. See OR, Reports, August 1864, 39, ser.l, pt.l, 468–484; Juan Rayner, "An Eyewitness Account of Forrest's Raid on Memphis," West Tennessee Historical Society *Papers* 12 (1958): 134–37; Jack D.L. Holmes, "Forrest's 1864 Raid on Memphis," *Tennessee Historical Quarterly* 18 (1959): 295–321.

52. OR, Report of Colonel Wallace Campbell on the Battle of Athens, 24 November 1864, 39, ser. 1, pt. 1, 520–523.

53. Hondon B. Hargrove, *Black Union Soldiers in the Civil War* (London, 1988), 191.

54. OR,, Report of Lieutenant J.D. Hazard, 17 October 1864, 39, ser.l, pt.l, 525.

55. James M. McPherson, *The Negro's Civil War: How American Negroes Felt and Acted During the War for the Union* (New York, 1965), 231.

56. Lovett, "Negro in Tennessee," 83–84; Lovett, "West Tennessee," 53, 70.

57. Hurst, *Nathan Bedford Forrest*, 198; O.R., W.T. Sherman to Edwin M. Stanton, 15 June 1864, 39, ser.l, pt.2, 121.

58. *New York Times*, 30 October 1877.

59. Henry, *As They Saw Forrest*, 189.

60. Report from General William A. Pile to Adjutant General Lorenzo Thomas, 21 May 1864, in Ira Berlin, Joseph P. Reidy, and Leslie S. Rowland, eds., *Freedom: A Documentanl History of Emancipation: 1861–1867: Series 2: The Black Military Experience*, (Cambridge, 1982), 251.

61. Lovett, "Negro in Tennessee," 95–109.

62. Hargrove, *Black Union Soldiers*, 193.

# MEMPHIS RIOTS:

## White Reaction to Blacks Memphis, May 1865–July 1866

### Bobby L. Lovett

The bloodiest reaction to black freedom and the quest for racial equality during Reconstruction occurred in Memphis, Tennessee, on May 1–2, 1866. White citizens went on a rampage and tried to destroy the new black community of South Memphis. This riot, which caused considerable loss of black life and property, was the result of a demographic revolution imposed upon Memphis by events of the Civil War. Moreover, the abrupt change in race relationships induced volatile racial friction in Memphis. Yet, the destructive riot turned out to be somewhat constructive in that it gave the Radical Republicans the excuse to assume control of Reconstruction from President Andrew Johnson. In addition, the riots helped convince national and state Republicans to pass protective civil rights legislation and citizenship for blacks.

The increase of enough blacks in Memphis to constitute for the first time a black community was the result of a demographic revolution. South Memphis, which had been created as a result of thousands of slaves and free blacks pouring into the area near Fort Pickering during the Civil War, was where the Army's Freedmen Department under John Eaton of Ohio had located two contraband camps, Fiske and Shiloh. Contraband Camp Dixie, holding over 2,000 fugitive slaves, was built upon President's Island west of the fort in 1863. Moreover, a small contraband camp was placed in North Memphis (Chelsea) in 1864. By 1865, lands in these camps were being leased or sold to the Negroes by former owners or by the Treasury Department in lieu of federal taxes.

The normal pattern for town slaves and free blacks up until Memphis fell to Union forces in 1862 was that "blacks lived in little patches within a perimeter of whites."[1] The high concentrations of blacks in former contraband camp areas violated this antebellum demographic pattern. Thus South Memphis in particular allowed its black residents a measure of freedom and cover from watchful white eyes not before enjoyed by slave or free black. Inevitably, conflict would rise between an expanded white urban population and a new black urban population.

The overnight growth of black residents in Memphis took white residents by surprise. Many white residents had fled when Memphis fell in June 1862, only to return from their Confederate havens in Mississippi and elsewhere during 1865 to find that the city's black population had increased from 3,882 to 10,995, according to a city council census. That census was quickly surpassed when the Memphis Freedmen's Bureau took its own census in August 1865 counting 16,509 blacks out of 27,703 residents.[2] Needless to say, it seemed to whites, that blacks intended to take over the city. Moreover, the majority of blacks lived outside of city jurisdiction, where they were not subject to Memphis's notorious black laws, and could do as they pleased notwithstanding state black codes.

Add to this social and demographic setting the factor that hatred of blacks and northerners was intense in Memphis in 1865, because the white residents were bitter over the results of the war and the occupation of their city by Union forces, especially black soldiers, and the result is a volatile concoction for riot or revolution. Confederate flags defiantly outnumbered American flags on display throughout the city. And southerners insulted white Yankees, black Yankees, and freedmen alike.

Was it not safer for southerners to focus their pent-up bitterness and frustration upon the symbol of defeat—the freed slaves in South Memphis—than upon the mighty white Yankee? One white refugee, Elizabeth Avery Meriwether, wrote down her reactions to the hordes of blacks found in Memphis upon her return:

> Negro squatters were everywhere. As we drew near Memphis the farm houses on the road side had been either deserted or burned to the ground. Some of the troops were black. They spoke no word to me, I spoke no word to them; their black faces and blue uniforms frightened me. In those days, just after the war, we did not know what the Yankees meant to do to the crushed and conquered Confederate soldiers. Those Negroes were armed; they would get leaves of absences; they could walk from Fort Pickering to Ridgeway in half an hour; no friends or neighbors were near me. Can you wonder, my children, that I was

uneasy? During my walks from one shop to another I sometimes had to get off the sidewalk into the street in order to make way for these Negro soldiers—they walked four and five abreast and made not the slightest effort to let white women pass. Sometimes one of them would say: "We's all ekal now. Git out o' our way, white woman." Any stranger seeing those Negroes would have supposed the blacks not whites were masters in the South.[3]

To Meriwether, and to other whites, it was unbearable to have former slaves shame and humiliate southerners right in front of Yankees. Meriwether even went to the point of trying to evict black squatters from her land, but five black soldiers came to protect the blacks and to tell her that blacks had "a right to this bandoned land"—her front yard. Such clash of Negro defiance with southern whites' attempt to reassert white social supremacy daily intensified the worsening racial climate in Memphis.

The summation of daily racial incidents, rumors, and newspaper accounts led whites to conclude that blacks were violating every southern black code imaginable—and it did not matter that most of these codes were now null and void.[4] Although Memphis and the State of Tennessee prohibited black education, by late 1865 Memphis blacks had twenty-two schools with 1,101 pupils in daily attendance, not including 1,549 black soldiers attending regimental schools at Fort Pickering.[5] Black soldiers and free black officers and leaders organized civil rights and suffrage movements, and sent a "Shelby County Delegation" to the October 1865 State Colored Men's Convention at Nashville's St. John A.M.E. Church. One of these delegates, Sergeant Henry Maxwell of Fort Pickering's despised Third United States Colored Artillery Regiment—the regiment assigned to patrol the streets and arrest white or black—gave a fiery keynote address that angered whites; in part, Sergeant Maxwell said:

> We came here for principles, and there will be no discension [sic]. We want the rights guaranteed by the Infinite Architect. For these rights we labor. For them we will die. We have gained one; the uniform is its badge. We want two more boxes besides the cartridge box—the ballot and the jury box. We shall gain them.[6]

For whites, this was going too far. For even interracial courtship and marriage were rumored to have taken place in black South Memphis.

The new black community became not only a social and political threat to white supremacy, but an economic threat as well. Although one-third or more of the blacks were unemployed and living off Freedmen's Bureau rations, what meager economic progress Negroes made in Memphis caused whites great alarm. Whites feared any expansion of independent black economics because black hack drivers, teamsters, skilled craftsmen, and ordinary laborers were already depriving whites of jobs. Moreover, the Union had dared to establish the Freedmen's Savings and Trust Company Bank on Beale Street in December 1865. Blacks like Buck Fuller, a drayman, Henry Gerry, a painter, Julius Nelson, a laborer, and Turner Hunt, a carpenter, took out accounts in the new bank, thereby demonstrating new wealth accumulating in the black community.[7]

Memphis authorities reacted by arresting Robert Church for keeping a saloon on DeSoto Street—a violation of the black codes. However, the newly re-established state courts, dominated by Republicans, overturned that conviction in the case of *Church* v. *State of Tennessee* (1866) on the grounds that the black codes were now null and void.[8] Church, who became an early twentieth century millionaire, was part of the Memphis black community's efforts to pressure the legislature into repealing the black codes that prevented black enterprise; they even sent a petition to the legislature regarding the matter.

By the early part of 1866, Memphis blacks had eight churches, 500 Negro-owned hacks, eight stores, several saloons, two fruit stands, two furniture stores, four lunchrooms, and enough barbershops to organize the Memphis Colored Barbers' Association. According to the Freedmen's Bureau Census of 1865, Memphis had 300 blacks worth $100–$500 in money and properties, eighteen blacks worth $500–$1000, four blacks worth $2,000 or more, and three blacks worth $5,000 or more.[9]

In light of the depressed economic conditions in 1865 and 1866, the many white refugees in the city, and thousands of Irish immigrants looking for employment opportunities, certainly the black economic advancement was deeply resented by the whites. Paradoxically, without regard to jealousy, the whites argued that freed blacks would become lazy, idle, worthless beggars unless they were relocated on the farms under white supervision.

Whites were convinced that blacks were only able to display this socio-economic defiance because of abolitionist Yankee help. Indeed, many northern organizations had come to Memphis to aid blacks, including the Chicago Sanitary Commission, the Boston American Tract Society, Cincinnati's American Missionary Association, New York's United Christian Commission, the Western Freedmen's Aid Commission of Ohio, and the Baptist Home Missionary Society of New York. Moreover, the

Freedmen's Bureau had come to town in 1865 to establish hospitals, schools, banks, orphan's homes, and labor contracts for the despised blacks.

As municipalities, like Memphis, regained civil control of government in 1865 and 1866, whites became bolder in striking out at these symbols of Yankee Black Republicanism. Moreover, daily newspaper accounts illustrated that this was the pattern taken by southerners all over the South during the latter part of 1865 and the early part of 1866. The citizens at Collierville, just east of Memphis, forced two black Memphis soldiers off a passenger train, and lynched one of them for shooting a white man who had pulled a gun and demanded the soldiers' seats. It soon became frequent that newspapers reported as much as forty-nine percent of daily Memphis police arrests were Negroes.[10] One respectable Negro gentleman was abused and fined for carrying a pistol after his life was threatened for daring to write a letter to the Nashville *Colored Tennessean* protesting the treatment of the black community by police and city authorities.[11] As more and more freedmen reported such abuses to the Freedmen's Bureau, it became apparent that a southern campaign had begun to force the Negro to leave Memphis or submit to white supremacy.

However, when blacks refused to be pushed, cursed, beaten, and outraged, the whites became bewildered. It took some time for whites to realize that the country slave's docility had been transformed by the city into arrogant defiance. Although he normally performed the role of Sambo to his day-time employers, to other whites on the streets he became sassy and belligerent. Thus by May 1865, the increased friction between black and white had reached the point of combustion.

Not until the arrival of a new post commander, General John E. Smith, in May 1865, did the army and the Freedmen's Bureau attempt to do anything significant about the dangerous racial situation in Memphis. General Smith quickly recognized the volatile nature of the situation. Military rule was soon to be replaced by restoration of civil government in Memphis.[12] General Smith communicated to the commander of the Union Army of Tennessee, General George H. Thomas at Nashville, that "the Negro must be held responsible to honor contracts with employers, and both races need yet to be controlled by the strong arm of federal authority."[13] Apparently, Smith had already consulted with the Freedmen's Bureau, which convinced him that placing blacks on plantations would reduce black-white friction.

Smith and Memphis Freedmen's Bureau superintendent General Davis Tillson organized a relocation program to force 6,000 unemployed blacks to work on West Tennessee, northern Mississippi, and eastern Arkansas plantations. Their efforts were endorsed by General Clinton B. Fisk, assistant commissioner of the bureau for Tennessee and Kentucky, who assured moderate whites "that your city will not be disgraced by the presence of a single black vagrant. Surplus blacks will be relocated in the countryside." As massive arrests commenced throughout the city, the Freedmen's Courts fined blacks for the least offence: selling cotton without a license, driving a hack on the sidewalk, disorderly conduct, fighting, stealing, cursing, and beating one's wife. Those who could not pay the fine were sent to work for whoever paid the fine, like a white farmer. Some bureau agents were accused of taking bribes from disloyal whites in order to hire out black prisoners. One black family was sent to Missouri to work on a plantation for a mere $15 fine.[14]

Black leaders and black soldiers resented this treatment of their people. William B. Scott, editor of Nashville's *Colored Tennessean*, said in an editorial on August 12, 1865, that the Freedmen's Courts should be dismantled because they violated the dignity and rights of blacks. A delegation of Memphis blacks registered a protest at Tillson's office, and convinced him to stop indiscriminate arrests of blacks in return for helping him to convince "idle, vagrant, and worthless blacks" to leave the city.[15] However, repeated abuses of blacks by police and soldiers caused a black delegation to present other lists of grievances to the bureau on Madison Street almost monthly and until just five days prior to the outbreak of the May 1866 riot.[16]

Because the black troops resented seeing their people, former slaves just like themselves, being shipped by trains and steamers to some former Rebel's plantation, they went about the city and told blacks to disregard the white man's order. Tillson quickly protested to General Smith, "Colored Soldiers interfere with their labors and tell free people that the statements made to them by [white] soldiers sent for the purpose are false, thereby embarrassing the operations of the Bureau...."[17] Smith ordered the black soldiers to cease interference with the relocation program. However, the black troops became more defiant and proceeded to interfere with police arrests of blacks, refused to arrest and transport black vagrants to the Memphis and Charleston Railroad Depot for shipment out of the city, arrested some white vagrants, and boasted openly that more black people would soon come into the city around Christmas time. Some black soldiers broke the ribs of one sassy white man, Thomas Betts, causing the *Memphis Argus* and the *Avalanche* to accuse colored troops of numerous crimes and atrocities against white citizens.[18]

In November and December 1865, some whites embellished the rumor that "Negro troops were overheard to say that as soon as enough blacks came into the city, probably around Christmas time, they would carry out a plot to take control of the city." Actually, the black arrivals were the result of white Mississippi militia attempts to disarm Negroes just below Memphis, because they feared a "Negro rebellion around Christmas time" too. The *Natchez Courier* in December 1865 said, "The Negroes are evidently preparing something and it behooves us to be on the alert and prepare for the worst." Moreover, the approach of Christmas and the off-season for farming brought trainloads of ragged—but dressed in their Sunday-best—blacks into town to shop and visit. Smith was unaware of this tradition; so he telegraphed Nashville for additional "white troops." He said, "The reason for this request is that the citizens of Memphis have become alarmed by the fear that an insurrection impends among the colored people, encouraged by the colored soldiers." When the rebellion did not occur, Smith blamed the *Avalanche* and other racists for "exaggerating affairs here."[19]

Nonetheless, Smith believed that replacement of black troops with white troops would bring peace to Memphis. He recommended that the Eighty-Eighth U.S. Colored Regiment and the Second U.S. Colored Light Artillery be consolidated with the Third U.S. Colored Heavy Artillery Regiment. He suggested that the hated white officers of the disbanded black regiments be dismissed from service. The prompt approval of these requests in December left only the Third U.S.C.H.A. and a company of the Sixteenth U.S. Regulars (whites) mounted. Still, General Smith had to rely on blacks for manpower and patrol duty.[20]

For this reason, Smith attempted to understand the feelings and concerns of his black garrison. In January 1866, he began to defend his men:

> In reference to the habitual conduct of colored soldiers upon the streets of this city, the statements of the *Argus* are undoubtedly prejudiced and false. Investigation develops the fact that provocations are frequently given the colored soldiers and resented by them. Their general deportment has been respectful and orderly. The fact cannot be concealed that the Negro soldiers, the Freedmen's Bureau, and the political freedom of the black are new conditions repugnant to the ancient prejudice of the South.[21]

General Smith arrested a city policeman for shooting a Negro man for allegedly trying to escape arrest. Smith now had realized that "there is a group of people in Memphis who are moved to provoke an outbreak among the colored people; the police force of the city is mostly Irish who are animated by a peculiar hatred and jealousy of the colored people."[22] The general's radical move was designed to stop the "use of arms and violence to effect the release of the colored prisoner," by the colored troops.

General Smith took further steps to bring the racial situation in Memphis under control. He imposed a curfew upon all black troops. He visited the barracks at night, and rode through the South Memphis saloon district to arrest any curfew violators. When these measures failed to reduce incidences between blacks and whites, Smith prohibited all Negro balls, dances, and fairs. This measure caused such loud black protest until General Tillson of the Freedmen's Bureau went to Smith in behalf of the black delegation to ask the general to lift the prohibition; however, Smith refused.[23] These measures by Smith brought more anger and defiance than discipline from the black soldiers and citizens in South Memphis.

To make matters worse, conflicts between Irish and black residents of Memphis began to come out into the open after being hidden for years during slavery times. It was not uncommon for slave masters to hire the Irish to perform tasks too dangerous to risk prime slave hands. Former slave Thomas Bradshaw said, "There were Irish draymen and colored draymen before the war; the Irish did not take the same privileges with the colored men at that time as they do now, because the owners would take a stick and maul them." Prince Moultrie, former slave and resident of the city of Memphis for ten years, said of Irishmen, "I think he is very much below me."[24] Irishmen viewed Negro teamsters, cooks, maids, and laborers as economic competitors who impeded the rise of their people to an economic status equal to that of other whites. The war had offered them a golden opportunity in Memphis, but the black soldiers were still the last obstacle to their taking over the city. Because most Rebel whites had been disfranchised, the Irish voters controlled the new elections in 1865. Irishman John Parks became the new mayor. The Irish took 167 of the 180 police positions and forty-two of forty-six fire station jobs.[25]

Both policemen and firemen prayed for the day when the last of the black soldiers would be disarmed and mustered out of military service. The hated Negro could then be put in his proper place and learn to treat Irishmen like regular white folk. And so it was that by April 1866, the racial problem in Memphis had many faces: the Negro opposed to the Bureau of Freedmen; the Negro migrant in conflict with the older, more established white residents of the city; immigrants and Irishmen against black soldiers and workers.

To make matters worse, General Smith was relieved by General George Stoneman on April 30, which caused the loss of continuity of control of the racial situation in Memphis. Stoneman made the mistake of giving the impression that he would maintain a *laissez faire* policy toward the civil government's dealings with the colored people. It took strong persuasion to wake General Stoneman to the fact that white racial campaigns were disguises for anti-Yankee and anti-Union campaigns. White attacks on the vulnerable Negro was simply psychological compensation for the southerner's inability to attack the mighty Yankee. Stoneman's visits into the city revealed American flags flying over a few places: the Freedmen's Bureau and related buildings, John Eaton's *Memphis Evening Post* building, the military facilities, and some black schools. Respectable citizens shunned him and his officers, and refused to invite them to social gatherings. The flag, the Union Army, and the Freedmen's Bureau were all associated with the hated Negro of South Memphis. Not until whites stood up and booed the flag at a local theatre did Stoneman become angry enough to react; he threatened to close down the place and arrest any person who displayed hostile actions toward the Union or Stars and Stripes.

It was the trend in late 1865, after the South's bitter defeat, for Southern whites to openly vent hatred and resentment against the Negro and the Union. In the military departments of Arkansas, Mississippi, and West Tennessee, commanders had to issue orders for the arrest of any person, man or woman, who displayed disrespect and open defiance for the Union and its symbols. However, whites boldly violated these orders in regard to the Negro. The *Memphis Argus* on April 29, 1866, said, "Would to God they were back in Africa, or some other seaport town—anywhere but here; they are a perfect nuisance, and forfeit all the regard that humanity can offer them in their present condition." The *Argus* on May 1, 1866, even accused the Freedmen's Bureau of making a fortune "selling marriage certificates to poor deluded blacks" od South Memphis. Actually the Bureau only charged a five cent fee for marriage certificates. Both the *Argus* and *Avalanche* resorted to sensational headlines to invoke racial hatred against blacks. One headline read "Cincinnati White Woman in Love with a Nashville Barber;" another read "Riots against Negroes Break Out in Norfolk and Richmond, White Youths Fire on Negro Civil Rights Parade."

In this environment of anarchism, the policemen of Memphis invoked a campaign of revenge against the blacks of Memphis. It is obvious they felt their self-styled terrorism would be questioned by no authority outside of city government—a government controlled by their countrymen. In this manner, the riot was conspiratorial in nature.[26]

April 30, 1866, was the day set by the war department for all of the remaining black regiments in Tennessee to muster out, including the Forty-Fourth Colored Infantry of Chattanooga, the Sixteenth Colored Infantry of Knoxville, and the Third United States Colored Heavy Artillery (U.S.C.H.A.) of Memphis. The latter regiment staged two elaborate dress parades at Fort Pickering where they received praise from the *Memphis Post* and black people.[27]

On the following day, Tuesday, May 1, most of the black troops were given their final pay, except for back-pay and bonuses. Except for some 150 black soldiers who remained at the fort waiting for such monies, the rest established homes in South

Memphis or took advantage of free government train transportation to return to their homes in other counties or nearby states. A few small gangs of black soldiers left the fort during the late morning hours and went into South Memphis's redlight district near Fourth and South streets. Having nothing else to do, these men, joined by many women and children, hung around the corner, drank whiskey, joked, sang, and in general tried to impress their black spectators.

This black celebration was spoiled when a small ragged squad of Memphis policemen appeared on the opposite side of South Street. At the sight of their hated enemy, the soldiers led the crowd in giving "Three cheers for Ole Abe Lincoln, the Great Emancipator." One of the policemen frowned and shouted nasty obscenities, including "Your father Abe Lincoln is dead and damned."[28] The black soldiers, mostly former slaves, defiantly returned the insults with insults: "Po white trash"; "You damned po buckaroos." Just as the blacks appeared to win the verbal battle against the ill-educated Irishmen, the policemen proposed to find a certain "damned nigger" who the day before had been involved in a jostle with four law officers, but had escaped into the safe environment of South Memphis, when some soldiers hit one of the policemen over the head and freed the prisoner. Unaware that the black troops had decided to take some action the next time those "po' boys beat on a nigger in South Memphis, the police, described by contemporaries as "loafers, drunkards, burglars, plunderers, robbers, and murderers," crossed South Street under the rule of "hot pursuit" and waded into the crowd of Negroes to arrest two black fellows.[29] The blacks were temporarily at a loss as to what to do about this insane act of boldness.

However, when the policemen started toward Memphis with their black prisoners, the black crowd, including women and children, became loud and trailed the police down to Causey Street. Apparently satisfied that the prisoners would not suffer police brutality, the crowd turned back to South Memphis; but during the calm before the storm, a thunderbolt struck. A black fellow, who had followed and observed the police closely, came running and exclaiming that the Irishmen had shot one of the black men. Black anger turned to hostile action. The crowd took off after the whites; soldiers pulled concealed pistols and fired into the air, causing the police to return the fire point blank. The blacks retreated.

It seemed that things were about to quiet down once more when another black came to inform the crowd that they had wounded one of those "po' white buckaroos." Encouraged by this, the blacks gathered their forces once more and continued the pursuit. It is not known whether the blacks shot the policeman or whether the policemen wounded their own man in the confusion. Nonetheless, the black crowd caused the frightened police to scatter in their attempt to get back into Memphis under the principle of every man for himself. Samuel Van Pelt, a black South Memphis resident, heard the commotion and came onto his porch on Hernando Road to see black soldiers and young boys chasing a lone white man while hollering: "Halloa, stop that white son-of-a-bitch."[30] Somehow, the whites, including two wounded, made it back into downtown Memphis in less than an hour-about 4:45 p.m.

At this point the incident took the form of a race riot. Black residents shut themselves in their homes. Black soldiers went toward the fort to get more arms, though the commander refused to issue any. Desperate and disposed to carry the contest to the bitter end, the blacks rounded up what arms were available in the black community. The county sheriff and city police decided to form a joint posse of 100 whites, and proceed toward South Memphis by 5:30 p.m. Using sticks, brickbats, and guns, the "posse" beat the heads of Negroes they met on the streets en route to the scene of the fight. Finding no black soldiers at Fourth and South Streets, the "posse" turned west toward the Mississippi River, where some black soldiers were sighted coming from the fort. The sheriff shouted for the blacks to surrender; the blacks refused.

Shooting erupted on both sides. Scattered skirmishes raged back and forth amongst the shanties and homes of South Memphis. The well-trained black troops were joined by other veterans who soon took the offensive. In order to avoid being cut off from any possible retreat, the whites moved to the east toward Morris Cemetery; but before they could get back to South Street by crossing the bridge, more black soldiers poured out of the fort, moved to the east, and began to successfully flank the inexperienced whites. It was evident that very few Confederate veterans were present at this point. A fireman, Henry Dunn, was hit and killed immediately as the whites fought intensely to cross South Street bridge. The blacks followed, crossing the bridge and pressing the whites all the way into Memphis up to the Second Presbyterian Church at Beale and Main Streets. But a mounted company of the Sixteenth United States Regular Infantry arrived to reinforce the "posse" and drive the blacks back toward the fort. The white soldiers ordered the blacks to disarm and go to their barracks within the fort.[31] The time was 9:00 o'clock.

Meanwhile, the defeated whites licked their wounds, their anger welled, and they retaliated by shooting in cold blood two black prisoners.[32] They shouted that they were going to go into Memphis and "kill the last damned one of the nigger race, and burn up the cradle, God damn them."[33] Reinforced by all sorts of ruffians and rabble, the "posse" headed back into South Memphis around 10:00 o'clock that night.

This mob hit South Memphis like a storm, broke into small groups, and fanned out through the black homes while carrying torches of destruction unknown even to Attila. Homes were broken into, pillaged, or burned. Women were insulted, beaten, and gang raped. One of the groups set fire to a Negro hut and permitted an invalid girl to burn alive as they stood by laughing, imitating Rebel yells, drunken with the taste of human blood. Soon the awful smell of burning flesh and fresh blood rose toward the moon. One northern missionary said, "The city was so brilliantly illuminated, the chief lights being the churches and schoolhouses of the colored people." As cries of anguish and frustration pierced the silence of the muddy Mississippi River, the U.S. Regulars arrived once more to put an end to the riot.[34] However, they too had no love for the "niggers and darkies," and so no white rioters were arrested.

Therefore, on the next morning, Wednesday, May 2, 1866, a delegation of 200 prominent black men went to Fort Pickering an hour before daybreak and requested protection or arms. General Stoneman refused, and threatened to arrest them if they did not leave the premises. Still he sent no troops to patrol the city, but Stoneman permitted Lieutenant B.F. Baker of the Third U.S.C.H.A. to go into South Memphis and round up the stray members of his regiment and bring them into the safety of the fort. Although about thirty blacks went along with Baker, some like black Sergeant Lewis Harst of Company H refused to abandon their families in South Memphis. As soon as black troops in the fort learned of the cowardly attack during their involuntary absence, they made a mad rush to break open the arms depot. The Sixteenth Regulars under Captain Thomas J. Durnin fired a volley above the heads of the blacks, and threatened to turn the fort's huge cannon upon them. Seeing that whites had no intention of permitting blacks to gain arms for killing white people, the black soldiers cooled their tempers and returned to their quarters. The officers permitted a few blacks to go up to the parapets in order to at least keep a watchful and hopeful eye toward their community to the east and south of the fort.[35]

Although things were quiet now at 9:00 in the morning some Memphis whites were determined to finish the job of running all blacks out of town. When word reached the city that black soldiers had attempted to arm themselves again, rumors were intentionally spread that the blacks of South Memphis had renewed the riot. Mobs formed quickly; thugs broke into Henry Fulsom's gunshop on Main Street, taking many guns.[36] Black workers were assaulted on the streets and in businesses. Mayor John Parks proved his incompetency to handle the matter by riding around the streets dead drunk and "making an ass of himself," said one contemporary witness.[37] And because Stoneman sent no troops to quell the new disturbance, anarchy took the place of law and order.[38]

All Union symbols became fair game to arsonists, murderers, and robbers. This drunken rabble shot two invalid blacks sitting on the porch of the Freedmen's Hospital at Main and Madison. White teachers, white officers of colored troops, and missionaries were cursed, pushed, spat upon, and threatened. When the Freedmen's Bureau superintendent went to the scene of the riots at the request of the prominent black delegation, which had been rejected by Stoneman, the whites threatened to kill him; he had to flee to the safety of Flynn House between Beale and Gayoso Streets. Stoneman sent troops to rescue him, and to prevent a mob from burning down the Republican *Post* building. Henry A. Rankin, one of the leaders of the 1865 State Colored Men's Convention and a northern missionary teacher, was struck with a horse whip as a white ruffian tried to beat the "black hide off that damned darkie"; but respectable whites prevented the man from shooting Rankin with a pistol. Although several attempts were made to burn down the main meeting place for blacks—Caldwell's Hall—neighboring whites put the fires out to prevent damages to their adjacent properties. Around 4:00 that afternoon the riot became so atrocious and barbaric that respectable whites became alarmed and former Confederate officers proposed to patrol the city. Black residents fled into the nearby woods; those not able to follow were beaten and arrested by the thousands.[39]

With no more opportunity to do some "nigger knocking," the rioters turned their attention to the funeral of one of the dead whites, Henry Dunn, an engineer for Fire Company No. 2. Dunn had lost his life fighting the soldiers near the South Street bridge the day before. He was buried in the Elmwood Cemetery. The *Memphis Daily Appeal* on May 3, 1866, commented:

> Dunn had belonged to the Crockett Rangers in the late war and was a peaceable, orderly, and good citizen, whose death will be deeply regretted by many friends. We have had too much of this lawless aggression on the part of vicious Negroes infesting South Memphis, and it is high time more strigent measures were adopted to either force them to behave themselves or leave the area.

Actually, investigation later revealed that Dunn had been shot in the back by another rioter named John Pendergast, a vicious racist who was heard to exclaim: "I have made a mistake, I thought it was a damned yellow [mulatto] nigger."[40]

In addition to the sobering effects of the funeral, several events had taken place to help bring about an end to the bloodshed. Although black troops had made another try around noon to take some arms, Captain Durnin had managed to restrain them. Durnin said, "They were pretty well excited and regretted that they had returned their arms and could not defend their homes." General Stoneman, who the night before had received a printed message from Mayor Parks requesting standby federal troops, finally came to his senses and placed the city under martial law. Rather than let Rebel officers take control of patrolling the city, Stoneman published this message:

> Gentlemen, circumstances compel the undersigned to interfere with civil affairs in the city of Memphis; it is forbidden for any person, without the authority from these headquarters to assemble together any posses, armed or unarmed, white or colored.

After Mayor Parks failed (or refused) to respond to Stoneman's written inquiries as to what was the condition of the 2,000 blacks arrested during the riot, or whether the city was able to give a guarantee that "the rights and privileges of the colored population shall be respected and protected," Stoneman sent a telegram to the army headquarters at Nashville requesting additional troops to arrive in Memphis by Saturday, May 6, 1866.[41]

Realizing that the riot would probably play into Radical Republican hands, southerners sought some consolation out of the results, and tried to place the blame upon the blacks. One woman said, "One good result of the Memphis Riot and Massacres was the improved behavior of the Negroes. Even the Negroes next door to us at No. 95 Union Street moved away to less respectable quarters."[42] The *Memphis Argus* commented on May 3, 1866, "This time there can be no mistake about it, the whole blame of this tragic and bloody riot lies as usual with the poor, ignorant, and deluded blacks." The *Argus* on May 5, 1866, said, "One of our city journals has tried to make it appear that we have been inciting this vandalism; we do not approve of these infamous deeds any more than the *Post*." The *Memphis Public Ledger* on May 3, 1866, and the *Memphis Avalanche* on May 5, blamed the situation on the use of blacks to patrol the white citizens.

This southern arrogance caused many Unionists to express desires to punish the city for damages. General Benjamin F. Runkles of the Memphis Bureau was so angry he said, "I wish that a tax will be levied upon the people of Memphis for every dollars worth of property destroyed, and every orphan, widow, or cripple they have made."[43] General Ulysses S. Grant and the Army Command at Washington debated the possibility of bringing certain white Memphians to military trial for these crimes. A Republican wrote to Governor William G. Brownlow on May 2, according to the *Nashville Daily Press and Times* of May 7, 1866, that he wished the government would "find and hang every murderer engaged in this foul business." On May 3, 1866, both the *Daily Press and Times* and the *Memphis Post* were very upset because the police had beaten many of the 2,000 arrested blacks "to a jelly."

General Clinton B. Fisk, the Assistant Commissioner for the Tennessee Freedmen's Bureau, was most disturbed about the riots. He telegraphed Freedmen's Bureau Commissioner Oliver O. Howard at Washington to relay General Stoneman's messages: "Buildings occupied by the agents of the Freedmen's Bureau have been burned down by the rabble. The preachers and teachers to the colored people are all leaving." Another Stoneman message read in part:

> I have given orders to send off all the discharged [colored] soldiers with their families who desire to leave. They have been stationed here a long time and are very much disliked by the lower classes of people whom they have had to control here.

On May 4, Fisk wrote to Howard: "I fear this is but the beginning of evil days. The Memphis press had labored faithfully and successfully in bringing about this day of wrath." Fearing that riots would spread into the countryside, Fisk sent his agents into rural areas to allay the fears of black workers in order to keep them from abandoning the new cotton crops. Heeding Howard's advice, on May 7, 1866, Fisk took the train to Memphis. He found that Stoneman had already formed an investigating commission that included Runkles of the bureau.

On May 15, Fisk ordered the fort's military prison to be readied and so "fitted up for the reception of those implicated in the late riots." Evidently, Stoneman vetoed the order. Fisk said, "I have been rather impatient to make an arrest of these leading conspirators but General Stoneman does not agree with me. General Stoneman doubts his power to convene a Military Commission for the trial of these villains." Fisk felt that a civil trial would be a farce because the chief witnesses were blacks who could not testify under law in Tennessee courts. He asked Howard if the rioters could be arraigned before the Freedmen's Courts. After that request was refused, Fisk suggested that a military receiver be appointed to collect reparations from Memphis whites. He said, "Nothing but a prompt, vigorous course under martial law will convince the people that the government is earnest in protecting the Freedmen." Apparently, the military did not agree; so nothing was done to initiate Fisk's radical measures.[44]

Naturally the lack of federal or state action against the rioters upset the leaders of the black community. On June 13, the Executive Committee of the 1865 State Colored Men's Convention called for another State Colored Men's Convention to meet in Nashville on August 11, 1866. Memphis blacks concurred and held a mini-convention at Caldwell's Hall on July 19, 1866. The mini-convention selected thirteen delegates to attend the Nashville convention. These delegates, including George King, Edward Merriweather, Berber Alexander, and Aldolphus Smith, were instructed to push for a State Equal Rights League and the black suffrage.[45]

In the meantime, national Republicans who desired to take control of Reconstruction got involved in the riot investigations. On May 22, a Joint Congressional Committee to Investigate the Memphis Riots arrived in town. The committee results showed that two whites and forty-six blacks died in the riots. Some seventy-five persons were injured, 100 persons robbed, five women raped, ninety-one homes burned, four churches burned, eight schools destroyed, and $17,000 worth of government properties stolen. Many of the dead were former black soldiers. George Cobb, Third U.S.C.H.A., Isaac Richardson and George Black also of the Third U.S.C.H.A., and James Mitchell of the Sixty-First U.S.C.T. were among the fourteen black soldiers killed. The Congressional Report was published and released by August, not for gaining sympathy for the black victims, but to show the disloyalty of President Andrew Johnson's home state, and to prove that the leader of the riots was the "Vice-President of the Johnson Club of Memphis, Tennessee."

Tennessee Republicans responded by placing the Memphis Police Department under the supervision of a new State Board of Police Commissioners. Mayor Parks, who complained that the new commission was a Radical Republican machine, was forced to relinquish control of the force. Newly hired officers were dressed in clean blue, military-style uniforms, mounted on horses, and placed under strict codes of discipline. They were not allowed to smoke, drink, gamble, and loiter on the job as the former police had done. The court under John C. Creighton, one of the most vicious of riot leaders, was replaced by a new Police Court. On Monday, July 2, 1866, the "Metropolitan Blues" marched to the *Memphis Post* building where Republican leader and editor John Eaton addressed them on principles of justice. The new force marched off under the sounds of cheers from blacks and whites and promptly arrested some Irish Democrats for vagrancy, loitering, gambling, public drunkenness, and disorderly conduct. They later arrested Parks and Creighton for "drunkenness and disorderly conduct"; Mayor Parks was escorted to his home and released, but Judge Creighton was taken to jail due to his arrogance and strong cursing.[46]

In the midst of these post-riot developments, the black community was rebuilt and given some civil rights concessions. Some 200 black carpenters were hired by the American Missionary Association, the Freedmen's Bureau, and others to rebuild schools and churches. Steamboats arrived daily with clothes and other goods from benevolent northerners. On July 4, 1866, the black community celebrated the revival of freedom by marching in the city parade—against the wishes of the Irish-controlled city government—giving a picnic at Caldwell's Hall on Third Street, chartering the steamer R.M. Bishop for an outing on President's Island (old contraband camp Dixie), and presenting a dance at Dennison's Grove on Vance Street. By the end of July, the blacks had received from the General Assembly all civil rights accorded to whites, ratification of the 14th national amendment, and the right to city services. By February 25, 1867, black suffrage for males was granted.[47]

Although the riots were over, people pondered the question, "Why did the riots occur in May 1866 and in the City of Memphis?"

Three scholarly articles have been written on the Memphis Riot, the first large scale race riot of the Reconstruction era of American history: two by Jack Holmes, "The Effects of the Memphis Race Riot of 1866," in West Tennessee Historical Society *Papers*, 12 (1958) and "The Underlying Causes of the Memphis Riot of 1866," in the *Tennessee Historical Quarterly*, 17 (1958); and one by James Ryan, "The Memphis Riots of 1866: Terror in a Black Community during Reconstruction," in *Journal of Negro History*, 62 (1977). Professor Holmes blamed the riots upon the use of black troops to patrol whites. Professor Ryan placed the blame similarly upon black soldiers, yet equally upon Mayor Parks and General Stoneman for losing control of the situation. Although correct in basic causes, both authors failed to assess the most complex cause, because they ignored the activity and reaction of the black community. This sort of historical writing has been traditional among American historians, who are unable or unwilling to view blacks as actors and initiators rather than as the object to be acted upon.

The real complex cause of the riots was the new phenomena of urban freedmen and the demographic revolution they helped to create in Memphis. Before the war, Memphis had less than 4,000 blacks, who lived among whites without being any socio-economic threat to white supremacy. However, the 16,000 post-war black residents ignored old race relationships in their attempts to assert manhood, independence, and equality. This was aided by new communities with a high concentration of blacks, such as South Memphis, which offered some sense of protection for black defiance, whereas rural blacks were constantly under the paternal control of a white landowner or the threat of white nightriders. Paradoxically, daily contact between the races magnified and personified rumors of black social rebellion. Undoubtedly, the riots became frustrated attempts to reassert white control over free blacks like before the Civil War.

Inevitably, former slaves and southern whites were bound to clash in urban centers. The rural freedmen, unlike pre-war free blacks and town slaves, had not lived directly under restrictive black codes, but only under the law of their masters. This same slave came to town expecting complete freedom, not knowing how to stay in his place, and not understanding that freedom was indeed "quasi" in regard to skin color; so his daily antics for displaying manhood and social equality angered whites. The pre-war free blacks and town slaves were aware of what it meant to be a partial citizen, but they knew it was best to gain complete citizenship and social equality through diplomatic and legal channels. However, they had no time to educate the ignorant country black to this reality.

Finally, let us dispel the myth that the black troops were solely responsible for this black arrogance and defiance that caused the riot. Because there was no real organized black leadership, except for the black soldiers, whites naturally focused the blame for the black attempts at social rebellion upon the colored troops. The African Methodist Episcopal Church was involved in the push for black equality, and the black troops mostly belonged to that church. The schools preached equality, and black troops had thirteen schools, including one taught by the black leader Henry A. Rankin. Moreover, reports in the *Avalanche*, *Appeal*, *Post*, and *Public Ledger* constantly reported crimes against whites that were attributed to black soldiers. Firstly, black troops were often blamed for crimes committed by other blacks or whites in blue uniforms. Former soldiers, government employees, and freedmen camp wards wore blue uniforms. For example, the Fifty-Fifth Colored Infantry arrived in Memphis from Vicksburg in January 1866 to await bonus monies; the Eighth Iowa Volunteers arrived in Memphis en route home on April 30, 1866.[48] Secondly, though some educated black noncommissioned officers for black regiments were leaders in the civil rights movement, most of the leaders of this movement were black ministers and free black businessmen, not black soldiers. Thirdly, the black soldier was a little better educated and disciplined than the average former slave upon the streets of Memphis.

The basic problem and cause of the riots was not black troops but urban blacks and their behavior in conflict with traditional race rules in the city. One cannot convict the blacks of misbehaving, but simply conclude that their behavior was inappropriate for the times. For even the Freedmen's Bureau, the Union Army, the Memphis Republican *Post*, and many Yankees opposed the black quest for complete social equality.

The events in South Memphis in 1865 demonstrated this well. Consider that when there were no more black troops to blame for misbehavior and arrogance, some whites continued to abuse and assault any blacks available. Between June and July 1866, for example, three blacks were murdered by whites during broad daylight in downtown Memphis, fifteen whipped in public, eight assaulted on city streets, and hundreds maltreated or fired without pay.⁴⁹ Such action was double psychological compensation for whites: first, it served to satisfy their desire to reduce the hordes of urban Negroes to a subordinate socio-economic status; secondly, it served to satisfy southerners' desire to strike back at a symbol of northern Unionism and Radical Republicanism.

*This article first appeared in the Spring 1979 issue of the* Tennessee Historical Quarterly.

1. Ronald A. Walter, "Oral History Interview with Blair T. Hunt on September 8, 1976," MS, Memphis Room, Memphis Public Libraries, Memphis.

2. Leigh D. Fraser, "Demographic Analysis of Memphis and Shelby County, Tennessee, 1820–1972," (MA thesis, Memphis State University, 1974), 9–10, 118; Shelby County Records: City of Memphis Census, 1865, Tennessee State Library and Archives (TSLA), Archives Division (AD), Nashville; Shelby County Records: City of Memphis Journal, 1865, TSLA, AD, Nashville; Davis Tillson to Clinton B. Fisk, Memphis, 18 August 1865, "Freedmen's Census of Memphis, 1865," in the U.S. Selected Records of the Tennessee Field Office of the Bureau of Refugees, Freedmen, and Abandoned Lands, 1865–1872 (hereafter quoted as BRFAL): Letters Sent by the Memphis District Office of the Superintendent, the Rental Agent, and the Sub-Assistant Commissioner or Agent, 30 June 1865–21 March 1868, part of Record Group 105, National Archives and Record Service (NARS), Washington, 1958; United States Eighth Census, 1860 (Washington, 1864).

3. Elizabeth A. Merriwether, *Recollections of 92 Years, 1824–1916* (Nashville, 1958), 164–67.

4. *A Digest of the Ordinances of the City Council of Memphis, 1826–1857* (Memphis, 1857), 123–26.

5. J. H. Cobb, *Report and Extracts Relating to Colored Schools in the Department of the Tennessee and State of Arkansas* (Memphis, 1864), Pauline L. Sneed, "The Education of the Negro in Tennessee during the Reconstruction Period." (MA thesis, Fisk University, 1945); *Extracts From Documents in the Office of the General Superintendent of Refugees and Freedmen, Memphis, Tennessee* (Memphis, 1865).

6. *Colored Tennessean*, Nashville, 12 August 1865; May 1866 missing.

7. Records of the Comptroller of the Currency: Registers of Signatures of Depositors in Branches of the Freedmen's Savings and Trust Company, 1865–1874, Memphis, Tennessee, Accounts 1–1995, 2000–6298, 28 December 1865–1 July 1874, Microcopy 24, part of Record Group 101, NARS, Washington, 1969.

8. *Nashville Dispatch*,12 July 1866, a clipping in the State Historian's Papers, Record Group 29, TSLA, AD, Nashville; *Senate Journal of the Tennessee General Assembly, 1865–1866* (Nashville, 1866 ), 656.

9. *Memphis Bulletin*, 7 January 1865; Jackie M. Thomas, "Economic and Educational Activities of the Freedmen's Bureau, 1865–1869," (MA thesis, Tennessee State University, 1960); John W. Blassingame, "The Union Army as an Educational Institution for Negroes, 1863–1865," *Journal of Negro Education*, 34 (1965), 152–66; J.W. Alvord, *Report on Schools and Finances, 1865–1866* (Washington, 1866), 18; David M. Tucker, *Black Pastors and Leaders: Memphis, 1819–1972* (Memphis, 1973); T.O. Fuller, *History of the Negro Baptists in Tennessee* (Memphis, 1936); Earle Whittington, *Centennial History of St. John's Methodist Church* (Memphis, 1960)—Collins Chapel Colored Methodist Church met in St. John's in 1865 and 1866; *Nineteenth Century Churches of Downtown Memphis* (Memphis, 1974); T.O. Fuller, *The Story of the Church Life among Negroes of Memphis* (Memphis, 1938).

10. *Memphis Argus*, 24 August 1865; Tennessee Prison Records, Military, Criminal, and Circuit Courts, 1831–1922, Record Group 25, TSLA, AD, Nashville; BRFAL: Complaint Books of the Freedmen's Court in the Memphis District, 24 July 1865–20 November 1866, NARS.

11. *Memphis Bulletin*, 13 February 1865.

12. BRFAL: List of Letters Sent by the Office of the Assistant Commissioner, Synopses, 23 November 1865–29 December 1866, vols. 8, 12, and Letters, 1 July–9 September 1865, vol. 6.

13. General J.E. Smith to General W.D. Whipple Chief of Staff for the Army of Tennessee, Memphis, 26 June 1865, Adjutant General's Office: Army of Tennessee, General Correspondence, 1865–1867, Record Group 21, TSLA, AD, Nashville; *Memphis Post*, 17 January 1866.

14. BRFAL: Letters Sent by the Office of the Assistant Commissioner for Tennessee, 2 October 1865–17 March 1866, vols. 7, 9–10, Complaint Books of the Freedmen's Court in Memphis, Letters Sent by the Office of the Assistant Commissioner for Tennessee, 17 March 1865–31 December 1866, vols. 11–14, and Letters Sent by the Office of the Chief Medical Officer for Tennessee, 26 August 1865–25 January 1869, vol. 39, NARS.

15. D. Tillson to J.E. Smith, Memphis, 26 August 1865, 29 September 1865, BRFAL: Letters Sent by the Memphis District, 1865–1868, NARS.

16. A.F. Reeves to C.B. Fisk, Memphis, 26 April 1866, Ibid.

17. D. Tillson to J.E. Smith, Memphis, 26 August 1865, Ibid.

18. Memphis BRFAL to Nashville BRFAL, Memphis, 23 May 1866, BRFAL: Reports and Affidavits Relating to Outrages and Riots, Oaths of Office, and Letters Relating to Appointments Received by the Assistant Commissioner, NARS.

19. J.E. Smith to Army of Tennessee Chief of Staff, Memphis, 9 November 1865, 31 December 1865, 23 September 1865, 9 January 1866, Adjutant General's Office: Army of Tennessee General Correspondence, TSLA.

20. J.E. Smith to Dept. of Tennessee, Memphis, 26 October 1865, Special Orders No. 165, District of Memphis HQ, 16 December 1865, Special Orders No. 320, District of West Tennessee HQ, Memphis, 29 December 1865, Ibid; 88th U.S.C.T., 2nd U.S.C.L.A., and 3rd U.S.C.H.A. in Compiled Service Records for Volunteer Units: U.S. Colored Troops, Record

Abstracts, NARS.

21. J.E. Smith to Dept. of Tennessee, Memphis, 9 January 1866, Adjutant General's Office: Army of Tennessee General Correspondence, TSLA.

22. Ibid.

23. D. Tillson to Nashville BRFAL, Memphis, 29 September 1865, A.F. Reeves to C.B. Fisk, Memphis, 26 April 1866, BRFAL: Letters Sent by the Memphis District, 1865–1868, NARS; J.E. Smith to Dept. of Tennessee, Memphis, 26, 27 January 1866, Adjutant General's Office: Army of Tennessee, TSLA.

24. Testimony of Thomas Bradshaw, U.S. Report of the Select Committee on the Memphis Riots and Massacres, 39th Congress, 1st Session, Report No. 101 (Washington, 1866).

25. *Memphis, 1819–1969: A Sesquicentennial Supplement to the Commercial Appeal*, 25 May 1969.

26. See Jack Holmes, "The Underlying Causes of the Memphis Riot of 1866," *Tennessee Historical Quarterly*, XVII (1958), 195–221, a different viewpoint.

27. The Pulaski Citizen, 16 April 1866; *Tennesseans in the Civil War: Organizations and Rosters*, 2 vols. (Nashville, 1964); *U.S. Eleventh Census: 1890 Schedules Enumerating Union Veterans of the Civil War, Tennessee*, (Washington, 1948); *The Medical and Surgical History of the War of the Rebellion*, 6 vols. (Washington, 1870); *Roll of Honor: Names of Soldiers Who Died in Defense of the American Union Interred in the National Cemetery at Memphis, Tennessee, and Chalmette, Louisiana*, vol. 21 (Washington, 1869).

28. Shelds McIlwaine, *Memphis Down in Dixie* (New York, 1948), 150; Judge J.P. Young, ed., *Standard History of Memphis, Tennessee: From a Study of the Original Sources* (Knoxville, 1912), 143–46.

29. *The Pulaski Citizen*, 4 May 1866; B. Runkles to C.B. Fisk, Memphis, 10, 23 May 1866, BRFAL: Reports and Affidavits Relating to Outrages and Riots, 1866–1868, NARS.

30. B. Runkles to C.B. Fisk, 23 Memphis 1866, Ibid; Testimony of Samuel Van Pelt, *Congressional Report* No. 101, 106–08.

31. *Paris Intelligencer*, 11 May 1866; Rev. M.E. Strieby to AMA, New York City, 21 May 1866, American Missionary Association Papers: Tennessee, Amistad Research Center, New Orleans (quoted hereafter as AMA Papers); *Riot of Memphis: Letter from the Secretary of War*, 39th Congress, 1st Session, House of Representatives, No. 122 (Washington, 1866).

32. *Memphis Argus*, 2 May 1866; *Memphis Post*, 2 July 1866.

33. *Memphis Post*, 2 July 1866, Young, *Standard History of Memphis*, 143–46; *Trace of Interior Crest of Fort Pickering, Memphis, Tennessee* (U.S. Army of Engineers, 23 May 1865); *Memphis and Environs: Map, 1865*, Memphis Room, Memphis Public Libraries.

34. *Memphis Post*, 2 May 1866; *Nashville Press and Times*, 3–5 May 1866; M.E. Strieby to AMA, New York City, 21 May 1866, AMA Papers.

35. Baker testimony, *Congressional Report* No. 101, 319.

36. *Memphis Public Ledger*, 3 May 1866.

37. *Memphis Post*, 12 July 1866; McIllwaine, *Memphis Down in Dixie*, 151–53; Young, *Standard History of Memphis*, 243–46.

38. Roberta M. Ratcliffe, "The Church Family in Memphis," (MA thesis, Tennessee State University, 1972), 1–9; various testimony, Congressional Report No. 101, 9, 10, 14–16.

39. Memphis Post, 2–5 May 1866; Congressional Report No. 101, 4, 9, 14–16; B. Runkles to C.B. Fisk, Memphis, 3, 6 May 1866, BRFAL: Letters Sent by the Memphis District, 1865–1868, NARS.

40. James C. Mitchell testimony, *Congressional Report No. 101*, 5–7; *Story of the Memphis Fire Department* (Memphis, 1945), 22; List of Elmwood Cemetery, Memphis Room, Memphis Public Libraries.

41. Durnin testimony, *Congressional Report No. 101*, 223–25; *Memphis Appeal*, 2–3 May 1866; *Memphis Argus*, 5 May 1866; B. Runkles to Major W.L. Porter, Memphis, 11 May 1866, BRFAL: Reports and Affidavits Relating to Outrages and Riots, 1866–1868, NARS.

42. Merriwether, *Recollections of 92 Years*, 182.

43. B. Runkles to C.B. Fisk, Memphis, 12 May 1866, BRFAL; Reports and Affidavits Relating to Outrages and Riots, 1866–1868, NARS.

44. C.B. Fisk to O.O. Howard, Nashville, 3, 4, 7 May 1866, C.B. Fisk to Howard, Memphis, 19 May 1866, BRFAL: Letters and Telegrams Sent by the Office of the Assistant Commissioner for Tennessee and Kentucky, 3 July 1865–30 April 1869, vols. 15–18, NARS; Lt. Col. J.E. Jacobs to B. Runkles, Memphis, 15 May 1866, BRFAL: Letters Sent by the Office of the Assistant Commissioner for Tennessee and Kentucky, 17 March–31 December 1866, vols. 11–14, NARS.

45. *Colored Tennessean*, 12 August 1866; *Nashville Daily Press and Times*, 6–11 August 1866.

46. *Memphis Argus*, 22–23 May 1866; *Memphis Post*, 2–3 July, 1 August 1866.

47. Ellen Cole to G. Whipple, Cincinnati, 10 May 1866, E. Smith to G. Whipple, Memphis, 20 June 1866, E. Smith to M.E. Strieby, Memphis, 8 May 1866, AMA Papers; *Paris Intelligencer*, 16 February 1867; *Nashville Daily Press and Times*, 3, 6 September 1866; *Pulaski Citizen*, 21 December 1866; *Clarksville Chronicle*, 25 January 1866; *Knoxville Whig*, 7 February 1867; *Colored Tennessean*, 18 July 1866; *Memphis City Directory, 1866* (Memphis, 1866).

48. *Nashville Weekly Union and American*, 1 March 1866; *Memphis Post*, 1, 20, 21 March,1866, 18–29 April 1866; *Colored Tennessean*, 29 April 29 1866.

49. "Outrages of Whites Against Blacks in the Memphis Sub-District for Months of June and July 1866," BRFAL: Reports and Affidavits Relating to Outrages and Riots, 1866–1868, NARS.

# "STAND BY THE FLAG"

## Nationalism and African American Celebrations of the Fourth of July in Memphis, 1866–1887

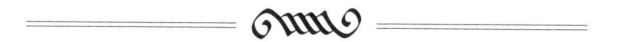

### Brian D. Page

On July 4, 1866, African Americans in Memphis, led by the Sons of Ham, a recently established mutual aid association, organized a parade and picnic to celebrate the birth of American independence, thus beginning a long and important cultural tradition within the African-American community.[1] They celebrated this national holiday in the shadows of the horrendous Memphis massacre of May 1, 1866, which had resulted in the death of forty-six African Americans.[2] This atrocity did not curb African Americans' assertion of freedom, or their affirmation of their rights within the social and political landscape of this southern city.[3] For the first generation after emancipation, celebrating the Fourth of July became a rite of identity, history, and memory for African Americans, who made the day their own unique event in contrast to the general indifference shown by local whites to the holiday. A careful examination of these holiday celebrations, in fact, uncovers important truths about the construction of nationalism and racial identity in the urban South after the Civil War.

For most white residents of Memphis, the traditional holiday of the Fourth of July lost much of its meaning during the war years. It seemed somehow inappropriate to celebrate nationalism in the midst of a war to destroy that nation. It especially seemed inappropriate to whites concerned about the reversal of race relations that accompanied the Federal occupation of the city. In June 1862 Memphis fell to Federal forces and the city soon became the destination for a large number of African

Americans. After the war, the *Memphis Daily Avalanche* commented that "the city is literally swarming with these ragged and dirty vagabonds, who are seriously looking for the sweets of freedom."[4] The number of African Americans in Memphis indeed rose from 3,882 in 1860 to 15,525 in 1870.[5]

The mere numbers of African Americans unnerved some whites. Eilzabeth Meriwether, a member of an affluent family in Memphis, noted the change in notions of power and equality among African American citizens after her return to the city following the war:

> Men but lately released from slavery, men but a degree removed from savagery sometimes do terrible things when suddenly entrusted with power... Any stranger, seeing those negroes would have supposed the Blacks, not the Whites, were masters in the South... As I saw those things that first morning in Memphis, and as I myself experienced them the thought came to me that, If negroes were to dominate life in the South, it would be better for us to emigrate.[6]

To whites such as Meriwether, African American occupation soldiers were especially a problem; they were an explicit reminder of the war and implied notions of equality. On January 23, 1866, the *Memphis Daily Avalanche* commented

> The system of Negro garrisons in the South carries with it its own commentary of uselessness and wantonness... It disturbs all the natural feelings of the white man; it corrupts the whole Negro population of the South; it puts before their eyes a picture of their race, which raises their expectations above all reason and discontents them with the plain tasks of labor.[7]

In March 1866, the *Memphis Daily Avalanche* even claimed that "riots and mobs were unknown among us until the Negro troops were quartered here."[8]

For many whites, the nation equated with black soldiers, which, in turn, meant social anarchy. These Memphis residents thus had little regard for either the Union or for any holidays celebrating the nation. At a congressional hearing following the May massacre, a Union general reported on a lack of patriotism. He commented that "if a love of the Union and the flag was considered loyal he would look upon a large majority of the people of Memphis as not being loyal." The general observed that the United States flag was only displayed at three locations in Memphis: army headquarters, the Freedman's Bureau, and at the office of the *Memphis Daily Post*. This lack of patriotism was found throughout the region. Retired Major General Carl Schurz commented after touring the South that there was "no national feeling" in the region.[9]

White rejection of the Fourth of July's celebration of the words of the Declaration of Independence did not soon disappear. In 1867, the *Memphis Daily Appeal* reported, "The Fourth can at present be appropriately celebrated by only one class in the South—the radicals, and as a partisan holiday."[10] The *Memphis Daily Post* reported, in 1869, that the Fourth was, "celebrated... only by our Germans and our colored citizens." Furthermore, the newspaper commented that "the rebel press groans about oppression and tyranny" and that white Southerners "do not have it in their hearts to celebrate as in the glory years of the past."[11] As late as 1888, it was noted that "since the late war between the States, the Fourth of July has become, in the South, a day of minor importance."[12]

It might have been a day of minor importance to whites, but to African Americans in Memphis, the Fourth of July was one of the major public holidays; the words of the Declaration of Independence finally seemed to be more than mere promises. There is a long history of African American celebrations that have their roots in slavery. In antebellum slave communities, for example, African Americans gathered to celebrate Pinkster Day and Election Day in the rural countryside and on the outskirts of cities. Urban African Americans celebrated West Indies Day or designated their own emancipation as a holiday.[13] Antebellum recognition of Independence Day had often been a method of protest. Frederick Douglass in his famous speech in Rochester, New York, on the character of this national holiday stated, "Your high independence only reveals the immeasurable distance between us," and "the blessings in which you, this day, rejoice are not in common." Furthermore, Douglass lashed out, "This Fourth of July is yours, not mine."[14] Prior to emancipation, the words of the Declaration proclaiming equality and freedom from tyranny rang hollow for most African Americans.

Then during the Civil War came the celebration of the Emancipation Proclamation. On January 1, 1867, for example, the Sons of Ham and other social and benevolent associations organized an emancipation celebration and led a parade through the city streets. Undoubtedly these individuals were energized by the promise of freedom. Many of the same organizations that participated in this event contributed to Independence Day celebrations in Memphis.[15]

The Fourth of July celebrations shared common characteristics with these earlier public demonstrations. African Americans celebrated with dancing and singing until the late hours of the evening, a common characteristic of slave festivals.[16] Historians have noted further a strong cultural connection between the traditional holiday barbecue and slave festivals.[17] Barbeques were used to celebrate the Fourth in Bartlett in 1882 and in Memphis in 1884.[18] In addition, the Independence Day events had direct precedents in other Reconstruction-era demonstrations. In Memphis on August 1, 1866, in recognition of West Indian emancipation, African Americans called for the right to vote, to serve on juries, and to hold office.[19] On February 27, 1867, Horatio Rankin, a local African American politician, urged African American citizens to "stand by the flag" in order to demonstrate "that they were worthy of complete equality."[20]

These Independence Day commemorations were more than patriotic expressions. They could be used to build a memory for the future as a promise of better days to come and a medium for encouraging moral improvement and preparing African Americans for citizenship. Free, but confronted with slavery and discrimination, African Americans struggled to define what it meant to be black and American.[21]

In Memphis, during the years 1866 to 1887, there were nineteen accounts of Fourth of July celebrations in local newspapers. Reference was made to these public events in every year except 1871 and 1886. Sixteen of the accounts made specific reference to the organizations that participated. Leading the way were the newly established mutual aid and benevolent organizations that had emerged from black churches throughout Memphis. These organizations pooled together their resources in order to help African American communities, creating a vital community framework.[22] In Memphis it is possible to construct a more complete picture of this institutional infrastructure from the limited amount of records left behind. From the years 1866 to 1874, over two hundred various organizations deposited money in the Freedmen's Savings and Trust Company. These deposit ledgers include the names of members who served as officers and some contain biographical information about the participants. Furthermore, names can be cross-referenced with Memphis city directories and relevant newspaper articles, presenting a more visible description about the nature of these organizations.[23]

The level of mutual aid society involvement in the Independence Day celebrations provides insight to the range of people, and the range of motives, involved in these public commemorations. In general Fourth of July celebrations emerged within the context of a large, poor, and unskilled African American population.[24] Armestead Robinson, in his study on African American organizations in Memphis, has previously identified a split between religious and benevolent groups and those engaged in political activity. While political leadership lay within the more skilled middle class, the community's institutional infrastructure was dominated by those organizations with a religious and benevolent purpose.[25] In addition, unskilled women led the majority of these associations.[26] In other words, not only was the black community able successfully to organize for the benefit of others, but it was also largely the result of leadership and involvement from unskilled African Americans, especially women.[27]

Two benevolent groups in particular dominated Independence Day ceremonies. The Sons of Ham and the Independent Pole-Bearers, in thirteen of these celebrations, materialized as the leaders and organizers of these public ceremonies. These two associations planned parades leading the participants down the streets of Memphis and organized picnics in various parks in the city. Other African American societies including both sexes in Memphis participated in these celebrations. Some groups that were particularly visible included the Daughters of Ham, the Daughters of Zion, the Sisters of Zion, the Sons of Zion, the Mechanics Benevolent Association, St. Johns Relief Society, and various other mutual aid and benevolent organizations.[28]

The Sons of Ham was formed prior to the Civil War and had a good deal of influence in Memphis during Reconstruction. In the early 1870s, members were able to carve out an influential space for themselves in local politics.[29] They were also one of the first to plan and lead a Fourth of July celebration in 1866 when they organized a picnic and parade.[30] The leaders of this association consisted of carpenters, drivers, porters, and upholsterers. However, officers were not solely limited to the skilled and economically stable. There were two accounts of unskilled working-class African Americans attaining an established position within the Sons of Ham. As a result, some general laborers, although it was rare, were elected as officers. In addition, many of the leaders could not be located in various city directories, suggesting that they may have been new to the area, most likely lacking a sufficient job, or that they did not hold a stable residence or job in Memphis. The leadership framework within the Sons of Ham, however, leaned toward the economically established.[31]

The Independent Pole-Bearers was another association that contested for a leadership role in African American celebratory events. Reference to the society first appears in 1868, when they participated in a parade organized by the Sons of Ham. Gradually, the Independent Pole-Bearers would eclipse the Sons of Ham politically and socially in Memphis.[32] By 1874, the Independent Pole-Bearers were leading the parades; they continued to dominate the Fourth of July celebrations into the 1880s.[33] The leadership structure of the Independent Pole-Bearers resembled the Sons of Ham in that it leaned heavily towards the skilled and middle-class members of the African American communities. However, here again, this did not rule out the possibility of a general laborer gaining an official office within this association. Of eight known members of the Independent Pole-Bearers, three represented the unskilled working class.³⁴ As a result, characteristics of these two groups suggest that the organization of Fourth of July celebrations was initiated by the more skilled and prosperous within the African American communities, but did not exclude members of the African American working class.

Other organizations participating in the parades, picnics, and sociopolitical gatherings underscore the inclusive character of these public celebrations. The Daughters of Zion was a very influential benevolent organization in Memphis during the Reconstruction era.³⁵ First mentioned in the 1867 parade organized by the Sons of Ham, they participated in many of these ritual events and even created their own celebrations. In 1875 and 1877, the Daughters of Zion organized a social gathering at the Exposition Building in Memphis.³⁶ The Daughters of Zion included many members of the African American working class. A number of the officers were unskilled daily laborers who washed and ironed clothes for money. Martha Ware, a washerwoman and a victim in the Memphis Massacre, was a prominent member. Some of the women also listed as their husbands unskilled men who cut wood or worked on farms to make a living.³⁷

The Sisters of Zion and the Sons of Zion also participated in the celebrations. The Sisters of Zion consisted of washerwomen, housekeepers, and cooks, whereas the Sons of Zion included farmers, daily laborers, draymen, bricklayers, barbers, and clerks.³⁸ A pattern that emerges in these associations reflects a trend towards the participating male organizations being led by members of the African-American skilled and middle class, while female organizations tended to be under the leadership of the unskilled working class.

Group affiliation provides some characteristics of the participants in these celebrations, but it is impossible to gauge how many people were in each of these organizations. The *Memphis Daily Post* suggested that the United Daughters of Ham consisted of over one hundred members in the 1868 celebration.³⁹ In 1868, the Daughters of Zion listed over three hundred members in their organization.⁴⁰

While exact numbers are lacking, it is possible to get a feel of these celebrations to determine just how large these public events were in Memphis. The information revealed suggests that these celebrations consisted of a rather large portion of the African American residents in the Memphis area, with thousands participating. The Memphis newspapers, for instance, frequently remarked on the size of the crowds that joined together on this national holiday. On July 4, 1866, the *Memphis Daily Post* reported, "The colored people turned out in mass to see them [the parade], and crowds accompanied them to the grove." In 1867, the paper estimated that two thousand were in attendance and in 1869, 1875, and 1877, the papers suggested that five thousand African Americans joined together to celebrate.[41] The accuracy of these numbers is unknown, but the numbers indicate a consistently large display of celebratory fervor.

In fact, there is some evidence to suggest that these Fourth of July celebrations helped construct a community from a dispersed population.[42] In 1872, the *Memphis Daily Appeal* reported that "several car loads with them [African Americans] arrived from Brownsville. Several other car loads with them [African Americans] arrived by the Charleston road." The paper also commented that they arrived by "foot, on horseback, by river, by wagon... and made an immense army."[43] At the very least, the Fourth of July in Memphis established bonds of fellowship and severed the distance between African Americans in the area.

The celebrations served other functions as well. They were fund raising events for the various mutual aid and benevolent organizations. In 1866, the Sons of Ham "organized for benevolent purposes," with the money raised used "to increase the benevolent fund." The Sons of Ham, in 1879, planned a picnic, "for the purpose of raising funds to replenish their treasury, the amount so received to be dispersed among the sick and... burial for destitute members."[44] By joining together and projecting an image of solidarity, African Americans could instill a sense of belonging and, in the process, build a community.

The different celebrations between 1866 and 1887 shared certain components. One of the most revealing was the parade, which would usually be the first event of the day followed by a public gathering at a park, picnic grove, or building.[45] A typical African American parade at this time followed a prescribed order. The 1869 celebration, which was organized by the Sons of Ham, proceeded in this order: the chief marshal of the day, the grand marshal of the different societies mounted on horseback, a musical band, the United Sons of Ham, the Benevolent Society No. 1, the Union Forever Society, and the Independent-Pole Bearers. From that point, the list of parade order continued, ending with the Gymnastic Society.[46]

On other occasions various military organizations such as the M'Clellan Guards led the parades. Parades are hierarchical by nature and undoubtedly reinforced the ranked order of the different societies. The working class or the socially marginalized would often use parades to secure respectability for their individual and collective identity. The standard norms of neatness, order, and patriotism served to mold other public ceremonies.[47] In Memphis the order and appearance of the participants were consistently noted. In 1866, the *Memphis Daily Post* commented, "All were neatly dressed in holiday attire."[48] The *Memphis Daily Appeal*, in 1879, reported the participants in the parade gave a "fine soldierly appearance," and in 1872, they noted that there was "not a single disturbance."[49] The attention to order and appearance in these celebrations was as much a self-conscious attempt to gain respect in society as it was a reflection of the standards of contemporary celebrations.[50]

A popular way to distinguish between groups, and classes, was the use of flags and banners. Each group designated itself with flags and banners. In 1867, the African American participants were "drawn up in line and decorated with regalia of their several orders." The African American associations, in 1869, marched in procession with "each society bearing a banner, with the name of the society and the date of organization. . . wearing the regalia of his order." Again in 1879, the various African American societies carried "flags and banners" as they marched through the city of Memphis. Certain individuals were often selected to lead theirorganizations. In some cases, one member of an African American society would be elected to head the whole parade, elevating him to a heightened level of pride and self-respect.[51]

Dress was also a distinction among the parade participants.[52] Frequently it would be mentioned that the participants were "neatly dressed in holiday attire" or dressed in an "endless variety of costumes." On the Fourth, various military organizations would parade "in their handsome uniforms." Other times the appearance and dress of the participants would simply be noted as being in "full regalia."[53] Regardless of the phrase used to depict the appearance of the African Americans who participated, clothing played a vital role in the picture they presented. Clothing could undoubtedly depict class and affluence, but also could be used to transcend a working-class experience. For the independent barber or blacksmith it could designate his position in the community. Likewise, for the washerwoman or laborer who paraded through the streets, dress could claim a position of respectability in their own community, and the larger society.

Another obvious distinction in the parades was between men and women. While both male and female organizations participated, the manner in which they paraded sometimes differed. In the 1875 procession, male and female societies paraded together but with a "carriage containing the queen of the day and maids of honor." In addition there were "twelve carriages containing female members of the societies."[54] This may have been a reflection of Victorian sensibilities designating the street as a male terrain. In most of the processions reference was not made to different modes of transportation; however, this did not mean that men and women paraded equally.

Another gender distinction in the African American parades was the time of the parade. On July 4, 1868, the female organizations paraded separately from the men. The *Memphis Daily Post* reported that the male societies gathered at a "later hour" than the female organizations. In 1869, the women assembled to parade at nine in the morning, while the men gathered together at eleven in the morning.[55]

A final difference was the length of the parade. In 1868, the female societies not only gathered at an earlier hour, but also traveled a shorter parade route. The route for women was considerably shorter in the celebration of 1869. The male organizations proceeded down a total of eight streets compared to three for the female societies.[56] No matter the differences in length, time, and transportation, African American women were included in these public occasions, but given a less visible public role. One can only speculate on the role these women played behind the scenes.[57]

The parades were not radical demonstrations, but they sometimes reminded whites that local African Americans had power and that they were willing to go beyond their traditional neighborhood boundaries. African American military companies, such as the M'Clellan Guards and the Zouaves cadets, with both names representing direct reference to the Union army during the Civil War, participated in these Independence Day celebrations, leading parades and congregating at the designated place for social gathering. On July 4, 1878, according to the *Memphis Daily Appeal*, the M'Clellan Guards "engaged in a competitive drill" and determined a winner at the end of the evening. The drill reflected traditional military standards of the day and the goal of precision and order, as they revealed "careful and good timing."[58]

The majority of the parades occurred in the northern part of the city beyond the traditional area for African Americans. The parade routes expanded on the emancipation celebration of 1867, enlarging their scope of the city. Of the sixteen parades mentioned during this period, the information revealed suggests that most of them followed the same pattern. These parades generally proceeded along streets north of Vance Street up to Poplar. This physical area can be understood as the core of Memphis during Reconstruction. The region south of this area contained the majority of the African American population. The southern part of these parade routes would usually be the point of origin, and, depending on the destination, the various African American societies would either proceed north or march north and return south at the end. The reports on these parades usually noted that the participants marched through the "principle streets" in Memphis. Some make reference to the actual streets in these processions. Their primary destinations reflect the character of these parades.[59]

The parade sometimes began at the hall of one of the African American organizations. In 1868, the participants gathered at the hall of the Sons of Ham on Gayoso Street and proceeded to march through the city. The parade often ended at another destination, Court Square. In 1875, the *Memphis Daily Appeal* noted that "in and around Court Square the Negroes congregated in great numbers." Again in 1887, it was reported that "the city was crowded with colored people yesterday [July 4] and Court Square seemed to possess a special charm for them."[60] The question to be raised is what exactly was this "special charm"? Court Square undoubtedly contained a number of conscious and subconscious meanings for the African Americans who occupied this space. Court Square was a seemingly established public place for the citizens of Memphis. Not only was it public, but it was also extremely visible to both black and white residents. Public spaces represented a common ground for African Americans to reinforce their rights as American citizens in the larger white communities. The Fourth of July provided an opportunity to celebrate freedom, but, more importantly, to affirm equal rights.

Another destination was the Exposition Building, a few blocks behind Court Square, where in 1875 and 1877, the Daughters of Zion led a Fourth of July celebration. These social gatherings differ from the others in that they occurred in an enclosed space. However, the building existed as a public accommodation for the citizens of Memphis. Therefore, African Americans were still able to celebrate in the public sphere and assert their rights.[61]

Other times the parade would come to an end at the Charleston Depot where the participants would take railroad cars to the Fair Grounds on the outskirts of the city. In 1867, the *Memphis Daily Post* reported, "A train of cars ran from the city to the picnic grounds at short intervals throughout the day, carrying immense crowds." The *Memphis Daily Appeal* noted in 1874 that the various African American societies "paraded the streets, finally hitting at the Charleston Depot, whence they were conveyed to the Fair Grounds."[62]

African Americans paraded down Main, Poplar, Second, Adams, Madison, and Union. The marches also paraded down Gayso, DeSoto, Beale and Vance.[63] Not only would the parades march past the Beale Street Church, a large African American church constructed shortly after the Civil War, but they would also continue though established white sections of town.[64] The marchers proceeded in full public view thus expanding the boundaries of their urban environment.

Additional celebratory events took place at parks and picnic groves in the city. The various African American societies congregated at Alexander Park, James Park, Estival Park, and Humboldt Park. Two parks, Alexander and James, were located on Vance Street in the southern part of the city, which seems to validate the conclusion that African Americans tended to congregate in socially prescribed areas. However, in 1869, the participants paraded to a Mrs. Preston's grove located at the head of

Court Street. While this was most likely a private area, the location of the picnic grove suggests it would have placed African Americans within reasonable visibility for the white residents of Memphis.[65]

What happened at the celebrations? Almost always, the organizers would read a copy of the Declaration of Independence. Then leading citizens addressed the crowd. A particularly useful year to study is 1867, in the midst of the political battle over African American voting rights in Tennessee, when celebrations took place at two different locations in Memphis. Presidents Island, the location of one of the largest contraband camps in the South during the Civil War, was the site of one gathering. Edward Shaw, a leading African American politician, addressed the crowd there, claiming that the holiday was a "celebration of the freedom of America." Furthermore, African Americans "could now join in with this celebration, and would show that they were worthy of their freedom." General W. J. Smith, a white Memphian and member of the Union army, stated "he was glad to see them [African Americans] out to celebrate the national day of American Independence." General Smith went on to comment that "all patriotic citizens, white and black, could meet on common ground and in a common cause."[66] White newspaper reporters gave a slanted view of the day's speeches; the *Memphis Daily Appeal* reported that the participants were led by "radical white politicians... designed for grinding the political axes."[67]

Another celebration, led by the Sons of Ham and other organizations, took place at the Memphis Fair Grounds.[68] This event drew a larger crowd than the one at Presidents Island, probably due to the nature of the participants. Presidents Island organizers were much more affluent than the majority of the African American population in Memphis. Edward Shaw, a future county commissioner, A. T. Shaw, a white law clerk, and John Harris, a black lawyer, led this gathering.[69] At the fair grounds, leadership came from the benevolent organizations.

Approximately five thousand citizens attended the 1869 celebration. After the parade, leading citizens of Memphis addressed the crowd. Reverend William Murphy urged his fellow African Americans to "stand up and be worthy of our freedom." Furthermore, Reverend Murphy suggested that instead of money for lawyers and doctors they should contribute to "building churches, schoolhouse, and dwellings for themselves."[70] Edward Shaw then delivered one of the most poignant interpretations of the meaning of the Fourth of July for African Americans. Shaw suggested that the Fourth of July was an African American holiday, stating, "I claim the privileges we now enjoy came through the Declaration of 1776." Reaffirming his place within American history, Shaw related, "I believe that I am as much included in that declaration as was General Washington." Furthermore, Shaw asserted, "Our duty is to show defense to the principles dear to the American people, and strive to elevate ourselves."[71]

What happened at Independence Day celebrations began to change by the mid-1870s. Affluent white residents of Memphis had been leading a charge to relinquish control from the current city government and thus to gain control of the African American voting class. In January 1874, an Irish and African American coalition had been able to make substantial gains in the election of city officials, sparking a political movement led by Memphis's leading citizens in order to gain command of local events. The People's Protective Union, led by members of the elite, urged for the repeal of Memphis's city charter on financial terms. One aspect of this elite movement was aimed at gaining the support of African Americans through political reconciliation. In December 1874, various African American leaders designated their support for the Democratic Party, marking a further political reconciliation.[72]

The nature of this new alliance became apparent in the 1875 Independence Day celebration. In some ways, that year's celebration was business as usual. The Independent Pole-Bearers and Hezkiah Henley, an African American blacksmith, led the Fourth of July celebration. It began with a parade including a variety of African American associations from the Sons of Ham to the Daughters of Zion. The event climaxed with a visible political gathering at the Memphis Fair Grounds with an estimated crowd of five thousand participants.[73] But, at the fair grounds, the new political reality became apparent through the variety of African Americans and white Americans, including General Nathan Bedford Forrest, who gave speeches. The *Memphis Daily Appeal* reported, "The Independent Pole-Bearers had invited a number of prominent Southern gentlemen" and "there was no little anxiety as to the probable result of this meeting." Furthermore, "from the number of societies and the display made by them, it was evident that the Negroes intended making at least jollity yesterday."[74]

By 1887, African Americans had celebrated the Fourth of July in Memphis for twenty-one years. On July 4, 1887, the Independent Pole-Bearers "marched along the principle streets," but judging from newspapers, they also rather quietly marched out of the history of Fourth of July celebrations.[75] African Americans in Memphis did not stop celebrating the Fourth of July altogether, but the nature of these celebrations changed. The long parades and large crowds disappeared, replaced by simple and small social gatherings of various members of the African American communities.[76] Two years later, in 1889, the *Memphis Daily Appeal* suddenly claimed "patriotism among the colored citizens was no less extant than with his Caucasian brother." There was a social gathering at the African American Carfield Orphan Asylum where "most of the colored divinities and celebrities attended and good feeling prevailed." After five more years, on July 4, 1894, the Memphis African American recognized the national holiday by "going way off by himself" to celebrate.[77] The evidence suggests that the Fourth of July seemed to have lost that "special charm," which made prior celebrations so unique, to the social and legal dictates of Jim Crow and second-class public citizenship.[78]

Social and political landscapes in Memphis changed markedly in the 1880s. In 1879, when Memphis lost its city charter, the political power of African Americans was diminished when the city became a taxing district of Shelby County under the auspices of the Tennessee legislature. The state government appointed various city officials and citywide elections replaced ward representation, hindering the impact of the African American vote. In 1883, the Civil Rights Bill was overturned in the Supreme Court, paving the way for segregation. Finally in 1889, the state of Tennessee successfully established Jim Crow, limiting the political and social rights of African Americans. In the 1880s, there emerged in the South what has been traditionally called the "nadir" period for African Americans. In Memphis, this sense of increased hostility in the South altered the nature of these Fourth of July celebrations.[79] Disfranchisement and Jim Crow segregation helped to pave the way for a rapid embrace of Independence Day by Memphis whites. In 1891, it was noted

> for many years after the war this legal holiday was not observed in the South, but as social bitterness engendered by that fratricidal struggle fades into forgetfulness, the observance grows more universal—and in a few years the day will be celebrated throughout the Southern land just as much as in the North.[80]

Again in 1894, it was stated that the Fourth of July "seems to mean more to the South as time rolls on than it did."[81]

But for Memphis African Americans, the Fourth of July once again became a far off promise of equality as the words of the Declaration of Independence were voiced, but proved to have little meaning, in the Jim Crow South.

The purpose of studying these events is an attempt to relate meanings of patriotism and citizenship within African American communities. After the Civil War, the Fourth of July emerged as an African American holiday demonstrating their nationalistic spirit. Furthermore, on this national holiday African Americans revealed their American characteristics by incorporating their history into the nation's identity. African American politicians and individuals of Memphis encouraged members of their communities to demonstrate race progress by standing by the flag. Perhaps as a testament to their nationalistic spirit, the *Memphis Daily Appeal* commented that independence "has a peculiar charm, now that they are released from servile bondage, and stand free as American citizens."82

On the Fourth of July, African Americans were able to carve out a space for their past in American history and a place for their experience in America's destiny. That they were unsuccessful is a testament to the powers of change. However, it does not mean that African Americans ceased to reveal their American identity, only that it materialized in different forms. African Americans continued to live in search of dignity and self-respect regardless of the historical situation. The very fact that we examine African American Fourth of July celebrations separately from the larger society is a reflection of the differences imposed on them from the dominant majority. As a generation of white southerners turned away from the Fourth of July, African Americans celebrated it fervently, reinforcing their perspective of freedom, but, more importantly, they commemorated this national holiday as Americans.

*This article first appeared in the Winter 1999 issue of the* Tennessee Historical Quarterly.

1. *Memphis Daily Appeal*, 5 July 1866, 5.

2. There has been a wide variety of historical literature written on the Memphis Massacre. The following were used in relation to this study: Walker Barrington, "'This is the White Man's Day': The Irish, White, Racial Identity, and the Memphis Riots," in *Left History* 5 (Fall 1997): 31–55; Kevin R. Hardwick, "Your Old Father Abe Lincoln is Dead and Damned: Black Soldiers and the Memphis Race Riot of 1866," *The Journal of Social History* 27 (Fall 1993): 109–128; Bobby L Lovett, "Memphis Riots: White Reaction to Blacks in Memphis, May 1865–June 1866," *Tennessee Historical Quarterly* 38 (Spring 1979): 9–33; Altina L. Waller, "Community, Class and Race in

Memphis Riot of 1866," in the *Journal of Social History* 18 (Winter 1984): 233–246. The massacre resulted in a Joint Congressional Committee Investigation, providing the most detailed information in the record of the 39th Congress. See 39th Congress, 1st Session, House Report 101 in *Memphis Riots and Massacres, Mass Violence in America* (New York, 1969).

3. I approach this subject in agreement with the fact that various public rituals contain implicit and explicit meanings that broaden our understanding of the history of a particular group of people or period of time. Not only do they help translate the social and political landscape for historical purposes, but they also serve as a viable method for constructing a collective memory. Parades and public celebrations are viable tools for uncovering history. Two studies influenced

my understanding of public rituals as historical evidence: Susan G. Davis, *Parades and Power: Street Theatre in Nineteenth-Century Philadelphia* (Philadelphia, 1986) and Mary Ryan, "The American Parade: Representations of the Nineteenth-Century Social Order," in *The New Culture History*, ed. Lynn Hunt (Berkeley, 1989). Ryan suggests that parades were used to impress "their group identity on the minds of countless bystanders," 138, 139. Parades can be used to define the urban landscape uncovering social and political realities. See Peter Gould and Rodney White, *Mental Maps* (Middlesex, England, 1974), 34; D.W. Meinig, ed., *The Interpretation of Ordinary Landscapes: Geographical Essays* (New York, 1979), 2–6. Also, two studies, in particular, discuss the use of African American public rituals used for claiming their right to civic space: see Elsa Barkley Brown and Gregg D. Kimball, "Mapping the Terrain of Black Richmond," and Shane White, "It Was a Proud Day," in *The New African American Urban History*, ed. Kenneth W. Goings and Raymond Mohl (Thousand Oaks, Cal., 1996), 73–76, 41–42. In addition, public celebrations are useful methods for constructing the collective memory of a particular group of people. See Genevieve Fabre, "African American Commemorative Celebrations," in *History and Memory in African American Culture*, ed. Genevieve Fabre and Robert O'Meally (New York, 1994), 72–91; Earl Lewis, "Connecting Memory, Self, and the Power of Place in African American Urban History," in *The New African American Urban History*, 116–141; Kenneth Moss, "St. Patrick'sDay Celebration and the Formation of Irish-American Identity," *Journal of Social History* 29 (#1, 1995): 126–129, 139, 140.

4. *Memphis Daily Avalanche*, 3 March 1866, 2.

5. Population Schedules of the 9th Census, 1870, City of Memphis, Wards 1–10. Several sources were used to develop a historical and demographic perspective of the city of Memphis. See Kathleen C. Berkeley, "'Like a Plague of Locust': Immigration and Social Change in Memphis, Tennessee, 1850–1880" (PhD Dissertation, University of California at Los Angeles, 1980), 111, 125; Gerald Capers, *The Biography of a River Town: Its Heroic Age* (New Orleans, 1966), 107, 108, 163; William D. Miller, *Memphis During the Progressive Era, 1900–1917* (Memphis, 1957), 5–7; Armstead L. Robinson, "Plans Dat Comed from God: Institution Building and the Emergence of Black Leadership in Reconstruction Memphis," in *Toward a New South? Studies in Post-Civil War Southern Communities*, ed. Orville Vernon Burton and Robert C. McMath, Jr. (Westport, Conn., 1982), 187; David M. Tucker, *Black Pastors and Leaders: Memphis, 1819–1972* (Memphis, 1975), 5–7; Howard Rabinowitz, *Race Relations in the Urban South, 1865–1990* (New York, 1978), 61

6. Elizabeth Avery Meriwether, *Recollections of 92 Years, 1824–1916* (Nashville, 1958), 164, 167.

7. *Memphis Daily Avalanche*, 23 January 1866, 2.

8. Ibid., 20 March 1866, 2.

9. *Memphis Riots and Massacres*, 32; *Memphis Daily Avalanche*, 3 January 1866, 1, 4 January 1866, 2.

10. *Memphis Daily Appeal*, 6 July 1867, 3.

11. *Memphis Daily Post*, 6 July 1869, 1.

12. *Memphis Daily Appeal*, 5 July 1888, 5.

13. William B. Gravely, "The Dialectic Double Consciousness in Black American Freedom Celebrations, 1808–1863," *The Journal of Negro History* 67 (Winter 1982): 303, 304; White, "It Was A Proud Day," 20–23; William Wiggins, *O Freedom: Afro-American Emancipation Celebrations* (Knoxville, 1987), XX, 26–32.

14. Frederick Douglass, *The Life and Writings of Frederick Douglass, Volume II: Pre-Civil War Decade, 1850–1860* (New York, 1950), 189, 190.

15. *Memphis Daily Post*, 2 January 1867, 4,

16. In these Fourth of July celebrations dancing and singing were consistently reported. See *Memphis Daily Post*, July 1866–1869; *Memphis Daily Appeal*, July 1867–1887.

17. William Wiggins has noted the persistence of cultural traditions in emancipation day celebrations. See Wiggins, *O Freedom*, 25–35.

18. *Memphis Daily Appeal*, 6 July 1884, 4; *Memphis Daily Appeal*, 6 July 1882, 4.

19. John Cimprich, *Slavery's End in Tennessee, 1861–1865* (Tuscaloosa, 1985), 104; William Gillespie McBride, "Blacks and The Race Issue in Tennessee Politics, 1865–1876" (PhD Dissertation, Vanderbilt University, 1989), 17, 118, 133; *Memphis Daily Post*, 2 August 1866, 8.

20. *Memphis Daily Post*, 27 February 1867, 8.

21. Fabre, "African American Commemorative Celebrations," 72–91; Gravely, "The Dialectic Double Consciousness in Black American Freedom Celebrations," 302–312; Benjamin Quarles, "Antebellum Free Blacks and the 'Spirit of 76'," *The Journal of Negro History* 41 (January 1976): 229–242.

22. Eric Foner, *Reconstruction: America's Unfinished Revolution, 1863–1877* (New York, 1988), 90, 95; Lawrence Levine, *Black Culture and Black Consciousness: Afro-American Folk Thought from Slavery to Freedom* (New York, 1977), 268, 269; Rabinowitz, *Race Relations in the Urban South*, 140–143, 198, 199,210. This pattern also resembled that of Free Black communities in the North prior to the Civil War. See Gary B. Nash, *Forging Freedom: The Formation of Philadelphia's Black Community, 1720–1840* (Cambridge, 1988), 5, 210, 259, 272, 273.

23. The Freedman's Bank was established in 1865 in Memphis, but went bankrupt in 1874. Many African Americans in the community lost all of their savings, including the various mutual aid and benevolent societies. See the Registers of Signatures of Depositions m Branches of the Freedman's Saving and Trust Company, 1865–1874, Memphis, Tennessee, National Archives, Record Group 101 (Memphis Public Library). Some of the biographical material, relating to the members of these societies, was obtained from the deposits slips of the Freedman's Saving and Trust Company. However, in most cases the deposit slips provided the names and the various city directories supplied their occupation. *Boyle and Chapman s Memphis Directory, 1876* (Memphis Public Library); *Edwards Annual Directory to the City of Memphis 1869, 1870,*

1874 (Memphis Public Library).

24. Robinson, "Plans Dat Corned From God," 47.

25. Ibid., 73, 91.

26. Kathleen Berkeley, "Colored Ladies Also Contributed," in *The Web of Southern Social Relations: Women, Family, and Education*, ed. Walter J. Fraser, Jr., R. Frank Sauders, Jr., and Jon L. Wakelyn (Athens, 1985), 194.

27. African American women were both African Americans and women, not one or the other. See Berkeley, "Colored Ladies Also Contributed," 184; Elsa Barkley Brown, "Negotiating and Transforming the Public Sphere: African American Political Life in the Transition from Slavery to Freedom," *Public Culture* 7 (Fall1994): 107.

28. *Memphis Daily Post*, July 1866–1869; *Memphis Daily Appeal*, July 1867–1887.

29. In 1869, it was reported that the Sons of Ham would be celebrating their eleventh anniversary. See *Memphis Daily Post*, 2 July 1869,4. The Sons of Ham were also influential in local politics during the early 1870s. See Tucker, *Black Pastors and Leaders*, 27.

30. *Memphis Daily Post*, 3 July 1866, 8; 5 July 1866, 8; 6 July 1866, 8.

31. The names and occupations of members of the Sons of Ham were obtained by cross-referencing the deposit slips of the Freedman's Savings and Trust Company with Memphis city directories. See note 23. Also, the Sons of Ham and their officers were listed in the 1874 and 1876 city directories. See *Boyle and Chapman s Memphis City Directory, 1876; Edwards Annual Directory to the City of Memphis, 1874*.

32. *Memphis Daily Post*, 7 July 1868, 4. In these celebrations the Independent Pole-Bearers gradually replaced the Sons of Ham as the leaders and organizers of these events. The Sons of Ham continued to have various picnics in the city throughout the 1870s. However, no mention is made to the Sons of Ham in the 1880s.

33. *Memphis Daily Appeal*, 5 July 1874, 4.

34. Unlike the other African American societies, information for the Independent Pole-Bearers came solely from the Memphis city directories. See *Boyle and Chapman s Memphis Directory, 1876; Edwards Annual Directory to the City of Memphis, 1874.*

35. Berkeley, "Colored Ladies Contributed," 181, 193, 182.

36. *Memphis Daily Appeal*, 6 July 1867, 3; 6 July 1875, 1; 6 July 1877, 1.

37. Information on the Daughters of Zion was compiled from the Freedman's Saving and Trust Company. See note 23. Martha Ware was a member of the Daughters of Zion and a victim of the Memphis Massacre. See *Memphis Riots and Massacres*, 344.

38. Information on the Sisters of Zion came from the deposit slips of the Freedman's Saving and Trust Company. However, information of the Sons of Zion came from both the Freedman's Saving and Trust Company and Memphis city directories. See note 23.

39. *Memphis Daily Post*, 7 July 1868, 4.

40. Ibid., 9 July 1868, 4.

41. *Memphis Daily Post*, 6 July 1866, 8; 5 July 1867, 8; 6 July 1869, 4; *Memphis Daily Appeal*, 6 July 1875; 6 July 1877, 1.

42. African American mutual aid and benevolent organizations not only provided support, but were also used to build a community. See Nash, *Forging Freedom*, 210.

43. *Memphis Daily Appeal*, 5 July 1872, 4.

44. *Memphis Daily Post*, 3 July 1866, 8; 6 July 1866, 8; *Memphis Daily Appeal*, 5 July 1879, 4.

45. *Memphis Daily Post*, July 1866–1869; *Memphis Daily Appeal*, July 1867–1887.

46. *Memphis Daily Post*, 2 July 1869, 4

47. Davis, Parades and Power, 21.

48. *Memphis Daily Post*, 6 July 1866, 8.

49. *Memphis Daily Appeal*, 5 July 1879, 4; *Memphis Daily Appeal*, 5 July 1872, 8.

50. It is important to realize that these celebrations were not radically different from other nineteenth century commemorations. Genevieve Fabre suggests that Independence Day celebrations could be used to offset white culture by creating a separate public ritual. However, in Memphis, African Americans also reflected contemporary festivities of the dominant society. Fabre, "African American Commemorative Celebrations in the Nineteenth Century," 76; Davis, *Parades and Power*. As African Americans embraced freedom they did so in their own image. Joel Williamson states that African Americans were the "most American of Americans." Joel Williamson, *The Crucible of Race: Black-White Relations in the American South Since Emancipation* (New York, 1984), 49.

51. *Memphis Daily Post*, 5 July 1867, 8; 7 July 1868, 4; 2 July 1869, 4; 6 July 1869, 1; *Memphis Daily Appeal*, 5 July 1872; 5 July 1879, 4. William Wiggins notes that the American flag was a popular symbol in Emancipation Day celebrations. See Wiggins, *O Freedom*, 95

52. In antebellum slave festivals dress was one way in which African Americans could transcend their marginal situation. In post-emancipation parades clothes became a way to designate class and status. See White, "It Was A Proud Day," 28; Brown and Kimball, "Mapping the Terrain of Black Richmond," 76; Robin D.G. Kelly, *Race Rebels: Culture, Politics, and the Black Working-Class* (New York, 1994 ), 50.

53. *Memphis Daily Post*, 6 July 1866, 8; Memphis Daily Appeal, 5 July 1872, 4; 5 July 1882. The "regalia" of the participants was often mentioned is some form or fashion. See *Memphis Daily Post*, 5 July 1867, 8; 7 July 1868, 8; *Memphis Daily Appeal*, 6 July 1867, 3.

54. *Memphis Daily Appeal*, 6 July 1875, l.

55. *Memphis Daily Post*, 7 July 1868, 4; 2 July 1869, 4.

56.. Ibid.

57. Historians have noted the communal aspect of voting that included female participation. See Darlene Clark Hine and Kathleen Thompson, *A Shining Thread of Hope: The History of Black Women in America* (New York, 1998), 158–160.

58. *Memphis Daily Appeal*, 6 July 1878, 4. 59. Reference was made to a parade in every year

except 1870, 1871, 1878, 1884, I1885, and 1886. In 1868 and I1869, the specific parade route was listed. See *Memphis Daily Post*, 3 July 1868, 4; 2 July 1869, 4.

60. *Memphis Daily Post*, 3 July 1868, 4; *Memphis Daily Appeal*, 6 July 1875, 1; 5 July 1887, 8.

61. Ibid., 6 July 1875, 1; 6 July 1877, I.

62. *Memphis Daily Post*, 5 July 1867, 8; *Memphis Daily Appeal*, 5 July 1874, 4.

63. Ibid.

64. Elsa Brown and Gregg Kimball have suggested African American parades proceeded past various establishments that designated "Race Progress." See Brown and Kimball, "Mapping the Terrain of Black Richmond," 83.

65. *Memphis Daily Post*, 2 July 1869, 4.

66. *Memphis Daily Post*, 5 July 1867, 8.

67. *Memphis Daily Appeal*, 6 July 1867, 3.

68. *Memphis Daily Appeal*, 6 July 1867, 3; *Memphis Daily Post*, 5 July 1867, 8.

69. *Edwards Annual Directory to the City of Memphis*, 1870.

70. *Memphis Daily Appeal*, 6 July 1869, 4.

71. Ibid.

72. The Fourth of July celebration in 1875 represented a break in African American support for the Republican Party. See Berkeley, "Like a Plague of Locust," 298–355. Joseph Cartwright concludes that the Reform movement initiated by the Memphis elite was, in fact, directed at limiting black political power. See Joseph Cartwright, *The Triumph of Jim Crow: Tennessee Race Relations in he 1880s* (Knoxville, 1976), 120. For a discussion on African American societies and reconciliation see Tucker, *Black Pastors and Leaders*, 31–34. For the most in depth analysis of this reform movement see Lynette Boney Wrenn, *Crisis and Commission Government in Memphis: Elite Rule in a Gilded Age City* (Knoxville, 1998).

73. *Memphis Daily Appeal*, 6 July 1875, 1. For information on Hezkiah Henley see *Edwards Annual Directory to the City of Memphis*, 1874. Also, for a discussion on the celebration of 1875 in the context of politics see Tucker, *Black Pastors and Leaders*, 32–34.

74. *Memphis Daily Appeal*, 6 July 1875, 1.

75. *Memphis Daily Appeal*, 5 July 1887, 8.

76. It must be remembered that just because there was no mention of an African American Fourth of July celebration does not necessarily mean that one did not occur.

77. *Memphis Daily Appeal*, 5 July 1889, 4; *Memphis Commercial Appeal*, 5 July 1894, 5.

78. This change may also reveal a shift in interests and focus within African American communities. Deborah Gray White states that African Americans, "accommodated racism by retreating to their own institutions." See Deborah Gray White, *Too Heavy a Load: Black Women in Defense of Themselves, 1894–1994* (New York, 1999), 26.

79. Cartwright, *The Triumph of Jim Crow*, 76, 119, 120, 138, 139, 145; Foner, *Reconstruction: Americas Unfinished Revolution*; Evelyn Brooks Higginbotham, *Righteous Discontent: The*

*Women's Movement in the Black Baptist Church* (Cambridge, 1993), 4, 5; Valeria W. Weaver, "The Failure of Civil Rights 1875–1883 and its Repercussions," *The Journal of Negro History* 54 (October 1969): 368–382.

    80. *Memphis Appeal Avalanche*, 4 July 1891, 4.

    81. *Memphis Commercial Appeal*, 4 July 1894, 5.

    82. *Memphis Daily Appeal*, 5 July 1876, 4.

# BLACK RECONSTRUCTIONISTS IN TENNESSEE

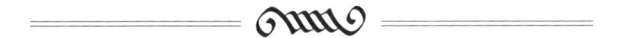

*Walter J. Fraser, Jr.*

During the last several decades historians writing about the role of the black political leaders in the ex-Confederate States from 1865 to 1876 have sharply revised the interpretations of the Redeemers and their sympathizers who characterized Reconstruction as an era of Negro rule and corruption. However, students of the subject have concluded that many questions remain unanswered. Who were the black leaders and office holders at the local level? Did Negro leaders resist intimidation and terrorism? Did they articulate the desires of the black masses? What was the relationship between the black leaders, the masses, and the white politicians? Investigations into these areas also may help to resolve the continuing controversy over the psychological effects of slavery.[1] Since few studies have probed these areas and no recent inquiry has raised these questions with regard to the first state readmitted to the Union, this paper will focus on Tennessee and in particular the western portion of the state and its urban center Memphis.[2]

Memphis, seat of Shelby County, was a rough, dirty, river city of approximately 21,000 whites and 14,000 Negroes in 1865. The latter included mostly ex-slaves, a few who were free men before the war, and Federal troops; the former included Union and ex-Union army men, government agents, northern merchants, and native whites. The ratio of blacks to whites in Shelby and the surrounding counties was nearly equal with the exception of Fayette, which counted nearly sixty percent blacks in its population.[3]

The press and clergy of Memphis reflected the racial animosity of the native white toward the black man. The *Daily Appeal* viewed the Negro as "unthrifty, lazy and wholly unreliable" while the *Avalanche*, ignoring legal emancipation, proclaimed that the Negroes "are still slaves in fact if not in name." One prominent minister told his congregation that he burned books holding that slavery was an evil; another advocated distribution of Bibles to blacks so that they might read of their inferiority.[4] Following the Memphis race riot of May 1866, a Federal investigating committee concluded that the violence was "actuated by the deadly hatred of the colored race."[5] In early 1867, when the self-serving Brownlow government at Nashville grudgingly enfranchised the Negro, the *Appeal* declared, "It would be better for the whole black breed to be" annihilated rather than given the vote.[6] A few months later the paper asserted that the Negro is "but a generation removed from the savage."[7] However, despite the strong racial antipathy, the violence directed at the Negro during and after the 1866 race riot, and the warnings of the Conservative press, Radical Republican black leaders emerged in West Tennessee.

Although by 1867 the lily-white Brownlow administration exercised extensive power across the state through urban police forces, commissioners of registration, and a state militia, white Conservatives vied with Radical Republicans for the black vote. The most powerful Radical faction in West Tennessee was the machine of Barbour Lewis and the Eaton brothers, John and Lucien. New England born, college-educated, zealous abolitionists, and Union army officers, they settled in Memphis after the war and established the *Post*, which advocated Negro civil and political rights and public schools. While the Eatons edited the propaganda arm of the machine, Lewis as chairman of the Memphis Republican party worked among the black voters through the Union Leagues of West Tennessee. State and local offices depended on the election of John Eaton, Jr., to the state superintendency of public instruction and Brownlow as governor in August 1867.[8]

One of the first Negro leaders attracted to the Lewis-Eaton organization was Captain Hannibal C. Carter. A native of Indiana and a free man before the war, Carter was well educated and working as a barber in New Orleans when the city fell to Union forces in 1862. A few months later he became the commanding officer of Company C, Second Regiment, Louisiana Native Guards, Corps de Afrique. Carter served in this capacity until he resigned from the unit in May 1863, due to service-connected disabilities. He soon moved upriver to Memphis where he became the proprietor of a saloon and gambling house. Light-skinned, above average in height, he frequently boasted of his white parentage on his father's side. When Carter joined the Lewis-Eaton machine he was about thirty years of age. In 1867 he founded the

Tennessee Colored Banking and Real Estate Association of Memphis with several other Negroes, two of whom, William Kennedy and Edward Shaw, also joined the Lewis-Eaton organization.[9]

William Kennedy was also a mulatto, in his early thirties and not a native of Tennessee. His profession was "speculator" and by 1870 he owned property valued at $10,000.[10]

Edward Shaw was born in Kentucky during the 1820s. It appears that he removed to Indiana at an early age and by 1852 as a free man he had settled in Memphis. He also became an owner of a saloon and gambling house. Shaw did not serve in the war and when asked publicly why he had not, he convulsed the audience by replyin,: "I was afraid I might get shot." Described as "a bright mulatto, six feet, and rather of the Indian appearance," he was "an able, forcible... earnest, and... eloquent speaker."[11]

During the summer of 1867, Carter, Kennedy, and Shaw worked closely with Barbour Lewis to organize and register blacks for the Republican Party. They warned Memphis Negroes at public rallies to beware of the "rebels" and former slaveholders who had "infamously degraded" the Negro race and were now pretending to be their friends in order to enlist their votes. Other black Radicals were attracted to the Lewis-Eaton machine and appeared with Carter, Kennedy, and Shaw on the hustings. One was John Harris, known by his friends as "a first rate stump speaker" but characterized by the Conservatives as "a carpenter from Texas," who "spends most of his time in low saloons." When Joe Helm also joined the machine, the press observed that although "the Negro Helm" had given his occupation as a "steamboat man, faro dealer would have been more correct."[12]

Negroes who allied themselves with Memphis Conservatives were sometimes harassed, "waylaid and beaten" by the black politicos of the Lewis-Eaton organization. When A. N. Thomas, described by Conservatives as "a very respectable colored man... quiet and well-behaved," began organizing Negroes to vote against Brownlow's reelection, he was followed, his home watched, and attempts were made to assassinate him. On June 17, 1867, Carter and Helm were arrested, charged with attempted murder, and held on $2,000 bond each for assaulting Thomas with a whip.[13] Other Negro Conservatives who publicly denounced Brownlow as a racist and urged Negroes to remain loyal to their true friends, the Southern people, testified that they were harassed by "Black Leaguers." Alarmed at the success of the black Radicals' intimidation of potential voters, the Memphis press in mid-June urged Conservatives to arm in order to protect themselves and their Negro allies.

Conservatives also tried to sow discord between the white and black members of the Eaton-Lewis machine. In July the *Avalanche* reported that Dr. S. H. Toles, a black

Republican, had accompanied Barbour Lewis by rail to speak at Bolivar in Hardeman County. On the train the conductor refused to allow Toles to take a seat beside Lewis and the doctor was then relegated to the "colored folks car"—a proceeding which Lewis condoned. Toles was so disgusted and disappointed with Lewis that he told the *Avalanche*, "De white trash don't care for niggers no how...."[14] In consideration of the attitudes subsequently revealed by the white members of the Lewis-Eaton machine toward the blacks, this incident, although patently reported by the Conservative press to divide the black and white Radicals, has the ring of truth.

The Conservative effort to win the black vote failed and Brownlow, John Eaton, Jr., Radical Republican legislators, and congressmen gained a large majority of the returns in Memphis and West Tennessee. Approximately five out of every six blacks voted the radical ticket in Shelby County. A Memphis Conservative wrote President Andrew Johnson that "the election leaves us under undisputed Brownlow and Negro rule.... " The combination of black and white Radicals comprising the Lewis-Eaton machine had marshaled the Negro voters and contributed to the Republican triumph. However, a rival Radical faction headed by James M. Tomeny, Federal marshal of West Tennessee, and S. B. Beaumont, chief of Memphis police, soon challenged the Lewis-Eaton organization for control of local, state, and Federal offices as well as the Negro vote.[15]

By late fall of 1867, both Radical factions were backing separate candidates in the Memphis mayoralty race. Before mass rallies of Negroes, Lewis, Edward Shaw, and ex-Union army general, scalawag, and state senator William Jay Smith denounced their Radical opponents while completely ignoring the Conservative candidate. On one occasion Shaw accused the Tomeny-Beaumont candidate of duplicity, and corruption as well as of "being... drunk in the... streets." Nonetheless, the Radical factionalism split the Negro vote and a Conservative won the mayoralty election in early 1868.[16]

Despite the setback, Carter, Shaw and Kennedy were now well aware of the power of the black vote and their own influence. Whetting their political ambitions was an act of the Tennessee legislature in January 1868 that declared "there shall be no disqualification for holding office... on account of race or color."[17] When the three black leaders began holding ward meetings in Memphis to test their strength as potential candidates in future elections, Barbour Lewis became worried. He wrote privately, "I know that I ought to go to some of [the meetings] and keep things moving on the right line.... Our colored people ought to be willing to wait awhile until they are competent but they are not." When he learned that Carter, Kennedy, and Shaw planned to meet with members of the rival Radical faction, he was even more concerned and he "went over to prevent mischief."[18] Lewis wanted to keep the Negro leaders and their influence among the black voters wedded to the Lewis-Eaton machine to insure the election of the machine's white Congressional candidate in 1868.

To keep the loyalty of Carter, Kennedy, and Shaw, the Lewis-Eaton organization gave them minor posts within the district Republican Party and held out the promise of public offices in the future. With the approach of the presidential and congressional elections, Lewis secured the appointment of the three black leaders to vice-presidencies in the Central Grant and Colfax Club and Carter and Shaw were made members of the Republican Executive Committee of the Congressional District.

During the summer and fall, Lewis and the three black leaders spoke at rallies across West Tennessee to rouse black support for the presidential ticket of Grant and Colfax and the Lewis-Eaton congressional candidate General William Jay Smith. They enlisted ex-slave David Brown to appear and speak with them. Again and again they reminded the Negroes of their obligation to the Republican party, praised the Grant and Colfax ticket, hailed Smith as "the champion of colored Radicals of West Tennessee," and warned against the siren calls of the "rebels" who had whipped the black man, kept him in ignorance, burned his schools and churches, and murdered or driven away the northern teachers, his white benefactors. They labeled colored Democrats as traitors to their race, denounced the candidate of the opposing Radical ring, and called for the state militia to protect black men on election day.[19]

Hoping to take advantage of the division among the Radicals once again, the Conservatives put forward a strong candidate and sought the Negro vote. Black leaders were enlisted to speak, Negro Democratic clubs were organized, and the *Appeal* urged its readers to patronize only black Conservative tradesmen. Meanwhile the Klan increased its terrorism against black Radicals.[20] In the late summer the Conservative standard-bearer wrote President Johnson, "The Negroes are showing every evidence of intending to... vote with us...."[21] When Edward Shaw learned that he had been marked for murder by an "assassination committee" of the Klan, he and other black leaders armed themselves. Seated on the speakers' platform in late August before a large rally of Memphis blacks, Shaw, Carter, and Kennedy were fired on by Klansmen; as quickly as they could draw their pistols they returned the fire "with a rattling volley," and when the Klan fled, the meeting continued.[22]

Even though the Radicals were divided and the Conservatives vigorously wooed the Negro vote, Memphis and Eighth District blacks overwhelmingly voted the Grant, Colfax, and Smith ticket. In Memphis and Shelby County, Smith received 4,212 black votes, but only 291 white. The Conservative candidate ran second with eighty-five Negro and 2,431 white ballots. The Radical incumbent got seventy-one black and 232 white votes.²³ The Lewis-Eaton machine was now in a position to obtain local, state, and Federal offices for its members.

Following the election Barbour Lewis privately acknowledged that Carter and Shaw, working "with efficiency and admirable tact and good judgment," had been of particular assistance in gaining the victory. He believed that with the continued alliance of the two men, "our party will soon be in a position to accomplish great good for the colored people, and our common cause." However, both Carter and Shaw soon became restive: they wanted fulfillment of white Republican pledges to secure the appointment or to aid in the support of Negroes for public office.²⁴ Edward Shaw would be bitterly disappointed.

By early 1869 Shaw decided that he had enough support among Shelby County blacks to be elected to the five-member board of county commissioners over which Barbour Lewis presided as chairman. But when Lewis heard of these plans, he and Congressman William Jay Smith privately decided to work against Shaw. They were willing to secure a lesser post for Shaw; the position they had in mind would "hardly make the trouble for us that the other... will." Shaw and others later charged that Lewis and Smith had conspired to defeat him "solely on the ground that he was a colored man."²⁵

When a Conservative candidate entered the race for commissioner the Conservative press called for Shaw's defeat; if a Negro were elected Shelby County would be "disgraced" the papers declared. However, on March 6 Shaw won the office by more than 400 votes, becoming the first Negro in West Tennessee and only the third in the state to ever win an elective post. His term of office was five years and his salary $2,500 per annum.²⁶

Angry with the white Republican-controlled Lewis-Eaton machine for opposing his election as a county commissioner, both Shaw and Carter threatened to join the opposing Radical faction. By this tactic they forced Lewis to reiterate his pledges to secure Federal posts for Negroes through Congressman Smith and John Eaton, Jr., recently appointed U. S. Commissioner of Education. In return Carter and Shaw buried their anger and promised to marshal support among the blacks to confirm the Lewis-Eaton candidates for Federal offices before the District Radical convention. Lewis wrote Eaton in early March, "I think Carter and Shaw will act with us hereafter.... At least they say they will." Ironically Lewis added, "If they would have the good sense and manliness to do so freely and honorably we could make a combination here that would keep our party in power for a long series of years."²⁷ The continued alliance of Carter, Shaw, and Kennedy was expected to keep the Negro masses wedded to the Lewis-Eaton machine and thereby neutralize the opposing Radical organization.

During the months of March and April, the three leaders held meetings among the District Negroes to enlist their support for the Lewis-Eaton nominees for Federal jobs. Members of the opposing Radical faction, both Negro and white, later testified under oath that Carter, Shaw, and Kennedy used money and physical intimidation to stack the convention in favor of the Lewis-Eaton candidates.[28]

When the District Radical convention met in Memphis in late April, the Negroes marshaled by Carter, Shaw, and Kennedy controlled the convention. Among the white nominees put forward and endorsed were Lucien Eaton for Federal marshal of West Tennessee and Barbour Lewis as appraiser in the U. S. Customs House at Memphis. The sole black nominated and confirmed by the convention was Hannibal C. Carter for assessor, U.S. Internal Revenue Department, West Tennessee. Through the aid of John Eaton, Jr., and Congressman Smith, Lucien Eaton was soon appointed marshal; however, when a white Radical was given the assessor's office, Carter had to settle for an assistant assessor's post. Both Carter and Shaw again felt betrayed. Both believed that Congressman Smith had not secured the position for Carter "because he was a colored man." Carter served briefly as an assistant assessor, but soon left the state. And when the Lewis-Eaton machine failed to secure a Federal post for Shaw, he let it be known that he was "mad and disgusted" that Lewis and the organization "did not do more for him" and the Negroes of West Tennessee.[29] Twice duped, he had been twice betrayed.

Adding to Shaw's political and economic frustrations was the loss of his $2,500 a year commissioner's post. When the Conservatives captured the governorship and the legislature in the elections of August 1869, the Board of Commissioners of Shelby County was abolished. By repealing other Radical legislation, abolishing judicial posts, and removing county registrars, the Conservatives quickly won control from statehouse to courthouse. With their influence severely diminished at the local and state level, white members of the Lewis-Eaton machine also worried about their being able to reelect Congressman Smith and thereby maintain their Federal ring. And when Edward Shaw joined the opposing Radical faction Barbour Lewis and Lucien Eaton felt that their machine was so endangered that they asked Shaw to "name his price" to aid in the Congressional campaign for Smith. However, still furious with the Lewis-Eaton machine, Shaw rejected the bribe. Lewis now believed that Shaw had been bought by their opponents; he wrote privately in disgust that local Radicals both "Negro and white... are mad for money..."[30]

Also leaving the Lewis-Eaton machine and joining the Radical opposition with Shaw was Giles Smith. A mulatto in his early thirties, above average in height, born in Tennessee, a "farmer" before the war, and an ex-Union Army private, Smith had secured an appointment as a mail agent with the U.S. Postal Service at Memphis through the aid of Congressman Smith. However, when charges of fraud were brought against Smith, he was fired from his post; both he and Shaw believed that he had been framed by the Lewis-Eaton machine to make room in the postal service for a white Republican. Giles Smith, like Carter and Shaw, felt that he too had been betrayed.[31]

Now working against his former allies, Shaw spoke before such Negro groups as the "Union Forever" Association, the Sons of Ham, and the Lincoln Aid Society, exhorting the blacks to be industrious and sober, to focus their energies on becoming landowners. He accused Lewis, Eaton, and Congressman Smith of using the Negro to gain office, and then forgetting the interests of the black man after the election. "We intend to teach such men that we are not to 'be led by the nose,'" Shaw told his audiences. "Colored men, go for everything pertaining to your welfare. The more I look at the rascality of those men, the more I despise and loathe them." Shaw sometimes concluded, to wild applause and cheers, "Teach them this: that you have rights to be respected."

As soon as Lewis learned of Shaw's attacks on the machine, he wrote to John Eaton, Jr., that Shaw, Giles Smith, "and a few other soulless hirelings" were meeting with Negroes of the district and attacking Congressman Smith and himself "in the meanest, roughest Ku Klux style." But despite the opposition of Shaw and Giles Smith, Lewis in late September still believed that Smith could be reelected. Important to the campaign would be William Kennedy, who had remained loyal to the machine, and the Negro leader Moses Hopkins.[32] Both Kennedy and Hopkins had received minor Federal posts through the Lewis-Eaton machine. A mulatto born in Mississippi, five feet eight inches tall, and a "farmer" before the war, Hopkins was a Union Army veteran who had risen quickly in the ranks to first sergeant during his service in the U. S. Colored Infantry.[33]

With Kennedy and Hopkins at their sides Lewis and Smith took to the hustings to defend the organization against Shaw's charges and to rally support for Smith's return to Congress. At a meeting held in early October in a Memphis Negro church, whose pastor was the Reverend William Brinkley, Lewis aimed a barb at Shaw who was in the audience. Lewis warned the crowd that there were Negroes posing as their leaders and working against Smith, but that their opposition was based solely on the ground that Smith had not secured Federal offices for them. Congressman Smith followed Lewis to the rostrum but when he tried to speak, Shaw leaped to his feet, declaring that Smith "should never again" be allowed to speak in Memphis. Fearing violence, the middle-aged Reverend Brinkley began putting out the lights. However, former police chief S. B. Beaumont, opponent of the Lewis-Eaton faction and now Shaw's ally, knocked Brinkley down and began kicking him. A general fight erupted and the meeting broke up.[34]

A few days later at a District Radical convention controlled by the opponents of the Lewis-Eaton machine, scalawag and former Congressman David A. Nunn described Edward Shaw, as a man of "honesty, courage and integrity" and nominated him for Congress. After being unanimously endorsed by the predominantly black convention, Shaw told the Negroes to stand together and throw off the yoke of Lewis and Smith. Neither man, said Shaw, "wants a nigger to run for office... and would kill them off faster than the Ku-Klux" if they could. Apparently unknown to Shaw and his Negro followers, Nunn had made a deal with local Conservatives who were backing ex-Confederate W. W. Vaughan for Congress. It was hoped that Shaw's candidacy would split the Negro vote and that Vaughan, gaining nearly all the white votes of the district, would win the election.[35] Edward Shaw would be the first Negro to run for Congress in Tennessee.

White Republicans in the Lewis-Eaton machine were convinced that Shaw had been bribed and was privy to the plan to divide the black vote. One member conjectured that Shaw would "get more money from them [Democrats] probably than he has ever begged in a similar speculation." Barbour Lewis believed that Shaw "might make a good fight. [The Democrats] furnish him funds quite liberally." Shaw's candidacy "may prove troublesome," Lewis wrote, "a black man's candidate is a specious cry among the ignorant and feeble minded blacks." Lewis knew that many Negroes were "indignant and angry," with the machine, but "they easily forgive and forget." And since Shaw "at present... has very few decent (black) followers," Lewis believed that with enough funds and good speeches, General Smith could be reelected.[36]

One of the tactics that Lewis employed against Shaw was the circulation of a hand-bill denouncing him for selling out the Negroes and the Republican Party to the Democrats. Lewis reported to John Eaton that the handbill "creates a mild sensation among our voters and is doing good. We have killed Shaw *dead*, by stabbing him constantly since he went over to our enemies." Infuriated by the charges, Shaw swore publicly "that he would shoot [Lewis] on sight!"[37] He refuted the allegations at rallies throughout the district in late October and turned on his accusers. Lewis and Smith are carpetbaggers, Shaw told the Negroes. They have used black votes to get "their arms into the Federal treasury."[38]

As the congressional race between Shaw, Smith, and Vaughan entered the final weeks, the Lewis-Eaton machine intensified its efforts to elect Smith. Again he was touted as the champion of Negro political and civil rights. When threats were made to assassinate Smith and members of his party if he spoke in Mason's Depot, Negroes offered him protection. A member of the Smith entourage that was traveling across the district in a lumber wagon wrote John Eaton's wife Alice E. Shirley Eaton (born in Vicksburg, Mississippi), not without a note of sarcasm, "I just love the col[ored] people at Masons, yes I do Alice.... 20 mounted men accompanied us to protect us. They called it Smith's cavalry."[39]

Once again factionalism among the Radicals, the charges and countercharges of Shaw, and the Lewis-Eaton organization confused and divided the Negroes; intimidation of the Negroes by the Conservatives and their control of the election machinery resulted in a small turnout of black voters. Of 8,000 Negroes registered in Shelby County, less than 2,000 voted. Although Vaughan beat Smith by more than 8,000 votes and Smith came in second in the race for Congress, the Lewis-Eaton machine considered it "a big victory" because "Shaw got only 165 votes in Shelby County" and ran a poor third.[40]

Following his defeat Shaw continued to work against the Lewis-Eaton organization holding meetings with Negroes across the district to gather signatures on a resolution notifying President Grant that Federal office holders in West Tennessee did not truly represent the Republican Party. United States Marshal Lucien Eaton notified John Eaton that Shaw "with a few of [his] dirty associates have organized... and seem to be... moving to do something about controlling the Federal patronage."[41] Yet when Barbour Lewis decided to run for Congress in the presidential election year of 1872 he believed that he needed Shaw's support to win and appealed to him for help. Aware more than ever that he had to support Grant and Lewis if he was to advance his own interests, and those of the black man, Shaw agreed to join with Lewis.

Shaw appeared at rallies across the district to tout the ticket of Grant, Wilson, and Lewis. He told his audiences that he was "heart and soul" for Lewis, a "faithful, true and zealous Republican." Aware of the movement in Congress for a civil rights bill, Shaw emphasized the urgent need for such a measure. He often observed that whereas Irish and German immigrant children have been admitted to public schools "the day after they landed," native American blacks have been set apart "tabooed and ostracized [sic]." Negroes have also been separated in railroad cars:

> where a lady of color though she be as refined as anybody in the land is sent into the Jim Crow car and there she meets the Jim Crow man, who puts his legs upon the seat behind her shoulders and puffs his stinking pipe or cigar and breathes out his stinking polluted breath.

Shaw told the predominantly black crowds that Negroes are neither allowed to associate with whites in hotels nor public places of amusement. As a slave the black man possessed no rights that the white man had to respect; but slavery is dead and such sentiments of inequality need to be buried. He condemned the Democrats for denying equality to the black man and for admonishing the Negro to be content with what he had. Therefore, when Congress reassembles, Shaw told his audiences, "We will demand that the Civil Rights bill shall become a law." Returning to an old theme, he averred that the black man must have "a fair share of the offices." With 9,000 potential office holders in the district, Negroes have not held one significant Federal post. After the elections, "we will demand some minor places" and "we expect [our] demands to be adhered to."

Shaw told the Negroes of the district that he had been falsely accused of going over to the Democrats. But he defied "any man living... to point where or when I was with the Democrats." Never could he have formed such an alliance, Shaw declared, because "I will never support any man who will not accord to me the self-same manhood he claims for himself." He admitted that he had opposed Congressman Smith but only because the latter refused to secure important Federal posts for the black man. Even Shaw's enemies described his style on the hustings as "eloquent" and his speeches as "orations after the MANNER OF CICERO."[42]

Conservatives were alarmed over the reconciliation of Shaw and Lewis. The press warned of the dangers of "Africanization," which could result from Lewis's election and the activities of the "wicked and designing... Shaw." Lewis and Shaw were accused of being up to their "dirty work" again among the Negroes and of trying to regain the strangle hold they once had over the District.[43]

Members of the old Tomeny-Beaumont faction also denounced Shaw among the Negroes. George S. Heyden, "a disgusted colored Republican leader," told Memphis blacks that Shaw had sold out to the Federal ring led by Lewis that had used the Negro voter for years. This was odd and disappointing, Heyden declared, in light of Shaw's previous charges against Lewis and considering "the many good fights Shaw has made for justice to himself and his people."[44]

When the Conservative candidate for Congress, Colonel Landon C. Haynes, a senator in the Confederate Congress during the war, used these themes on the hustings against Lewis, both Shaw and Lewis replied. Lewis reiterated that he had spent his life advocating equal rights and moral elevation for the Negro. Shaw warned the Negroes who were denouncing Lewis and himself that they were causing "division in our ranks." They are practicing "treason to the... party" and thereby strengthening "its enemies." He called for "union in our ranks now and forever."[45]

The ticket of Grant, Wilson, and Lewis was elected over their Democratic opponents in West Tennessee despite the Conservative press and the division among black and white Radicals. Lewis received 13,783 votes and beat Haynes by nearly 3,000 ballots. In the district there were nearly 1,500 white Radicals who probably voted for Lewis. Therefore, black men had cast approximately 12,000 votes for him. The *Memphis Appeal* asserted that Lewis's victory was due to his consolidation of the "ignorant... inferior" black Republican voters.[46] Certainly a major factor in Lewis's win was Edward Shaw. He had agreed to bury the past and join with Lewis to marshal the black voter in return for Lewis's pledges to work for equal rights for the black man and an educational system to assure all "a fair start in life." About a year after the Congressional race, Shaw was elected wharfmaster of Memphis and had become the leading Negro advocate in Tennessee of the Civil Rights Bill before Congress.[47] Congressman Barbour Lewis would become also a vigorous proponent of the bill.

In December 1873, amendments to the Civil Rights Bill of 1866 were introduced into Congress calling for the integration of public schools, inns, public conveyances, and "places of amusement." Immediately a rabid opposition arose in the South aimed particularly at the "mixed school clause." To counter this opposition, Republicans urged Negro leaders in the South to meet in convention and urge Congressional support of the Civil Rights Bill. Under Edward Shaw's leadership, Shelby and sixteen other counties elected delegates to a State Colored Convention at Nashville in late April 1874. Chosen president of the convention, Shaw lamented that only seventeen counties were represented, a fact which he attributed to white harassment of black leaders in the more rural counties.[48]

Shaw opened the convention with a ringing appeal calling for the Republicans in Congress to pass the Civil Rights Bill in the form in which it was introduced. If the "mixed school" clause were struck, the measure would be of little consequence; as long as there were separate schools for white and black, Shaw told the assembled delegates, "so long would the latter be taught their inferiority to whites."[49]

The convention passed resolutions asserting that Tennessee Negroes were treated with "insidious proscription" by being denied equal accommodations in public facilities and conveyances and that particularly the state's segregated school policy encouraged a "spirit of caste and hate." The failure of the Republican Party to secure passage of the bill before Congress would be "a baseless surrender of the rights of humanity to our insidious foe" who contests the Negroes' civil rights as vigorously as he did emancipation.[50]

After the convention adjourned, Shaw returned to West Tennessee and began to meet with Negro groups to secure their endorsement of the Nashville resolutions.

At the same time the Memphis press launched an attack on the actions of the "political zealots" of the State Colored Convention. Newspapers warned the Negro masses to beware of office-seeking black men whose "threatening demands" would jeopardize the public schools. The press charged Shaw with advocating a bill which encroaches "upon the domain of social and domestic life as fearlessly as... if the Anglo-Saxon race is a myth...."[51]

Stung by the condemnation of himself and the Nashville meeting, Shaw publicly answered the *Avalanche*. Place yourself in my position, he asked the Memphis editor, "with your pride of manhood, and ask yourself if another could be justifed in calling you a political zealot in laboring for your civil rights.... " The Negroes do not desire their children to be educated with whites, Shaw wrote, but "it is our wish to be from under the stigma of inferiority." Tennessee law, he pointed out, "states that a colored child shall not enter a white school, not that a white child shall not enter a colored school. This is intended to teach the colored child that it is inferior, and this we dislike." Mixed schools will not destroy public education but rather "hasten to destroy that school of prejudice... that teaches the colored child is inferior." Good government, Shaw concluded, is based on principles of justice and laws which defend the weak and powerless.

In speaking before Negro groups Shaw focused on the "mixed school" clause as the main provision of the bill. He pointed out the inequities of the segregated system of schools in Tennessee: the high teacher-to-pupil ratios in black schools, the low ratio in white, the markedly fewer black schools and months of operation, the irregularity of pay for the black teacher as compared with the regularly paid white one. Only a single school system will "give our children equal chances," Shaw emphasized, and permit them to learn to spell, read, and write and grow into literate men and women. But if there is such "prejudice in the breasts of Southern gentlemen to break up the public school system because I ask that my child may have the same privileges that theirs have, I say, in God's name let them break it up." Blacks had little to lose, but much to gain.[52]

The press characterized Shaw's addresses as "insolent, impudent harangues" designed to stir "their baser passions." And in the early spring Memphis newspapers fueled wild rumors that the blacks were about to launch class warfare. Aware of the rising tensions between black and white, a member of the Lewis-Eaton machine wrote that there is a great amount "of prejudice created here against the public school system by the Civil Rights Bill—It is very strong and I fear the result."[53]

When Shaw met with Barbour Lewis during the summer to map their strategy for the Congressional race of 1874, Lewis knew that West Tennessee Negroes wanted all portions of the Civil Rights Bill enacted, especially the "mixed school" clause. The Conservative press, however, denounced the bill as one aimed at enforcing social equality. And any white man not opposing the bill "is a disgrace to his race." In the late summer an editorial in the *Appeal* reflected the rabid racially-based hostility to the bill. White parents will not see "their lovely children with pure Caucasian blood throbbing through their pure white veins... intermix with dirty, lousy pickaninnies," the editor wrote. And Southern whites have sworn opposition to seeing

> their beautiful daughters sandwiched at the theater, in a public conveyance, or at the dinner table, between the stench of two musty Africans, whose hideous blackness only reflects the whiteness and beauty of the lovely object they would defile by the unnatural and loathsome contact. God almighty never intended such a profanation.[54]

In view of such virulent opposition to the "mixed school" clause, Barbour Lewis wavered in supporting this portion of the bill during his campaign for reelection to Congress. Once again Edward Shaw felt betrayed. Even the Memphis press announced that Shaw was a truer representative of the feelings of his race on the "mixed school" clause than Lewis, who "dodges" the issue. Delighting in Lewis'S "crawfishing" and knowing that Shaw and the Negro voters favored integrated schools, the press inquired: "Colored voters, what do you think of your sweetscented champion now?"[55]

The rabid campaign against the Civil Rights Bill by West Tennessee Conservatives and the confusion and factionalism created among the Negro masses by Shaw's advocacy and Lewis'S "craw fishing" on the "mixed school" clause, contributed to the latter's defeat. As a "lame duck" congressman, Lewis did vote for the bill after the "mixed school" clause was changed to read "separate but equal" school facilities. Not only was the heart of the bill as envisioned by Shaw and his Negro followers excised, but the Tennessee legislature promptly killed the remaining provisions by making them unenforceable.[56]

Although Shaw continued active in West Tennessee politics for a few more years, his influence on the Negro masses slowly declined. As his political power diminished both black and white Conservatives publicly rejoiced and a Radical Republican of the Lewis-Eaton ring privately exulted, "It [is]... very gratifying to have so many respectable white men taking hold."[57]

Edward Shaw eventually retired from "political life in seeming disgust." During the last years of his life he studied law and was admitted to practice before the Memphis bar. All his clients were Negroes.[58]

Hannibal C. Carter, William Kennedy, Edward Shaw, John Harris, Joe Helm, Dr. S. H. Toles, Giles Smith, Moses Hopkins, and David Brown were the nine Negroes identified as working at one time or another for the political machine directed by the Radical white Republicans Barbour Lewis, and John and Lucien Eaton. The five most prominent black politicos were Carter, Kennedy, Shaw, Smith, and Hopkins, all mulattos and free men at the outbreak of the Civil War. Four were born outside of the state. Four were considerably above average in height and young men in their early thirties. Three had served in the Union army; three owned property and founded a banking firm in Memphis after the war. All five were noted for their public speaking abilities. They were aggressive, ambitious men on the make for themselves but at the same time they had the interests of the black masses in mind when they publicly championed land ownership, educational opportunities, and civil and political rights for the Negro. To gain their political ends they attempted to unify the often fragmented Negro masses by using vituperative language, bribes, and physical violence against both black Conservatives and white Radicals. They also publicly denounced white Conservatives, resisted Klan terrorism by arming themselves, and on at least one occasion traded volleys with members of the Ku Klux Klan; on another occasion Negroes armed themselves and formed "Smith's cavalry" to guard the white Republican Congressman from assassination.

These black leaders allied themselves with the Lewis-Eaton machine because they believed it was the most expeditious route to secure county, state, and Federal offices for themselves and civil, political, and educational rights for the black masses. To hasten the realization of their ambitions they used the lever of threatening to bolt to the Radical opposition. But they soon discovered that despite the abstract idealism of Lewis, the Eatons, and Congressman Smith, these white Radical Republican leaders, like their Conservative counterparts, had a racially-based bias against black men that was particularly reflected in their refusal to aid Negro politicos to gain important public offices. Frustrated and betrayed, several of the Negro leaders eventually joined the opposition, but here too they soon realized that they were being duped and used. Only Edward Shaw gained an influential public post, winning two county elective offices *in spite of* the white Radicals.

All nine Negro leaders lived most of their lives in the caste system of the antebellum or postbellum South. Carter, Kennedy and Shaw were free men for years before the war and Smith and Hopkins were evidently free men at the outbreak. But as Smith and Hopkins were "farmers" in areas of high slave populations, they may have been slaves at one time during their lives. There is insufficient data to determine if Harris, Helm, or Toles were ever slaves. David Brown remained a slave into the early years of the Civil War. In any case, the actions and speeches of Brown and the other eight were not characteristic of the mentalities of concentration camp inmates or those who spent most of their lives in a rigid, authoritarian caste system. Their denunciations of Southern whites and their resistance to intimidation do not go hand in hand with docility and infantilism.

In sum, these black black leaders failed to achieve their ambitions for themselves or the goals they set for the Negro masses. However, with no prior political experience, consistently denounced, intimidated, and divided by white Conservatives who wanted to perpetuate the antebellum caste system, and duped, used, and betrayed by white Radicals, they did aggressively pursue their aims for years. Thus their significance lies not in their failure, but in that they waged the fight at all.[59]

*This article first appeared in the Winter 1975 issue of the* Tennessee Historical Quarterly.

1. John Hope Franklin, "Reconstruction and the Negro," in Harold M. Hyman, ed., *New Frontiers of the American Reconstruction* (Urbana, 1966 ), 63–64; August Meier, "Comment on John Hope Franklin's Paper," ibid., 79, 84–86; August Meier, "Negroes in the First and Second Reconstructions of the South," *Civil War History* (June, 1967), 127; John Hope Franklin, *Reconstruction: After the Civil War* (Chicago, 1961 ), 133–38; Joel Williamson, *After Slavery: the Negro in South Carolina during Reconstruction, 1861–1877* (Chapel Hill, 1965); Joe M. Richardson, *The Negro in the Reconstruction of Florida, 1865–1877* (Tallahassee, 1965); E. L. Thornbrough, ed., *Black Reconstructionists* (Englewood Cliffs, 1972), 19–20; Robert H. McKenzie, "The Shelby Iron Company: A Note on Slave Protest After the Civil War," *Journal of Negro History* (July, 1973), 341–48; Jerrell H. Shofner, "Militant Negro Laborers in Reconstruction Florida," *Journal of Southern History* (August, 1973), 397–408; Peter Kolchin, *First Freedom: The Response of Alabama Blacks to Emancipation and Reconstruction* (Westport, 1972), xix.

2. Alrutheus Ambush Taylor, *The Negro in Tennessee, 1865–1880* (Washington, 1941); James Welch Patton, *Unionism and Reconstruction in Tennessee, 1860–1869* (Chapel Hill, 1934); Mingo Scott, *The Negro in Tennessee Politics and Governmental Affairs, 1865–1965* (Nashville, 1964); Thomas B. Alexander, *Political Reconstruction in Tennessee* (Nashville, 1950); Joseph H. Cartwright, "Black Legislators in Tennessee in the 1880's: A Case Study in Black Political Leadership," *Tennessee Historical Quarterly* (Fall 1973), 265–284. Perhaps the dearth of recent studies focusing on the black man in Tennessee during this period is partly accounted for by the fact that the state was readmitted to the Union before the Reconstruction Acts of 1867 and experienced only a brief period of Radical control during which no black man was elected to Congress. [Tennessee did not elect its first African American Congressman until 1974, Harold Ford, Sr., of

Memphis.] The first black to serve in the state legislature was elected in 1873. Fourteen Negroes were elected to the state house in the 1880s and one in the late 1890s but after their tenure of office a black would not be elected to the legislature until 1964.

3. Taylor, *Negro in Tennessee*, 27–28; Joseph E. Walker, "The Negro in Tennessee dring the Reconstruction Period," (University of Tennessee, M.A., 1933), 84; Gerald M. Capers, Jr., *The Biography of a River Town, Memphis: Its Heroic Age* (Chapel Hill, 1939), 162–64; Ernest Walter Hooper, "Memphis, Tennessee: Federal Occupation and Reconstruction, 1862–1870," (University of North Carolina, PhD, 1957), 132.

4. *Memphis Avalanche*, 3 March 1866, as quoted in Lawrence J. Friedman, *The White Savage: Racial Fantasies in the Post bellum South* (New Jersey, 1970 ), 24; Hooper, "Memphis, Tennessee," 244–45.

5. Franklin, *Reconstruction*, 63.

6. "Taylor, *Negro in Tennessee*, 45; Alexander, *Political Reconstruction*, 129–31.

7. *Memphis Appeal*, as quoted in *Memphis Daily Post*, 15 July 1867.

8. J. W. Leftwich to Andrew Johnson, 21 April 1867, Andrew Johnson Papers, Hoskins Library, University of Tennessee, Knoxville; Walter J. Fraser, Jr., "Barbour Lewis: A Carpetbagger Reconsidered," *Tennessee Historical Quarterly* XXXII (Summer 1973 ), 155; Walter J. Fraser, Jr., "John Eaton, Jr., Radical Republican; Champion of the Negro and Federal Aid to Education," *Tennessee Historical Quarterly* XXV (Fall 1966), 239–42.

9. Records of the Veterans Administration, Pension Application Files: Civil War, National Archives, Record Group 15; Records of the Adjutant General's Office, Colored Troops Division, 1863–1889, Letters Received, Record Group 94, National Archives; *Memphis Appeal*, 13 July 1867, 10 September 1870; Taylor, *Negro in Tennessee*, 159.

10. Census of 1870, Schedule 1, County of Shelby, State of Tennessee, National Archives.

11. Ibid.; *Memphis Avalanche*, 13 July 1867, 25 October 1870, 10 May 10 1874; *Memphis Appeal-Avalanche*, 22 March 1891.

12. *Memphis Avalanche*, 26 May, 13 and 20 July 1867; *Memphis Post*, 17 July 1867; Hooper, "Memphis, Tennessee," 205–206.

13. *Memphis Avalanche*, 16 and 18 June,13 July 1867; Hooper, "Memphis, Tennes-see," 206.

14. *Memphis Avalanche*, 21,26,27 June, 16,19, and 31 July 1867; *Memphis Appeal*, 13 June 1867; *Memphis Post*, 17 July 1867; Taylor, Negro in Tennessee, 48–50; Hooper, "Memphis, Tennessee," 206.

15. J. W. Leftwich to Andrew Johnson, 2 September 1867, Johnson Papers; Hooper, "Memphis, Tennessee," 208–209; Walker, "Negro in Tennessee," 43–44; Fraser, "Barbour Lewis," 155.

16. Barbour Lewis to [John Eaton] 25 November 1867, Lucien Eaton to John Eaton, 14 October, 6 November 1867, John Eaton, Jr., Papers, Hoskins Library, The University of Tennessee, Knoxville; *Memphis Post*, 24, 25, and 27 October, 14 December 1867; *Memphis Appeal*, 4

December 1867, January 3, 1868; Capers, *Biography of a River Town*, 173, 174; Hooper, "Memphis, Tennessee," 210.

17. Taylor, *Negro in Tennessee*, 57.

18. Barbour Lewis to John Eaton, 5 February, 6 May 1868, Lucien Eaton to John Eaton, 6 May 1868, Eaton Papers; *Memphis Post*, 24 July, 27 August 1868.

19. H. E. Hudson to John Eaton, 21 September 1868, Barbour Lewis to [John Eaton], 25 July 1868, Eaton Papers; *Memphis Post*, 28 July, 4, 27, and 31 August, 30 September, 3, 8, 16, and 29 October 1868; *Memphis Appeal*, 28 July, 16 October 1868.

20. Hooper, "Memphis, Tennessee," 211; Taylor, *Negro in Tennessee*, 60–61; *Memphis Appeal*, 8 August 1868; *Memphis Post*, 28 July, 14 August 1868; Allen W. Trelease, *White Terror: The Ku Klux Klan Conspiracy and Southern Reconstruction* (New York, 1971 ), 176–77.

21. John W. Leftwich to Andrew Johnson, 27 July 1868, Johnson Papers.

22. *Memphis Post*, 1 May, 27 August 1868; *Memphis Appeal*, 6 August 1868.

23. *Memphis Post*, 4 November 1868; *Memphis Appeal*, 4 and 5 November 1868; O. F. Vedder, *History of the City of Memphis and Shelby County Tennessee* (2 vols.; Syracuse, 1888), II, 592.

24. Barbour Lewis to John Eaton, 15 and 26 November 1868, Horace Andrews to John Eaton, 1 February 1868, Eaton Papers; *Memphis Post*, 6 January 1869.

25. Barbour Lewis to John Eaton, 6 February 1869, Eaton Papers; *House Miscellaneous Documents of the House of Representatives for the Second Session of the Forty-First Congress 1869–1870*, Miscellaneous Document No. 143, 144.

26. *Memphis Appeal*, 24 and 26 February, 4, 6, and 7 March 1869; *Memphis Post*, 24 February, 8 March 1869; Scott, *Negro in Tennessee Politics*, 219–220.

27. Barbour Lewis to John Eaton, 1 March 1869, Eaton Paper.

28. Lucien Eaton to John Eaton, 14 March 1869, Barbour Lewis to John Eaton, 16 March 1869, Eaton Papers; *House Miscellaneous Documents No. 143*, 139–48.

29. Barbour Lewis to John Eaton, 18 April 1869, Lucien Eaton to John Eaton, 7 June 1869, Eaton Papers; Fraser, "Barbour Lewis," 161; *Memphis Appeal*, 12 July 1872.

30. Barbour Lewis to John Eaton, 4 May, 28 September 1870, Eaton Papers; *Memphis Appeal*, 7 and 15 August, 9 and 16 November 1869, 12 July 1872; see Shaw's letter-to-the-editor; *Memphis Avalanche*, 5 November 1870.

31. Census of 1870, Tennessee; Records of the Adjutant General's Office, Colored Troops Division, 1863–1889; *Memphis Avalanche*, 5 November 1870; *Appeal*, 12 July 1872.

32. Barbour Lewis to John Eaton, 28 September 1870 and attached clippings of *Avalanche*, [?] September 1870 and *Public Ledger*, [?]September 1870, Eaton Papers; *Memphis Avalanche*, 13 and 14 April 1870.

33. Records of the Adjutant General's Office, Colored Troops Division, 1863–1889; *Memphis Appeal*, 12 July 1872.

34. Horace [Andrews] to John Eaton, 6 October 1870, Eaton Papers; *Memphis Avalanche*,

4 October 1870.

35. Horace [Andrews] to John Eaton, 6 October 1870, James A. Moon to John Eaton, 13 March 1872, Eaton Papers; *Memphis Avalanche*, 6 October 1870.

36. Horace [Andrews] to John Eaton, 6 October 1870, Barbour Lewis to John Eaton, 6 October 1870, Eaton Papers.

37. Barbour Lewis to John Eaton, 24 October 1870, Eaton Papers; *Memphis Avalanche*, 5 November 1870; see Shaw's letter-to-the-editor.

38. *Memphis Avalanche*, 25 October 1870.

39. [Horace Andrews] to John Eaton, 4 November 1870, Eaton Papers.

40. Ibid., 9 November 1870, Eaton Papers; *Memphis Avalanche*, 9 November 1870.

41. Lucien Eaton to John Eaton, 16 June, 6 September 1871, Eaton Papers.

42. *Memphis Avalanche*, 27 June, 2 October 1872; see Shaw's letter-to-the-editor; *Appeal*, 11 August, 25 September 1872.

43. *Memphis Appeal*, 28 and 29 June, 7 and 24 July 1872.

44. *Memphis Avalanche*, 1 and 5 October 1872; see George S. Heyden's and P. D. Beecher's letters-to-the-editor.

45. Ibid., 21 and 25 September, 1 and 2 October 1872, see Shaw's letter-to-the-editor for the latter date; *Memphis Appeal*, 5 and 7 July, 25 and 26 September 1872.

46. *Memphis Appeal*, 8 and 10 November 1872; *Memphis Avalanche*, 7 and 18 November 1872.

47. *Memphis City Directory* (1874).

48. Barbour Lewis to John Eaton, 9 May 1874, Eaton Papers; Alfred M. Kelly, "The Congressional Controversy Over School Segregation," *American Historical Review* LXIV (April 1959), 552–55; John Eaton, Jr., *Grant, Lincoln and the Freedmen* (New York, 1907), 263–64; Taylor, *Negro in Tennessee*, 251–52; *Memphis Avalanche*, 14 May 1874.

49. *Memphis Avalanche*, 1 May 1874; see Shaw's speech as reprinted from the *Nashville Banner*, 30 April 1874.

50. Ibid., 10 May 1874; Taylor, *Negro in Tennessee*, 251–252.

51. *Memphis Avalanche*, 4,8, and 10 May 1874.

52. Ibid., 10 May 10 and 14, 1874.

53. Horace Andrews to John Eaton, 6 June 1874, Eaton Papers; *Memphis Avalanche*, 9 and 10 June 1874.

54. *Memphis Avalanche*, 24 June, 26 and 29 July, 2 and 4 August 1874; *Memphis Appeal*, 7, 15, 16, and 25 July, 22 September 1874.

55. *Memphis Avalanche*, 29 July, 21 and 26 October 1874; *Memphis Appeal*, 22 September, 6,7, and 21 October 1874.

56. *Memphis Appeal*, 4 and 5 November 1874; *Memphis Avalanche*, 4 and 5 November 1874; *Congressional Record, 43rd Congress, 2nd Session*, 998–999, 1011; Cartwright, "Black Leg-

islators in Tennessee," 267.

57. Lucien Eaton to John Eaton, 3 May 1876, 30 January 1878, Eaton Papers; *Memphis Appeal*, 7 January, 3 November, 9, 12, and 23 December 1874, 25 July 1875, 14 and 15 January 1876.

58. *Memphis Appeal-Avalanche*, 22 March 1891; see Shaw's obituary.

59. For conflicting interpretations see Eugene D. Genovese, "The Legacy of Slavery and the Roots of Black Nationalism," *Studies on the Left*, Vol. VI (1966), 2–25; Vernon Lane Wharton, (New York, 1965), 190.

*(Clockwise from bottom left)*

David G. Cooke (Courtesy of Rob Kinsey)

William G. Brownlow (Tennessee Historical Society)

Barbour Lewis (From *The American Government*... Forty-Third Congress, 1874)

John Eaton, Jr., (Library of Congress)

Clinton B. Fisk (Tennessee State Library and Archives)

*(Counter-clockwise from bottom right)*

J. C. Napier (Special Collections, Fisk University Library)

Jabez Philander Dake, Nashville (From *Davidson County, Tennessee*, 1880)

John Hope (Robert W. Woodruff Library, Atlanta University)

Ewing Ogden Tade (Courtesy of Teresa Duncan Spitzer)

Unknown USCT Soldier, Knoxville (Tennessee State Museum)

"Negro Recruits Taking the Cars for Murfreesboro" (*Frank Leslie's Illustrated Newspaper*, May 17, 1864)

"Confederate Massacre of Federal Troops after the Surrender at Fort Pillow"
(*Frank Leslie's Illustrated Newspaper*, April 1864)

"Scenes in Memphis, Tennessee, during the Riot—Burning the Freedmen's School-House"
(Harper's Weekly, May 26, 1866)

"Scenes in Memphis, Tennessee, during the Riot—Shooting Down Negroes on the Morning of May 2, 1866"
(*Harper's Weekly*, May 26, 1866)

LE & CHAPMAN'S MEMPHIS DIRECTORY. 51

*(left)* African American Benevolent Societies (From *Boyle, Chapman & Co. Directory of the City of Memphis for 1876*)

Y SHOOTING
Planters' Building.
call. P. H. Bryson,
erriman, vice presi-
nd, secretary.

R BRUDER BUND
Halle, 184 Main.
ay each month. J.
ent; J. Brown, vice
Glaentzer, secretary;
er.

LUB — Hall, Coch-
Main. Meets first
nth. H. Eschmann,
mmerman, vice pres-
cheibler, secretary;
reasurer.

LUB—Meets subject
nion, corner Second.
sident; L. Iglauer,
L. Strauss, recording
hlberg, financial sec-
as, treasurer.

RUETLI-VEREIN
, 184 Main. Meets
ery month. John
ent.

MAENNER-CHOR
, 184 Main. Meets
ery month. J. L.
ent.

UNIONE E FRA-
LIANA—Hall, 260
first Thursday each
Montedonico, presi-
sta, vice president;

### Colored.

INDEPENDENT POLE BEARERS — Hall, Washington, southwest corner Second — Meets first and third Monday in each month. S. Farris, president; J. H. Keely, secretary; I. Dickens, treasurer.

DAUGHTERS OF ZION—Meet first Tuesday in each month, Avery Chapel, Gayoso, northeast corner Hernando. Rachael Polk, president.

SISTERS OF ZION—Hall, Church, south side Beale, east of DeSoto. Meet first Monday in each month. R. Green, president; W. Radford, secretary; M. Henderson, treasurer.

SONS AND DAUGHTERS OF HAM No. 1—Hall, south side Gayoso, east of DeSoto. Meet first and third Tuesday of each month. R. A. Patterson, pr
secretary; R.

SONS AN
HAM No. 2—
south side G
first and th
month. R.
Sailer, secreta
urer.

MILITAR

BERSALI
Lorenzi Sola
Bellusmini, fi

*(right)* African American Military Companies in Memphis (*Harper's Weekly*, 1878)

*(above)* African Americans Presenting Grievances in State Capitol, 1876 (*Frank Leslie's Illustrated Newspaper*, March 6, 1876)

*(left)* Off to School (Detail from Thomas Nast, *The Emancipation of the Negroes*, January 1863)

Fisk University (HABS, 1970, Library of Congress)

Jubilee Singers (American Missionary Society, Library of Congress)

Roger Williams University (*City of Nashville Illustrated*, 1890)

# STATE COLORED CONVENTIONS OF TENNESSEE, 1865–1866

## Judy Bussell LeForge

In 1865 and 1866, Tennessee blacks convened state colored conventions to secure political liberty and full equality. A speaker at the first convention explained why these assemblies were not called Negro conventions in Tennessee. During an interview with the *Colored Tennessean* on August 8, 1865, the Reverend James Lynch reminded newspaper reporters of the mixed blood of the delegates. "We are not ashamed of the term 'negro,' but to call it a 'negro convention' is a lie... it is very hard to tell whether there is any pure blood or not, because white men used to love colored women very much...."[1] These conventions served as a sounding board for grievances, a platform to inform the Congress of their plight, and a springboard for aspiring black political leaders. During these assemblies, black leaders realized they would have to turn to the federal government to secure redress for their grievances. Therefore, these meetings represented the origins of the "early" civil rights movement in Tennessee.

Since the antebellum years, Tennessee courts did not consider free blacks to be truly free citizens. In a legal sense, they became no more than inmates on parole. As a result of this qualified freedom, the status of free blacks proved to be uncertain and subject to change.[2] In 1839 the Tennessee Supreme Court in *State v. Claiborne* declared, "The laws have never allowed [free Negroes] the enjoyment of equal rights, or the immunities of the free white citizens."[3] Legal exclusion from certain occupations occurred often. For example, an 1858 law declared that no free Negroes be employed as engineers for Tennessee railroad companies. State law also considered it dangerous for free blacks to sell liquor; hence they could not operate tippling houses. Other endeavors unavailable to free Negroes included operating a grocery. However, at least in Nashville violation of this "anti-peddling provision" occurred with some frequency. In 1865 free blacks conducted business from booths at the public market house.[4]

The political awakening of the black community required not only the communication and organization of political interest but also a sense of worthiness to exercise political rights. When Union forces invaded Tennessee in 1862 runaway slaves fled to large cities and towns where federal troops were stationed. Large contraband communities soon appeared in Memphis and Nashville. The urban contraband communities created enclaves that nutured black racial pride and political consciousness. Blacks soon held mass meetings for the articulation and communication of their new attitudes. On October 1, 1863, blacks rallied in Nashville to encourage enlistment in the Federal army. By January 1, 1864, a crowd of Memphis blacks assembled in a black Baptist church to celebrate the anniversary of the final Emancipation Proclamation. Besides mass meetings, urban black leaders also held marches to celebrate special events. On the Fourth of July in 1864, Nashville blacks held a separate parade when black regiments were not invited to march in the city government's parade. Participants in the parade displayed banners with mottos such as "They Rebelled against Right," "Free and Equal," and "Liberty or Death."[5]

The demonstrations and rallies of 1863 and early 1864 set the stage for the state colored conventions. By 1864, blacks began to unite to air the question of full rights. When Tennessee's military governor Andrew Johnson began to re-institute civil government in 1864, black leaders wanted to know what legal status would be granted to them once the federal military withdrew. Blacks wanted legal guarantees, fearing that once a civil government took charge, free blacks might again be treated as quasi-free persons.[6]

The impetus for the colored conventions began in Nashville on August 10, 1864, when a group of local black leaders organized a rally at Fort Gillem (the future location of Fisk University). William Sumner, Wade Hickman, Jerry Stothard, Peter Lowery, Ransom Harris, Nelson Walker, W. Alex Sumner, Ben J. Hadley, and Samuel Lowery encouraged "every colored man, woman and child come and spend one day in the cause of human Freedom and human equality... for the future freedom of our race."[7] A newspaper article the next day labeled the event a success. "Altogether, the affair was creditable to the colored people. They manifested a devotion to the Government which many white people in this city would do well to imitate."[8] This event also included a parade with hacks filled with well-dressed freedmen.[9]

According to contemporary newspaper accounts, seventy-three black leaders played important roles in political activities in Tennessee during 1864 and 1865. Nashville's major papers, the *Times and True Union*, the *Dispatch*, the *Press and Times*, and the *Colored Tennessean*, reported that forty-five leaders resided in Nashville, nineteen in Memphis, and nine in Knoxville.[10] The greater availability of information on black political activities in Nashville may account for the large number of leaders from that city. While many of the Nashville leaders were freemen, Wade Hickman, Ben J. Hadley, Henry Harding, and Abram Smith were runaway slaves. Both leaders from Knoxville, Alfred E. Anderson and David Scraggs, were freemen. Of the Memphis leaders, only Morris Henderson was identified as a runaway slave. Businessmen constituted the largest group of identifiable leaders. Clergymen also figured prominently among the leadership. While sergeants from U.S. Colored Troops (USCT) spoke at some mass meetings, their military duties seem to have prevented any deeper involvement. Because the legal status and occupation of all forty-three leaders cannot be identified, it is possible that the remainder could have been runaway slaves. If this is true, free blacks in Tennessee may not have monopolized the early political leadership positions in black communities.[11]

During the presidential election campaign of 1864, Tennessee blacks called for black suffrage and actively supported the Lincoln and Johnson ticket. In contrast to the Union Party's platform pledging emancipation, the Democratic candidates, George B. McClellan and George H. Pendleton, opposed any significant changes in race relations. Although the Union Party's platform included emancipation, the party did not endorse the idea of political equality for blacks. Andrew Johnson appreciated the Nashville blacks' endorsement of his vice presidential candidacy, but he refused to support black suffrage in return. According to the Knoxville *Whig and Rebel Ventilator*, Johnson asserted, "The negro [sic] must assume the status to which the laws of an enlightened, moral and high-toned society shall assign him."[12] Though disappointed with this decision, the state's black leaders continued their efforts for suffrage.

For advice and encouragement these leaders looked to their Northern counterparts, who had been agitating for suffrage for a while. On two occasions, Nashville's black leaders sponsored public speeches by John Mercer Langston, a prominent Ohio black. Langston, an accomplished speaker, traveled extensively advocating for black male suffrage. Elected as president of the National Equal Rights League in 1864, he persuaded Andrew Johnson to continue the process for a constitutional prohibition of slavery in Tennessee.[13]

Seeking to learn from black leaders in the North, Nashville and Memphis blacks sent delegations to the first truly National Convention of Colored Men in Syracuse, New York, from October 4 to 7, 1864. Nashville delegates Peter Lowery, Abram Smith, and Ransom Harris joined Memphis delegates Morris Henderson and Horatio N. Rankin in representing Tennessee. Although none of Tennessee's delegates spoke on the convention floor, each of them served as an officer or committeeman. These delegates at Syracuse demanded immediate abolition of slavery, equal rights and equal pay for the United States Colored Troops, prohibition of involuntary colonization, Negro settlement on America's public lands, immediate Negro suffrage in the District of Columbia, and the assertion of full confidence in the fundamental principles of American government.[14] One of the most poignant statements published by this 1864 national convention was its *Declaration of Wrongs and Rights*, which described the indignities blacks had suffered:

> We have for long ages been deeply and cruelly wronged by people whose might constitute their right; we have been subdued, not by the power of ideas, but by brute force, and have been unjustly deprived not only of many of our natural rights, but debarred the privileges and advantages freely accorded other men. We have been made to suffer well-nigh every cruelty and indignity possible to be heaped upon human beings; and for no fault of our own. . . . As a people, we have been denied ownership of our bodies, our wives, homes, children, and the products of our labor; we have been forced to silence and inaction in full presence of the infernal spectacle of our sons groaning under the lash, our daughters ravished, our minds violated, and our firesides desolated, while we ourselves have been led to the shambles and sold like beasts in the field. Now we declare that all men are born free and equal; that no man or government has a right to annul, repeal, abrogate, contravene, or render inoperative, this fundamental principle [of human freedom and equality]....[15]

To secure these goals the convention founded the National Equal Rights League with auxiliaries and subordinate associations in the different states. The league's purpose was "to encourage sound morality, education, temperance, frugality, industry, and promote every thing that pertains to a well-ordered and dignified life." The league also sought "a recognition of the rights of the colored people of the nation as American citizens."[16]

Upon returning to Nashville, the delegates shared their ideas and enthusiasm with their fellow black leaders. Their first plan of action was to organize a parade that traveled to the state capitol to petition Military Governor Andrew Johnson. The parade took place on October 24, 1864. Although some pro-Confederates threw rocks at a few freedmen, Johnson displayed compassion toward blacks when he stated, "I, Andrew Johnson, do hereby proclaim freedom, full, broad, and unconditional freedom to every person in Tennessee." The governor said he wanted to strike against that "corrupt [and] damnable [slave] aristocracy."[17] Tennessee's black leaders, perhaps mildly encouraged by Johnson's statement, decided to take the cause of freedom a step further.

Peter Lowery and Ransom Harris formed a Nashville chapter of the National Equal Rights League. Harris was elected to the league's national executive board. Another Nashvillian, Abram Smith, became the organization's vice president for Tennessee.[18]

After the election Johnson and the Tennessee Union Party turned their attention to restoring civil government. Beyond fulfilling an election commitment to emancipation, the party had no clear plans for redefining the blacks' legal status. In early January 1865, the state constitutional convention met to vote on two amendments: one abolishing slavery and the other forbidding the legislature from making any law recognizing it. These amendments made no reference to black rights. On January 9, the colored citizens of Nashville petitioned the convention to give blacks the right to vote and for protection in the courts.[19] They asked to be no longer treated as "an inferior degraded class," and reminded the Union Party that black voters would help sustain its dominance. Their document declared: "The government has asked the colored man to fight for its preservation and gladly has he done it. It can afford to trust him with a vote as safely as it trusted him with a bayonet." Regarding protection in the courts the petitioners asked, "Will you declare in your revised constitution that a pardoned traitor may appear in court and his testimony be heard, but that no colored loyalist shall be believed even upon oath? If this should be so, then will our last state be worse than our first, and we can look for no relief on this side of the grave."[20] Although the convention debated a proposal to give the franchise at least to black soldiers, no action was taken on the petition.

With its work complete, the convention sent the proposed amendments to the people and provided for the election of a governor and legislature. In a carefully orchestrated election, William G. "Parson" Brownlow became the governor of Tennessee. The constitutional convention nominated Brownlow as the only candidate. Because of his reputation as a man of loyalty and devotion to the Union, Brownlow seemed the natural choice. On February 22, 1865, the state of Tennessee abolished slavery—the first Southern state to do so voluntarily. To show their appreciation for Andrew Johnson's efforts in the emancipation movement, Nashville's black leaders, Buck Lewis, Wade Hickman, Benjamin Hadley, William Sumner, Daniel Wadkins, Henry Harding, and Felix Hynes, gave Johnson a gold watch. Tennessee's ratification of the Thirteenth Amendment on April 5, 1865, provided blacks with further cause to celebrate. Parades, mass meetings, and special church services were common.[21]

The newly elected legislature convened on the first Monday in April. On April 6, 1865, black leaders petitioned the new General Assembly on the matter of legal rights. One of the leaders proclaimed to the new legislature:

> We know the burdens of citizenship and are ready to bear them. We know the duties of the good citizen and are ready to perform them cheerfully, and would ask to be put in a position in which we can discharge them more effectually. We do not ask for the privilege of citizenship, wishing to shun the obligations imposed by it.[22]

As with the January 9 petition, these leaders again asked for the legal right to testify upon oath in courts. Even though blacks could testify in Freedmen's Courts under the Freedmen's Bureau, the prohibition against their testifying in civil courts gave them no protection against white violators of black person and property.[23]

The legislature struggled with defining the legal status of blacks. It granted "persons of African and Indian descent" the right to appear in court as witnesses, but not as jurors.[24] This House legislation concerned many Republicans outside of Tennessee. Under the caption: "A Warning from Tennessee," *Harper's Weekly* criticized that body for passing a series of black laws. It stated:

> The whole series shows indeed that the *Spirit* of slavery does exist. No contract between a white and a black citizen is to be binding unless witnessed by a white person. In the courts the colored citizens may be witnesses against each other only. On failure to pay fees after imprisonment colored citizens, whether orphans or not, may be bound out to white persons at the option of the court.[25]

The legislature did approve a black suffrage law, but offered little on the issue of equal rights. While white Conservatives resented the suffrage law, since it also barred former supporters of the Confederacy from voting, blacks were disappointed over the failure of the legislature to enfranchise them.[26]

Black leaders circulated a notice in May and June 1865 asking all counties to select delegates for the state's first colored convention. The signers of the notice included Jerry Stothard, Samuel Lowery, William Sumner, Nelson Walker, and Peter Lowery. The notice stated, "Great efforts are being made to oppress and reenslave us."[27] These leaders announced that the "colored people of Tennessee will hold a State Convention in the city of Nashville on the first Monday in August (the 7th), 1865."[28] According to the *Nashville Dispatch* on June 2, 1865, a number of "colored gentlemen representing Nashville, Memphis, and Knoxville... (urged) every county, town, hamlet, and village to be represented in this important meeting... to secure the political liberty and equality in Tennessee of the black man."[29]

The first State Colored Convention of Tennessee convened at ten o'clock in the morning on August 7, 1865, in St. John's African Methodist Episcopal Church. According to the *Colored Tennessean* and the *Nashville Daily Press and Times*, this church stood near the Nashville and Chattanooga railroad depot. A total of 140 delegates from twenty-two counties and six USCT regiments attended the four-day convention. Most of the delegates appeared to be former slaves.[30]

The Reverend Nelson G. Merry, a Baptist minister, opened the assembly with prayers and hymns.[31] The delegates then created committees to carry out their business. They formed three regional committees (East, Middle, and West Tennessee) and charged them with monitoring the progress of rural freedmen. According to the *Colored Tennessean* of August 12, 1865, the regional committees, comprised of three members from each section of the state, had the responsibility of "publishing an address to the blacks in which they were urged to govern their lives by the principles of industry, education, economy and Christianity." The committee members included A. McKinney, H. Alexander, and Sergeant H. Hardison of the Fortieth United States Colored Troops for East Tennessee; N.G. Merry, Richard Harris, and Ranson Harris for Middle Tennessee; and J.J. Jones, A. Motley, and H.A. Rankin for West Tennessee.[32]

A central committee conducted the fight to gain political privileges and civil rights. William B. Scott, editor of the *Colored Tennessean,* served as a member of the central committee as did Nashvillian Abram Smith. The delegates also created committees to address such issues as finance, transportation, and agriculture. Members of these committees included John T. Rapier of Maury County, B.P. Frierson of Rutherford County, H. Alexander of Knox County, C.A. McKinney of Hawkins County, F. Maxwell of Washington County, and H. R. Rankin of Shelby County. Following the creation of the major committees, Sergeant Henry J. Maxwell, Third United States Colored Heavy Artillery Regiment, Company B, Fort Pickering, Memphis, gave the day's keynote address. A highly respected and articulate free black soldier, Sergeant Maxwell claimed rights as an American citizen and believed, from the black soldier's point of view, that he was entitled unconditionally to these rights:

> By this music we march to victory. We shall be heard before Congress and before the legislature. We came here for principles, and there will be no dissension. We want the rights guaranteed by the Infinite Architect. For these rights we labor; for them we will die. We have gained one—the uniform is its badge. We want two more boxes besides the cartridge box—the ballot and the jury box. We shall gain them. Let us work faithfully unto that end.[33]

Next, Reverend James D. Lynch of Baltimore addressed the convention. Regarded as an intelligent and able man, Lynch had recently traveled through the South as a missionary.[34] This church leader urged black delegates to push vigorously for racial equality and the right to vote. His fiery speech set the tone of the assembly:

> We simply ask for those inalienable rights which are declared inalienable. Why should we not have them? In the past struggle when the nation stood trembling upon the verge of the precipice, the black man came to the rescue; his manhood was recognized in that hour of national trial, and why? From necessity—and I tell you my hearers that necessity will secure us our full recognition as freemen and citizens of this glorious republic.... There has been by implication unfriendly legislation in Tennessee but Tennessee has a master. That master is the United States.[35]

This bold warning by Reverend Lynch showed that blacks now looked to the federal government rather than to state government as the main guarantor of their rights.

Another influential speaker during the convention was James T. Rapier. He too railed against the failure of the state's Republican Party to address rights for blacks. Rapier, the grandson of Sally Thomas and the son of John P. (Thomas) Rapier, moved to Nashville from his native Alabama in 1864. A short time later, he moved to nearby Maury County to become a planter. Eventually, he returned to Alabama where he won election to Congress in 1872. Rapier's participation in this convention proved to be an interesting Alabama connection.[36]

During the late afternoon session, the delegates approved resolutions inviting General Clinton B. Fisk of the Freedmen's Bureau and Governor William G. Brownlow to address the assembly. Although Brownlow's ill health apparently prevented him from accepting the invitation, General Fisk agreed to speak to the convention.[37] The delegates also chose officers for the organization. Nelson Walker, a prominent and wealthy free black Nashvillian, was named president. According to Walker, the convention sought "to draft resolutions informing the Legislature of Tennessee and the President of the United States of the grievances of the Negroes in Tennessee, and to claim their right to exercise of suffrage in all elections held within the State."[38]

On the fourth and final day of the convention, General Fisk spoke to the assembly. He commended black leaders for standing up for their rights and told them of the difficulty of trying to secure social rights for the rural freedmen. Fisk said he welcomed any cooperation from the Colored Convention's county and regional committees in order to provide education and aid to rural blacks. The delegates listened and then acted on his request. They passed a resolution instructing the committees to cooperate as closely as possible with local Freedmen's Bureau offices. They also directed the regional committees to conduct an economic census of all blacks and their assets in the state[39]

Before adjourning on August 10, 1865, delegates also approved a letter of gratitude to Congress for creating the Freedmen's Bureau; a proclamation naming the first of January as the "Day of Jubilee" for blacks throughout Tennessee; and a note of thanks to General George H. Thomas for train transportation for the delegates. Finally, the convention petitioned Congress stating, "The Colored people of the State of Tennessee respectfully and solemnly protest against the congressional delegation of this state being admitted to seats in your honorable bodies [the Senate and the House of Representatives] until the legislature of this state enacts such laws as shall secure our rights as citizens."[40] The convention's report, published by the *Colored Tennessean* on August 12, 1865, stated that: "Intelligent [elite] colored men should have the rights that are allowed intelligent white men."

The convention's Congressional petition found receptive ears in Washington, D.C. In December 1865, Congress refused to recognize Tennessee's delegation until the state was declared by Congress to be formally back in the Union. In many ways, this action represented an amazing success for blacks in the state and provided them a grant of legitimacy from the Congress.[41]

During September and October 1865, the elected officers of the convention began to visit rural freedmen communities and assess their living and working conditions. In Shelbyville, Daniel Wadkins, Ransom Harris, and Nelson Walker addressed a mass meeting. Harris, the articulate pastor of Nashville's Colored Christian Church, served as the principal speaker at this gathering. On another occasion, Wadkins and Walker addressed the annual freedmen's picnic in the Edgefield area of Nashville. Everywhere the black leaders visited, the freedmen eagerly told of widespread white violence. When the legislature disfranchised most supporters of the defeated Confederacy, conservative unionists accused the Union Party of plotting to elevate blacks at the whites' expense. White hostility to black advancement began to swell. Because of this violence, the leaders decided to petition the governor.[42]

According to an October 1865 speech, Governor William G. Brownlow instructed the General Assembly to "examine our entire code, so far as it is shaped by the institution of slavery, and adapt it to the requirements of a free state." Brownlow's plan of adaption, however, proved conditional. In his view, only a certain class of blacks should be able to vote. "I am free to admit that, for the present, we have done enough for the Negro, and, although Negro voting cannot suit my natural prejudice of caste, there is a class of them I would be willing to see vote at once." His reluctance to grant all blacks the right to vote also appeared in his speech to the legislature. "A large class, ignorant, docile, easily led by designing men, and not safely trusted with political power, I am not willing to see at the ballot box."[43] Although Governor Brownlow and most Unionist leaders were aware of the Republicans' commitment to protect the freedmen, they realized they could not alienate supporters over the issue of race. Apparently, the prevailing attitude of emancipation, which had elevated slaves to free Negro status, represented a significant and sufficient improvement. Laws pertaining to the freedmen remained a state matter and no further action regarding ex-slaves seemed necessary beyond the granting of the "bare right to their freedom."[44] At this time, Brownlow saw no need to address the issue of violence against blacks.

As historian Bobby Lovett observed, "It took more than a gathering of blacks to persuade the conservative Tennessee legislature and Brownlow to give blacks anything."[45] Apparently, Brownlow and the General Assembly feared that liberal laws would cause out-of-state blacks to view Tennessee as a haven.[46] Although the Volunteer State refused to admit her freed population to full civil rights, the legislature in January 1866 extended black rights in courts of law. The General Assembly legalized all black marriages and passed a bill called "An Act to Define the Term 'A Person of Color'." The act identified such persons as those with African blood, including mestizoes.[47] On May 26, 1866, the state legislature gave all persons of color the right to make contracts, sue, inherit property, and have equal benefits with the whites in respect to laws for the protection of life and property. Despite this new equality in court and law, social equality remained absent. Blacks could not serve on juries, attend school with white children, hold public office, vote, or intermarry with whites.[48]

At the national level, radical Republican members of the United States Congress rapidly gained influence. They argued that Congress, not the president, should control Reconstruction and insure the rights of blacks. Reports of violence against unionists and blacks, along with news that southern legislatures had begun to enact "black codes," convinced Congress to pass the Civil Rights Act of March 1866.[49] Many Republicans believed that the bill would legitimize the Thirteenth Amendment. The Civil Rights Act declared that all persons (except Indians) born in the United States be recognized as citizens with full civil and legal rights. The army possessed the authority to enforce those rights.[50] Although President Andrew Johnson vetoed the bill, Congress mustered enough votes to override his decision.[51] On June 13, 1866, Congress enacted the Fourteenth Amendment. While Congress's stated purpose for the amendment was to ensure citizenship, equal protection, and due process of the laws for black citizens, it also sought to resolve any doubts concerning the constitutionality of the Civil Rights Act of 1866.[52] Ratification of the amendment became a prerequisite for former Confederate states to be readmitted into the Union.[53]

Despite Governor Brownlow's misgivings about extending certain rights to blacks, he gladly supported the proposed Fourteenth Amendment because it could help continue the disenfranchisement of former Confederate leaders and allow Tennessee to disown the former Confederate state government's debts.[54] In an effort to restore Tennessee to the Union, Brownlow, on June 19, 1866, called a special session of the General Assembly to vote on the proposed amendment. Although Conservatives in the House tried to prevent a quorum during the vote, the General Assembly eventually approved the amendment on July 19, 1866. As a result, Tennessee became the first southern state to pass the Fourteenth Amendment and the first southern state to rejoin the Union.[55] Because of the latter distinction, Tennessee, unlike other southern states, avoided the Military Reconstruction Program imposed by the Congress in 1867.[56]

From 1865 to 1866, black citizens of the state had witnessed the abolition of slavery with passage of the Thirteenth Amendment, passage of the Civil Rights Act of 1866, and recognition of citizenship under the Fourteenth Amendment. Tennessee's black leaders had cultivated black pride and political consciousness, and had perfected tactics of agitation that made the white populace and state governmental officials fully aware of their demands.[57] Despite new equality in court and law, no social equality existed. Blacks, now citizens of Tennessee, possessed all rights except suffrage.

Even before Tennessee ratified the Fourteenth Amendment, black leaders began a campaign on their own to convince the legislature to grant suffrage to blacks. Dissatisfied with the slow pace of change in blacks' legal status, the state's black leadership sought a more aggressive approach.[58] In a newspaper notice, members of the 1865 central committee called for State Colored Convention delegates to convene on August 6, 1866. Clearly, they realized the seriousness of the situation:

> While we feel a deep sense of gratitude to those benevolent societies which have done much for the freemen, still we recognize the fact that we must learn to rely upon ourselves, and that the world is looking to us for a demonstration of our capacity to perform the parts of useful, intelligent citizens. Though our county committees are aiding the poor and education, we must do more.[59]

The second State Colored Convention met in Nashville at St. John's African Methodist Episcopal Church from August 6–11, 1866. Seventy-six delegates from fourteen counties attended.[60] All four major cities sent representatives. One DeKalb County delegate told the audience that only by accident had he obtained a copy of the announcement in the *Colored Tennessean*. Delegates from rural areas told of depressed wages, widespread economic abuse, and racial violence against the freedmen.[61]

According to the *Nashville Daily Press and Times*, the assembly sought "to discuss the question of Education, Agriculture, Manufactures, and Mining with immediate reference to the welfare of the colored people." Nashville Mayor Matt Brown, a Conservative, "suggested" that the convention adhere strictly to these topics in hopes "that this city may not be visited and degraded by such proceedings as have recently been witnessed in sister cities...."[62] Apparently, the mayor threatened to prevent the convention from meeting if his suggestion were not taken seriously. On behalf of the Colored Man's State Central Committee, Reverend Daniel Watkins assured the mayor that questions touching on the issue of political rights would not be discussed. While the Conservative press praised the agreement reached by Watkins and Brown, black leaders such as Peter Lowery of Nashville and Ed Shaw of Memphis criticized it. Citing the increased frequency of mistreatment of blacks by whites, Lowery and

Shaw argued that only through black suffrage would their interests be protected. In their view, blacks were perfectly justified in discussing political matters.[63]

Once assembled, delegates elected M.J.R. Gentle, a Knoxville minister, president of the convention. Early in the proceedings, several members wanted to discuss a more forceful approach to securing political rights. However, Reverend Daniel Watkins cautioned delegates to avoid the question of political rights for fear of giving rise to political posturers who merely wanted to be "big men." This statement caused some restiveness among delegates, but Watkins ignored their reaction to argue the importance of providing educational facilities for the freedmen so that they could elevate themselves. With this opening discussion, the convention divided into two virtually equal camps, one of which favored political action and supported the Equal Rights League, the other of which desired educational and economic improvement and a continuation of the Central Committee.[64]

On the first day of the convention, the education and economic camp controlled the debate. A committee was created to collect statistics concerning schools in the three sections of the state. In addition, the assembly passed a resolution asking the state legislature to make annual appropriation of public funds adequate to secure to black children the advantages of a common school education.[65] During the Reverend G. W. Levere's speech on education, "a disorderly company of persons outside, who had resurrected an old drum and fife, and a few old rusty swords and dirty uniforms" paraded "around the church."[66] Eventually, this noise "disturbed the proceedings in no small degree." A messenger approached the party to inform them of the "decided wish of the Convention that they would either stop their noise or withdraw." According to one of the delegates, "as the noise suddenly ceased, we presume the wish of the Convention was granted by the frolicking party."[67] With order restored, the business of the assembly resumed.

During the evening session of August 7, divisions over the strategy and tactics employed by the State Central Committee became more clearly defined. When a motion was made calling for a union with the Equal Rights League, an ensuing debate occupied the remainder of that day and all of the next.[68]

The debate reached a decisive stage when Daniel Watkins launched a rambling attack on the league. He argued that its constitution "read strangely" because it used such terms as "military dictator and supreme judge" to describe its officers. Paraphrasing Isaiah 28:15, Watkins warned against putting faith in the agreements of men and making a "covenant with death, and a league with hell."[69] Others who opposed the league maintained that sectional parties would better represent blacks in the state. This debate prompted the Reverend A.E. Anderson to express his opinion:

> A League gave birth to the Convention one year ago.... We want fingers linked in a long chain, stretching from North to South. A League will do it.... Let all honest men unite on this broad platform. Are success and progress attained by sectional parties, or by being leagued together?[70]

Eventually, delegates approved the proposal for a state league and adopted a constitution for the new permanent organization. The vote, 35–29, favored uniting with the Equal Rights League.[71]

On the fourth day of the convention, delegates addressed the question of specific political rights. The assembly asked Congress to give Tennessee "a republican form of government, to enroll Negroes in the state militia and to enfranchise adult Negro males."[72] Ed Shaw, A.E. Anderson, and Samuel Lowery proposed that the convention thank Governor Brownlow and the General Assembly for ratifying the Fourteenth Amendment and to petition these state officers for the right to vote and serve on juries. Although the Fourteenth Amendment did not directly address suffrage for blacks, its definition of citizenship prohibited states from denying the right of suffrage to male inhabitants over twenty-one years of age who had not participated in the late rebellion.[73] Because Tennessee had already ratified the amendment, the convention's resolution proved to be tremendously important. Any state found guilty of violating these provisions became subject to loss of representation in Congress in proportion to the number of male inhabitants denied the right to vote. Brownlow, fearing a reduction in the state's representation in Congress, now realized that only black suffrage could sustain the Republican Party in Tennessee.[74]

Despite the often heated debates, delegates understood the importance of unity and diligence in efforts to elevate blacks in society. A Mr. Rexford, a member of the Nashville Bar, reminded delegates "character and capacity will be the tests." He cautioned:

> Don't ask greater political rights than white men have, but you are entitled to all the rights they have. You are here not by choice, by God, for wise ends, has placed you here. You ought to assert your rights, not to be better than any other, but to be equal to any other, not arrogantly, but humbly, looking to God for help. Throw away all sectional, all personal feelings.... Stand shoulder to shoulder in a common cause... and make the most of your newborn privileges.[75]

Although discussion of education and economic issues initially dominated the convention, the focus of the assembly later shifted to political questions. Many white-owned-and-operated Nashville newspapers did not like the changes. The *Nashville Dispatch* criticized delegates for their "petty squabbles" and failure to take any action on economic matters; the Nashville *Union and American* declared "evil influences had been brought to bear upon members to defeat the laudable ends which the Convention was framed to promote." Contending "politics is idleness for the negro and a barrier to progress," the *Union and American* refused to cover the remainder of the convention. Even the *Nashville Daily Press and Times* commented it had hoped that blacks would prove themselves to be above "petty feuds."[76] Such comments in the white press seem to suggest that it still sought to exercise some influence over the black community by defining the proper focus of the assembly's debate.[77]

On the last day of the convention, General Clinton B. Fisk of the Freedmen's Bureau addressed the delegates. Fisk counseled against demanding equal rights: He contended that the legislature had made all men equal before the law "as regards crime." At present, he believed that was sufficient. Fisk declared that pushing for political rights would "unnecessarily inflame his [the planter's] passions," and make matters worse for "all concerned." However, he did challenge his listeners to stand up for their rights as citizens: "Congress and the Tennessee legislature may legislate for you every day in the year, but at best the results lie with you. Stand up like men—turn your faces to the stars.... I will help you to your rights before the law...." In standing up for their rights, Fisk admonished blacks to "try to live well with the whites. Tell them you want to live with them in peace... and all will be well."[78]

General Fisk did commend the delegates for running their own convention, asserting that no one could claim outside influence. Although he acknowledged that there "had been a little sparring here," he remarked, "Men can't think alike." Fisk encouraged delegates to focus their efforts on education, which, he contended, offered the key to progress. The general challenged the black community to establish schools in every county town and offered one hundred dollars to each and every fund to build schools to replace those destroyed by arsonists. He also promised to use the military to protect the schools if civil authorities proved unwilling or unable to do so. At the conclusion of his speech, Fisk received a round of applause and a vote of thanks from the delegates. As the convention came to a close, the hymn "Blow yet the trumpet, blow" was sung and the assembly declared adjourned.[79]

Six months after the 1866 State Colored Convention on February 27, 1867, Tennessee passed the enfranchisement law. Prior to the debate and vote on this legislation, large numbers of blacks were present in the gallery of the General Assembly. According to the *Knoxville Whig*, "The gathering clouds of dusky humanity which settled down in the gallery of the house early in the day, plainly portended a storm.... Sambo could not be otherwise than an interested spectator." The mockery displayed by this Republican paper probably reflected the anxiety felt by those who opposed black suffrage. More than an interested spectator, the black man had in many ways initiated this action. While this law granted black suffrage, a section of the measure disqualified them from holding office or sitting on juries. Blacks contended that their right to vote involved both of these.[80] In the other ten southern states the Military Reconstruction Act of 1867 guaranteed for blacks the right to vote and to hold office.

Governor Brownlow also disapproved of this "odious sixteenth section" of the enfranchisement law and challenged the General Assembly to change it. On January 31, 1868, the legislature approved a bill entitled "An Act to Remove All Disabilities for Holding Office and Sitting on Juries on account of Race or Color."[81] Although blacks in Tennessee now had the rights they had fought so long to obtain, some elements of the population refused to accept, or even acknowledge, the legislation.[82]

The irreconcilable faction of the Conservative press condemned black suffrage. An editorial in the *Memphis Appeal* reflected the attitude of some:

> It would be better for the whole black breed to be swept away by pestilence. This may sound harsh but it is true... If one had the power and could not otherwise prevent that curse and inconceivable calamity, in many of the southern States, it would be a solemn duty for him to annihilate the race. The right to vote might just as safely be given to so many Southern American monkeys as to the plantation Negroes of Mississippi and Louisiana.[83]

Such ravings did not deter black Tennesseans from continuing to organize themselves. On February 21, 1867, black loyalists met in Nashville at the gun factory on College Hill to show their loyalty to Governor Brownlow and the *Nashville Daily Press and Times* for defending their rights. Although most blacks seemed content with the radical element of the Republican Party, a few were upset because they had not become office holders in the Brownlow administration. This small group decided to hold a "conservative" convention of their own in Nashville on April 6, 1867. Members of this assembly stated, "The spirit and tendencies of radicalism were unfavorable... (and) we take our stand with the true Union conservatives of Tennessee, and invite our race throughout the state to do the same."[84]

Six days later on April 12, a larger and less conservative group of blacks held a "Grand Pow Wow Meeting" at the capitol building in Nashville. One of the speakers at this gathering proclaimed, "If it had not been for the radicals we would be slaves today. To vote for a Conservative is to vote for the chain of slavery to be riveted on your necks."[85] The majority of black Tennesseans agreed with the message of this assembly and continued to support the radical element of the Republican Party, with certain stipulations.

Blacks, who comprised about three-fourths of the political strength of Tennessee's Republican Party at this time, sought promotion by political appointment and election within the party.[86] Their plea was a reasonable one. After all, during the gubernatorial election of 1867 over half of the votes for Brownlow were from newly enfranchised blacks. In addition, Republicans captured all the congressional seats, all the state senate seats, and all but three of the state house seats.[87] Anticipating a more active role in the party, black Tennesseans became involved in Union Leagues. These leagues organized blacks politically, promoted loyalty and good citizenship, and helped secure votes for the Republican Party.[88]

Reacting to black voting rights, the 1867 Republican sweep, and the success of the Union Leagues, disenfranchised former Confederates utilized an effective and frightening weapon, the Ku Klux Klan. This organization proved to be a powerful tool to intimidate blacks, especially during elections. Following widespread coverage in the newspapers, the Klan began to achieve social and political power. During the November 1868 national election, Klan violence increased. Determined to deny Tennessee's electoral votes to Republican U.S. Grant and the state's congressional seats to Republicans, the Klan instituted "a reign of terror." Governor Brownlow asked the General Assembly for more power to combat this hooded menace. As a result, the Ku Klux Klan Act empowered the governor to use unlimited military force against the Klan and to impose stiff penalties for political terrorism. By March, 1869, the Imperial Wizard directed that the Klan be dissolved and disbanded. However, organized violence against blacks in Tennessee did not end.[89]

In February 1869, Brownlow resigned the governorship to take a seat in the United States Senate. He appointed Speaker of the State Senate Dewitt Clinton Senter as acting governor. Although a Republican, Senter supported an end to disenfranchisement of former Confederates. Enfranchisement of this group, Senter believed, would heal the animosities that existed in the state. The acting governor also advocated the ratification of the Fifteen Amendment to the U.S. Constitution as a way to guarantee blacks the rights of citizenship and equality before the law. During the 1869 state election, Senter won the governorship and conservative Democrats gained control of the General Assembly. This shift in political power resulted in the dismantling of earlier legislation and spelled the end of the Republican era of Reconstruction in Tennessee.[90]

This turn of events upset blacks because Democrats in the General Assembly repealed a number of laws affecting them. For instance, the General Assembly repealed the Common School Law that meant that black children were without public educational opportunities. The repeal of the Common Carrier's Act no longer allowed "colored ladies and gentlemen" holding first class tickets to sit in first class railroad cars. Repeal of the Ku Klux Klan Act constituted one of the most devastating acts of the legislature. As a result, the governor's power to control organized violence was curtailed. However, the General Assembly did pass some legislation benefiting blacks. "An Act to Provide for the Children and their Descendants of Colored Persons to Inherit the Estate, Real and Personal, of their deceased parents" went into effect on January 24, 1870.[91]

A call for a constitutional convention represented the most important legislation of the session. Electors overwhelmingly favored the convention that began on January 10, 1870. Of the seventy-five convention delegates, sixty-five were Democrats and ten Republicans. No blacks served as delegates to this assembly. As a matter of fact, Tennessee was the only Southern state not to have a Reconstruction constitution written by black and while citizens. To black Tennesseans, this new constitution must have seemed like another battle of the Civil War.[92]

In the midst of this movement for Conservative control of the government of Tennessee, Republicans launched a counter attack on January 28, 1870. They accused the General Assembly of passing laws oppressing both white and colored Unionists and the constitutional convention of replacing members of the judiciary with ex-Confederates.[93] Two days after Republicans began their offensive, the legislature, in an effort to suppress increasing violence across the state, enacted "An Act to Preserve the Public Peace." However, Governor Senter considered this law inadequate to accomplish the desired ends. As a result, he asked the General Assembly to amend the law to enable the state's chief executive to enforce suppression of violence and disorder. The legislature failed to act on this request. Seeking to arrest the reign of terror in the state, Senter appealed to the president of the United States to send federal troops into Tennessee.[94]

Governor's Senter's request for federal troops, to be used in restoring order in Tennessee, presented state Republicans and their supporters with a special opportunity. Now they were in a position to persuade Congress to reconstruct Tennessee because the state government had, in the Republicans' view, disregarded federal Reconstruction acts.[95]

Black Republicans in the state began to work closely with white Republicans to unseat the state government. A black delegation, comprised of Dr. J.B. Young of Knoxville, J.C. Davis of Newmarket, and M.R. Johnson, J.H. Sumner, and J.C. Napier of Nashville, presented a memorial to the president of the United States and testified before the Congress's Reconstruction Committee concerning the state of emergency that existed in Tennessee.[96] This memorial, framed by the State Convention of Colored Men who met in Nashville, on February 21, 1870, represented the report of the convention's committee on crimes. The black delegation reported to the Reconstruction Committee that atrocities had been committed against the lives and property of the colored population of Tennessee. "The Rebel party," they asserted was "unchristian, inhuman, and beyond toleration." In their opinion, blacks and other Unionists could find relief only through military reconstruction.[97]

The Reconstruction Committee made a detailed inquiry into the condition of affairs in Tennessee. It examined numerous witnesses. The committee questioned a delegation of prominent Nashville citizens, notable Tennesseans from other sections of the state, the speakers of both houses of the General Assembly, and the governor of the state.[98]

Apparently, the testimony of Governor Senter and other state officials convinced the majority of Republicans in Congress that further Tennessee Reconstruction was not necessary. As a consequence, the movement to unseat the state government gradually lost support. According to historian Lester C. Lamon, blacks in Tennessee "resisted the deterioration of their status but found improvement hard to obtain." As federal authorities turned an increasingly deaf ear to their plans, the Republican Party slowly abandoned its "southern strategy" and found it less expedient to court black voters. In economic matters, blacks became dependent upon unsympathetic whites for their livelihood. Black leaders in the state continued to fight for equal rights, but had very limited resources and leverage.[99]

In assessing the overall effectiveness of the 1865 and 1866 State Colored Conventions, a number of questions come to mind. For example, did this decision by the Reconstruction Committee of Congress dampen future hopes of blacks obtaining full political and social rights in Tennessee? Were the State Colored Conventions influenced mainly by leaders within Tennessee or at the national level? Did other states hold colored conventions or was Tennessee unique in that regard?

Although black leaders in Tennessee were disappointed by the decision of the Reconstruction Committee, their efforts to win black rights continued. Between 1871 and 1873 two important State Colored Conventions met in Tennessee to discuss increasing educational and office holding opportunities for blacks. In 1874, another State Colored Convention convened specifically to address the civil rights guaranteed by law to all. By 1875, Congress passed the supplemental Civil Rights Bill. From 1870 to 1875, Tennessee's State Colored Conventions continued to serve as the prime means through which the Congress and the public were informed of the plight of blacks. In 1876, Tennessee blacks hosted the Colored National Convention in Nashville.

Leaders at the national level did influence the movement for black rights in Tennessee. During the 1865 State Colored Convention, the fiery speech by Reverend James Lynch of Baltimore reminded Tennessee that its "master" was the United States. In other words, black leaders now looked to the federal government as the guarantor of their rights, not the state government. Certainly, the Thirteenth, Fourteenth, and Fifteenth Amendments exemplify the role played by the federal government in the matter of civil rights.

Other states besides Tennessee held colored conventions. At least eight other southern states convened such gatherings: South Carolina, Virginia, Georgia, North Carolina, Arkansas, Alabama, Louisiana, and Texas. As a matter of fact, Texas held an assembly as late as 1895. The border states of Kentucky and Maryland also convened these conventions. State colored conventions also met in northern states: New Jersey, Connecticut, Indiana, Illinois, Massachusetts, Ohio, and New York. Interestingly, California held one of the earliest state colored conventions in 1855. The origin for these assemblies can be traced back to the National Negro Convention Movement, which began in 1830 and ended in 1864.

Although Tennessee's State Colored Conventions of 1865 and 1866 did not accomplish the goal of obtaining full social, economic, and political rights for blacks in the state, their efforts were, nonetheless, foundational for the movement that developed in the 1950s. In many ways, these assemblies of 1865–1866 represent the development of the "early" civil rights movement in Tennessee.

*This article first appeared in the Fall 2006 issue of the* Tennessee Historical Quarterly.

1. *Colored Tennessean*, 8 August 1865. Since the early 1860s, Maryland born James Lynch had distinguished himself as one of the rising stars of the AME (African Methodist Episcopal) Church.

2. Bobby Lovett, "The Negro in Tennessee, 1861–1866: A Socio-Military History Of The Civil War Era" (PhD dissertation, University of Arkansas, 1978), 191–193; Roger Raymond Van Dyke, "The Free Negro In Tennessee, 1790–1860," (Ph.D. dissertation, Florida State Uni-

versity, 1972), 95. From 1796 to 1834, however, free black men were allowed to vote under the Tennessee Constitution.

3. Helen T. Catterall, ed., *Judicial Cases Concerning American Slavery and The Negro*, II, (Washington, 1926–1937), 507–508; *Journal of the Convention of the State of Tennessee, Convened for the Purposes of Revising and Amending the Constitution thereof* (Nashville, 1834), 37.

4. James W. Patton, *Unionism and Reconstruction in Tennessee, 1860–1869* (Gloucester, Mass., 1966), 124.

5. John Cimprich, "The Beginning of the Black Suffrage Movement In Tennessee, 1864–65," *Journal of Negro History*, 45 (Summer 1980): 185–186; *Nashville Dispatch*, 18 August, 1864; *Nashville Times and True Union*, 6 July, 18 August, 25 October, 1864; *Memphis Bulletin*, 7 June, 2 August, 1864, 3 January 1865; *Nashville Press*, 2 January, 1865. These marches were usually led by black regiments with black businessmen frequently serving as parade marshals. Black ministers, military employees, benevolent society members, craftsmen, and school children sometimes walked together as units. Although the Emancipation Proclamation exempted Tennessee from its provisions, it did represent an endorsement of emanicipation by the federal government.

6. Bobby Lovett, *The African-American History of Nashville, Tennessee, 1780–1930* (Fayetteville, Ark., 1999), 200; Lovett, "The Negro in Tennessee," 191–193.

7. *Daily Times and True Union*, 11,12,16, 20 August, 1864. According to Bobby Lovett, "On the present site of Fisk University's Jubilee Hall, Fort Gillem (later named Fort Sill) was constructed. Fort Gillem was built by a native of Jackson County, Tennessee, Gen. Alvin Gillem, and the Tenth Tennessee Volunteer Regiment." Bobby Lovett, "Nashville's Fort Negley: A Symbol of Blacks' Involvement with the Union Army," in Carroll Van West, ed., *Essays in Tennessee's African American History: Trial and Triumph* (Knoxville, 2002), 121.

8. Ibid.

9. Lovett, *The African American History of Nashville*, 201.

10. (Boston) *Liberator*, 29 January 1864; Nashville *Times and True Union*, 30 December 1864, 4 January, 25 February, 1865; *Nashville Dispatch*, 16 August 1864; (Nashville) *Colored Tennessean*, 12 August 1865; *Nashville Press and Times*, 29 May 1865. Cited in Cimprich, "The Beginning of the Black Suffrage Movement," 193.

11. Manuscript Returns of the Eighth Census of the United States for Davidson, Knox, and Shelby Counties, Schedule I—Free Inhabitants, National Archives; *Nashville Press and Times*, 4 April 1868; Earnest W. Hooper, "Memphis, Tennessee: Federal Occupation and Reconstruction, 1862–1870" (PhD dissertation, University of North Carolina, 1957), 154–155. Cited in Cimprich, "The Beginning of the Black Suffrage Movement," 193–94.

12. *Knoxville Whig and Rebel Ventilator*, 23 April 1854.

13. John M. Langston, *From the Virginia Plantation to the National Capitol*, (Hartford, Conn., 1894), 200–231.

14. Lovett, *The African American History of Nashville*, 201; *Nashville Dispatch*, 16 August,

19 October, 1864; *Nashville Times and True Union*, 14 November 1864, 4 January 1865; *Memphis Bulletin*, 1 October 1864; National Convention of Colored Men, *Proceedings* (Boston, 1864), passim; *Freedmen's Bulletin*, I (July 1865), 136.

15. *Proceedings of the National Colored Men's Convention, Syracuse, New York, October 4–7, 1864* (Boston, 1864), 1–62; Howard Bell, ed., *Minutes of the Proceedings of the National Negro Convention, 1830–1864* (New York, 1869), 30, 40, 62.

16. Bell, *Minutes of the Proceedings*, ii, 36.

17. Andrew Johnson Papers, 1808–1875, Tennessee State Library and Archives, Nashville. In October 1865, President Johnson announced that he opposed any congressional legislation on black suffrage. He did approve, though, of a gradual extension of the vote to Tennessee's black men through state legislative action. The president suggested that black suffrage qualifications might be based upon military service, literacy, and property.

18. Lovett, *The African American History of Nashville*, 202; David Bowen, "Andrew Johnson and the Negro," *East Tennessee Historical Society Papers*, 40 (1968), 28–49; Cimprich, "The Beginnings of the Black Suffrage Movement," 185–95; *Minutes of the Proceedings of the National Negro Convention 1830–1864*, 1–62; Nashville *Dispatch*, October 1864; *Nashville Times and True Union*, 4 January 1865.

19. Alrutheus Ambush Taylor, *The Negro in Tennessee, 1865–1880* (Washington, D.C., 1941), 2; *Nashville Union*, 1 March, 13 May 1865; *Memphis Bulletin*, 14 April 1865; *Tennessee House Journal*, 1865–67 General Assembly, 1 Session, p. 133 (May 29, 1865). Aware of the prevalent racial prejudices among whites, black leaders protested that they did not want social equality. They contended that blacks preferred social associations with other blacks and that voting with whites would not change this.

20. *American Annual Cyclopedia*, 1865, 6 (1865), 778, cited in Taylor, *The Negro in Tennessee*, 2; *Proceedings of the Liberty and Union Convention, Which Assembled at the Capitol, in Nashville, Tennessee, on the 9th of January, 1865* (Nashville, 1865). The *Nashville Times* printed the official record of this convention in January 1865; *Nashville Times and True Union*, 18 January 1865. During this constitutional convention, Military Governor Andrew Johnson and (soon to be civil governor) William G. Brownlow successfully urged the deletion of black soldier suffrage from the slate of proposed amendments. Emancipation proved to be the only solid benefit the convention proposed for blacks.

21. Lovett, *The African American History of Nashville*, 202. The Thirteenth Amendment to the Constitution abolished slavery in the United States.

22. *Nashville Daily Times*, 18 January 1865. The 9 January and 6 April petitions apparently were similar, if not identical documents. The new General Assembly of 1865 convened on 3 April 1865.

23. Lovett, "The Negro in Tennessee," 195.

24. *House Journal*, 34th Tennessee General Assembly, 1st Session, 1865, 35; Eugene G.

Feistman, "Radical Disfranchisement and the Restoration of Tennessee, 1865–1866," *Tennessee Historical Quarterly*, 12 (1953): 135–51.

25. *Harper's Weekly*, 19 June 1865. This quote also appeared in *The* (Gallatin) *Examiner*, 21 October 1865.

26. Because Brownlow's radical partisans dominated the General Assembly, the administration had no trouble disenfranchising former supporters of the Confederacy. *Senate Journal*, 34th Tennessee General Assembly, 1865, 3–26.

27. W.E.B. DuBois, *Black Reconstruction in America, 1860–1880* (New York, 1962), 571–75.

28. *Nashville Dispatch*, 2 June 1865. Other city papers also printed this announcement

29. Ibid.

30. Taylor, *The Negro in Tennessee*, 8; Lovett, *The African American History of Nashville*, 203.

31. Taylor, *The Negro in Tennessee*, 8.

32. Lovett, *The African American History of Nashville*, 203; *Nashville Daily Press and Times*, 9 August 1865; *Nashville Dispatch*, 8 August 1865; *Colored Tennessean*, 12 August 1865; Taylor, *The Negro in Tennessee*, 9. Nelson Merry pastored First Colored Baptist Church in Nashville.

33. *Colored Tennessean*, 12 August 1865.

34. Taylor, *The Negro in Tennessee*, 8.

35. *Colored Tennessean*, 12 August 1865.

36. Lovett, *The African American History of Nashville*, 203–204.

37. *Colored Tennessean*, 12 August 1865.

38. *Nashville Daily Press and Times*, 9 August 1865; *Nashville Dispatch*, 8 August 1865.

39. *Colored Tennessean*, 12 August 1865; *Chicago Tribune*, 15 August 1865. Fisk advocated a suffrage system based on literacy. This was a condition few adult black Tennesseans could meet at that time.

40. *Colored Tennessean*, 12 August 1865; *Congressional Globe*, 38th Congress, 1st Session, p. 107 (21 December 1865); Lovett, *The African American History of Nashville*, 204. Richard Harris of Nashville opposed petitioning Congress not to seat Tennessee's delegation unless the state legislature first granted black suffrage. He feared that white Tennesseans would never give them the vote and that an appeal to Congress would probably backfire in their faces. On the other hand, Ransom Harris, the Equal Rights League official, retorted that if white unionists had enough moral consciouness to abolish slavery, then firm prodding would eventually win suffrage for the state's black men.

41. Lovett, "The Negro in Tennessee," 199; *Congressional Globe*, 38th Congress, 1st Session, p. 107 (21 December 1865); Tennessee's black leaders arranged for the presentation of their petition by Sen. Charles Sumner, a prominent radical Republican and an opponent of rapid readmission for the former Confederate states. Before Sumner could introduce the petition, Congress had already refused to seat the delegates from all former Confederate states, including Tennessee.

42. *Colored Tennessean*, 7 October 1865; Lovett, *The African American History of Nashville*, 204.

43. Tennessee, *Senate Journal of the General Assembly, 1865–66* (Nashville, 1866), 11–16; Lovett, *The African American History of Nashville*, 204; John B. Neal, *Disunion and Restoration in Tennessee* (New York, 1899), 39–41; *Daily Press and Times*, 5 April 1865; E. Merton Coulter, *William G. Brownlow: Fighting Parson of the Southern Highlands* (Chapel, N.C., 1937), 109.

44. William G. McBride, "Blacks and the Race Issue in Tennessee Politics, 1865–1876" (PhD dissertation, Vanderbilt University, 1989), 50–51; *Tennessee Senate Journal, 1865–67 General Assembly, 1st Adjourned Session*, pp. 10–13 (3 October 1865). Brownlow also was aware that the blacks' suffrage movement endangered the Tennessee Union Party's local hegemony. The federal government might respond to the blacks' complaints by intervening in their behalf. This possibility tormented conservatives and former Confederates as well as Union Party leaders.

45. Lovett, "The Negro in Tennessee," 199.

46. *Nashville Dispatch*, 4 May 1866.

47. *Senate Journal of the Tennessee General Assembly, 1865–66*. This bill was passed on 11 May 1866; Neal, *Disunion and Restoration in Tennessee*, 40.

48. *Acts of Tennessee*, 34th General Assembly, Adjourned Session, 1865–1866, 65; Neal, *Disunion and Restoration in Tennessee*, 40; Phillip Hamer, ed., *Tennessee: A History, 1673–1932*, 4 vols. (New York, 1933), II, 612. That same year, the worst outbreak of anti-black violence in Reconstruction Tennessee broke out in Memphis. In fact, the Memphis Race Riot of 1–2 May 1866 is considered one of the bloodiest and most destructive race riots in American history.

49. Forrest McDonald, *States' Rights and the Union* (Lawrence, Kan., 2000), 211. The Civil Rights of 1866 sought to repeal the racial codes imposed on blacks in the former Confederate states. In Tennessee, one such code restricted black business enterprise in Memphis. However, in the 1866 case of *State v. Robert Church* the court, citing the Civil Rights Act of 1866 ruled that a free man could not be punished that way. The principles of the Civil Rights Act of 1866 were incorporated in the Fourteenth Amendment.

50. Ibid; Mary Frances Berry, *Military Necessity and Civil Rights Policy: Black Citizenship and the Constitution, 1861–1868* (Port Washington, N.Y., 1977), 85–86. Most supporters of the Civil Rights Act favored equal rights without suffrage for blacks.

51. McDonald, *States' Rights and the Union*, 212. One of Johnson's declared reasons for vetoing the Civil Rights Act was that it embodied unprecedented intrusion of the federal government into the exclusive domain of the states.

52. Berry, *Military Necessity and Civil Rights Policy*, 97–98. The Fourteenth Amendment also sought to make the approach that the protection of the rights of freedom be left primarily to state governments and a part of fundamental law.

53. Lovett, *The African American History of Nashville*, 205.

54. Ibid.

55. *Tennessee Senate Journal of 1866*, Extra Session, 49. Tennessee was readmitted to the Union on 24 July 1866. After the required number of states ratified it, the Fourteenth Amendment went into effect on 28 July 1868.

56. Paul H. Bergeron, Stephen V. Ash, and Jeanette Keith, *Tennesseans and Their History* (Knoxville, 1999), 158.

57. Cimprich, "The Beginning of the Black Suffrage Movement In Tennessee," 192–193.

58. McBride, "Blacks and the Race Issue in Tennessee Politics, 1865–1876," 192–193.

59. *Colored Tennessean*, 18 July 1866; *Nashville Daily Press and Times*, 6–11 August 1866; *Memphis Evening Post*, 13 July, 15–16 August 1866. Apparently the *Post* and *Daily Press and Times* were the only Tennessee newspapers openly friendly to blacks. Republicans edited both. The *Colored Tennessean's* issues for the months of May through September 1866 are missing; therefore, it is difficult to gauge black opinion of the 1866 Colored Convention or the Memphis Race Riot of 1–2 May 1866.

60. Delegates from the following counties attended: Bedford, Blount, Davidson, DeKalb, Giles, Hamilton, Knox, Marshall, Montgomery, Rutherford, Shelby, Sumner, Williamson, and Wilson. The home county, Davidson, had the largest delegation present with twenty-two delegates, including Samuel W. Keeble, D. Watkins, and Nelson Walker. Memphis's blacks had met on 19 July 1866 and held their own mini-convention for the purpose of selecting thirteen delegates to the State Colored Convention. These included Berber Alexander, George King, Edward Merriweather, and Adolphus Smith. According to the *Nashville Daily Press and Times* on 7 August 1866, Edward Shaw also served as a delegate to the convention from Shelby County. Knox County, the site of Tennessee's third largest city, sent seven delegates, including Alfred E. Anderson, and E.D. Livingston. Hamilton County sent only one delegate, the Reverend C.P. Letcher. *Memphis Evening Post*, 16 August 1866; Lovett, "The Negro in Tennessee," 202–203.

61. *Memphis Evening Post*, 15–16 August 1866; Lovett, *The African American History of Nashville*, 205.

62. *Nashville Daily Press and Times*, 4, 6, and 10 August. This may have been a reference of the New Orleans race riot.

63. Ibid, 6 August 1866. While many delegates bristled at the mayor's suggestions, the Civil Rights Act of 1866 guaranteed colored citizens the right to meet in convention and discuss the question what they pleased except secession.

64. *Nashville Daily Press and Times*, 7 August 1866; McBride, "Blacks and the Race Issue in Tennessee," 138. M.J.R. Gentle defeated Daniel Watkins for president of the convention.

65. Taylor, *The Negro in Tennessee*, 21.

66. *Nashville Daily Press and Times*, 7 August 1866; According to the *Nashville Dispatch*, 7 August 1866, the group of marchers was from the Colored Soldiers League, ostensibly parading in support of the convention. Interestingly, the assembly voted to disavow any connection with the Colored Soldiers League, hoping that this would protect them from blame should the march trigger a riot.

67. *Nashville Daily Press and Times*, 7 August 1866.

68. Ibid., 8, 9, and 12 August 1866.

69. Ibid., 9 and 12 August 1866.

70. Ibid., 8 August 1866. The 1866 State Colored Convention recommended to the State Equal Rights League of Tennessee the appointment of a lecturer, whose duty it would be to visit the various counties and precincts of the state, and instruct the freedmen. Samuel Lowery was named president of the organization. Although a call for a state convention under the auspices of the new organization was set for 18 September 1866, a cholera epidemic prevented the State Equal Rights League from convening at that time. The first convention of the State League was held in 1867.

71. Ibid., 9 and 12 August 1866; McBride, "Blacks and the Race Issue in Tennessee Politics," 143.

72. *Nashville Daily Press and Times*, 7, 8, and 9 August 1866.

73. *United States Constitution, Fourteenth Amendment*, Sec. 1–2; Mingo Scott, *The Negro in Tennessee Politics and Governmental Affairs* (Nashville, 1964), 11.

74. Scott, *The Negro in Tennessee Politics*, 11. On 5 November 1866, during a special session of the legislature, Governor Brownlow declared that the Tennessee representation in Congress would be reduced to six without black suffrage and increased to nine by enfranchising black citizens. *Acts of Tennessee*, 34'h General Assembly, 2nd Adjourned Session, 265–266. While Tennessee had accepted the principle of black suffrage, it had not provided the machinery to implement the federal law. Members of the State Colored Convention were well aware of Tennessee's peculiar situation.

75. *Nashville Daily Press and Times*, 10 August 1866.

76. Nashville *Dispatch*, 8 August 1866; *Nashville Union and American*, 10 August 1866; *Nashville Daily Press and Times*, 9 August 1866.

77. McBride, *Blacks and the Race Issue in Tennessee Politics*, 146.

78. *Nashville Daily Press and Times*, 11–12 August 1866.

79. Ibid. 12 August 1866. The next scheduled meeting of the State Colored Convention was to take place during the first week in September 1867 in Knoxville.

80. *Knoxville Whig*, 6 February 1867; *Nashville Daily Press and Times*, 23 September 1867.

81. *Acts of Tennessee*, 35th General Assembly, 1ts Session, 1867–1868, Chapter XXXI, 32–33. This act provided: That every male inhabitant of this state, of the age of 21 years, a citizen of the United States and a resident of the county wherein he may offer his vote, six months next preceding the day of the election shall be entitled to the elective franchise, subject to certain exemptions and disqualifications which do apply to Negroes. Section sixteen provided that nothing in the act should be construed to allow Negro men to hold office or sit on juries. *House Journal*, 34th General Assembly, 2nd Adjourned Session, 1865–1867, 271–278.

82. *Nashville Daily Press and Times*, 22 February 1867.

83. *Memphis Appeal*, 26 February 1867.

84. *Nashville Daily Press and Times*, 18 April 1867.

85. Ibid., 14 April 1867.

86. Ibid., 8 February 1868; *Tennessean Tribune*, 6 March 1870.

87. *Journal of the House of Representatives of the State of Tennessee*, 1867–1868, 25.

88. May Alice Harris Ridley, "The Black Community of Nashville and Davidson County, 1860–1870," (PhD dissertation, University of Pittsburgh, 1982).

89. *Nashville Daily Press and Times*, 21 February 1869. The nine counties placed under martial law were: Overton, Jackson, Maury, Giles, Marshall, Lawrence, Gibson, Madison, and Haywood; J.C. Lester and D.L. Wilson, *Ku Klux Klan, Its Origin, Growth, and Disbandment* (New York, 1905), 129. The Imperial Wizard of the Tennessee Klan was a former Confederate, Nathan Bedford Forrest.

90. F. Wayne Binning, "The Tennessee Republicans in Decline, 1869–1876," (Part I) *Tennessee Historical Quarterly*, 39 (Winter 1980),474; Taylor, *The Negro in Tennessee*, 67, 72; Judy Catherine LeForge, "Tennessee's Constitutional Development, 1796–1870: A Conservative Struggle Toward Democracy," (Ph. D. dissertation, The University of Memphis, 2002), 170.

91. *Acts*, 36th Tennessee General Assembly, 1869–70, 92; Nashville *Union and American*, 20 March 1870; Taylor, *The Negro in Tennessee*, 74, 80.

92. Taylor, *The Negro in Tennessee*, 74; LeForge, "Tennessee's Constitutional Development," v.

93. *House Journal*, 36th Tennessee General Assembly, 1st Session, 1869–70, 671.

94. *Acts*, 36th Tennessee General Assembly, 1st Session, 1869–70, 67–68; *Senate Journal of the State of Tennessee*, 36th Tennessee General Assembly, 1st Session, 1869–70, 353–355; *House Journal*, 36th Tennessee General Assembly, 1st Assembly, 1869–70, 606, 842; Nashville *Republican Banner*, 12 April 1870.

95. Nashville *Republican Banner*, 18 March 1870; Taylor, *The Negro in Tennessee*, 77–78.

96. Nashville *Republican* Banner, 12 April 1870.

97. Robert E. Corlew, *Tennessee: A Short History* (Knoxville, 1981), 349–350.

98. Taylor, *The Negro in Tennessee*, 80. The Congressional Reconstruction Committee heard testimony from 11 March to 19 April 1870.

99. Lester C. Lamon, *Blacks in Tennessee, 1791–1970* (Knoxville, 1981), 49.

# WE BUILT BLACK ATHENS

## How Black Determination Secured Black Education in Antebellum Nashville

### Crystal A. DeGregory

As the home to several of the American nation's oldest and most distinguished historically black colleges and universities, Nashville's late nineteenth century reputation as the "Athens of the South" is unquestionably owed in no small measure to its copious opportunities for both white and black higher education. New South proponents increasingly touted white colleges such as Vanderbilt University (established in 1873) and George Peabody College for Teachers (1875–1979) and Fisk University (established in 1866), a black school founded and funded by Northern missionaries, as evidence of the city's commitment to educational and cultural progressiveness. By the early twentieth century, however, Nashville's New South idealists increasingly drew on these schools as well as an extended cohort other local schools including several black colleges such as Roger Williams University, formerly known as Nashville Normal and Theological Institute (1866–1929), Central Tennessee College, later renamed to Walden University (1865–1925), and Meharry Medical College (founded 1876), as evidence of the city's social and cultural distinctiveness. These schools, like many educational centers across the post-war South, became part and parcel of the campaign to reconstruct the mind of the South.

However, as Don Doyle has pointedly noted, the city's distinction as an education center "was more an outgrowth of Nashville's recent collaborative role during the war," than an "educational complex built on antebellum precedents."[1] Despite offering measured support to white Northern missionaries in the wake of the Civil

War, the efforts of New South proponents to develop black education have been characterized as merely supportive rather than truly collaborative in nature. Nashville was no exception to this rule, as southern reformers relied heavily on the success of Northern-sponsored institutions to demonstrate their commitment to an educational campaign for both blacks and whites. Consequently, most histories of black education in the South begin with the arrival of Northern missionaries who traveled to the war-torn South to establish education for slaves-turned-freedmen. They extol the sacrifices of Northern missionaries who often abandoned their lives of relative comfort to venture into the Deep South to serve as teachers in black schools and demonstrate that the success of these educational endeavors was due in no small measure to the leadership of Northern missionaries.[2]

It is therefore, predictable, even easy, to suggest that white missionaries created educational opportunities for Southern blacks. But such an assertion is largely one-dimensional since it does not acknowledge James D. Anderson's research on how the freedmen's educational movement was undergirded by black "self-reliance and [the] deep-seated desire [of blacks] to control and sustain schools for themselves and their children."[3] Such a contention has particular resonance in the case of Nashville, where the history of black education began decades before the arrival of the first Northern missionary and, similarly, almost three decades before the shots that began the Civil War rang out. At a time when even rudimentary instruction was exceptional for most white children, free and enslaved blacks in Nashville joined together to provide educational opportunities for black children through a string of independent, black-operated, and black-owned schools.

Dubbed "native schools," the narrative of the clandestine black educational centers unfolded against a consistently shifting backdrop of local, state, and national race relations and involved the intricate amalgamation of black agency, secrecy and white patronage and/or complicity. There is perhaps nowhere that this history is clearer than in the case of Nashville, where white opposition, violence and even hysteria—despite regularly causing the temporary closure of native schools—never permanently derailed black educational efforts. Their story is also one of extraordinary commitment, sacrifice, and determination. But it is a not only a story of black triumph over tremendous odds. Nor is it merely a testament to their willingness to fight racial inequality through self-determination. It signals the central place of education as social insurgency in the black community long before the coming of white missionaries with their protestant ethic. It demonstrates the conceptualization of education among blacks as the best means to both personal advancement and to racial uplift as well as a call to the service of others.

By chronicling the process of how education by-and-for black people in Nashville unfolded in the decades preceding the Civil War, this article hopes to demonstrate that the victories of Northern whites were won on the educational battleground that black Nashville had begun to till decades before their arrival and independent of Northern philanthropic and missionary support. These schools serve as the earliest indicator of the desire among black locals to secure educational self-sufficiency. Their thirty years of operation also created an incubator for the city's black teacher tradition. Black educators before the Civil War sought to offer a generation of black students more than academic instruction; they sought to imbue them with self-esteem and racial pride. Those teachers and the generation of students they produced, not only assumed influential positions in black communities including black Nashville, they popularized their black educational experiences. For all these reasons the story of black education in antebellum Nashville constitutes the foundation of black Nashville as a leading educational center and as "Black Athens."

> Very little that is noteworthy occurred in the founding of Fisk School. The battle for the education of colored children by white missionaries from the North had already been won by Rev. J.G. McKee, who had the honor of being first on ground in Nashville, and of bearing the brunt of the opposition to the opening of colored schools.—H.S. Bennett, in *A History of Colored School of Nashville, Tennessee*[4]

It is difficult to believe that white Northern missionary and Fisk University theology professor H. S. Bennett penned these words in the face of the longstanding history of self-determination in the education of black Nashville, a history that began three decades before McKee opened his school on October 13, 1863. Sometime in March 1833, Alphonso M. Sumner, a free black barber whose violent expulsion from Nashville would later lead him to Cincinnati where he was an abolitionist and served as publisher of that city's first black newspaper, founded a clandestine school for black children. Sumner belonged to black Nashville's small elite class of mulattoes, free blacks, and quasi-independent slaves who, as historian Bobby Lovett observed, had "special relations with Nashville elite whites [who] frequently looked the other way when these privileged Negroes bent the racial rules."[5] As the black barber of an exclusively white male clientele, Sumner was probably regularly privy to private conversations among whites on the issues affecting all Nashvillians.

Whether or not Sumner was customarily silent when rendering his services, Quincy T. Mills's characterization of "shaving time" as occasions where "white men sat in the barber's chair and submitted to the sharp straight razor at the hands of black barbers" offered free barbers like Sumner a particularly important place of power and privilege.[6] Such a "place" was however, not without ambiguity. It is plausible that despite the power he wielded over the life and death of each patron that sat in his chair, Sumner knew the limits of such power. In fact, it is very likely that when Sumner did speak in the presence of whites, his responses were both solicited and measured in order to preserve most obviously his business, but also to protect his life and ensure the welfare of his family and community. Even as a privileged free black entrepreneur, Sumner and others like him knew that no matter how close their relationship to the white world, their fate rested with the rest of the black community.

While there are few primary sources that chronicle Sumner's life and work in Nashville, one can understand the gravity of his choice to open this school for free black children given the context of the times. Across the nation, thousands of white Americans had been swept up in the tide of evangelism known as the Second Great Awakening. Adherents of this emergent Protestant doctrine stressed personal salvation in places such as Tennessee, where the Great Revival was popular and planted deep, permanent roots. In addition to bringing people closer to God and their frontier neighbors, the awakening had important (and perhaps unintended) consequences for American social life including antebellum reforms such as abolitionism.

However, the rise of abolitionist sentiments was fragile and whites began a particularly violent reign of terror following Nat Turner's 1831 uprising in Southampton County, Virginia, the era's bloodiest slave rebellion. Turner, who was a black preacher, had been taught to read by one of his master's sons. His religious conviction and religious leadership of other slaves who looked up to him was, arguably in part, due to the zeitgeist of the age. Their inclusion in the worship experience exposed many slaves to the Bible and these slaves increasingly identified with the oppressed peoples in biblical stories.[7] Similarly, the antislavery character of Methodist and Baptist doctrines, which in particular drew many slave converts, allowed their churches to meet their slave membership's call for black ministers who "combined African heritage, their common experience as slaves, and elements of biblical teaching to fashion a distinctly African American brand of Protestant Christianity."[8]

Ministers like Turner not only exposed other slaves to these biblical stories; they provided these stories as "a powerful motive for slaves to gain literacy."[9] In the wake of the Southampton uprising, such sentiments may have resonated with sympathetic whites in the North, but in the South, white fears of future protest among blacks led to increased restrictions on all blacks, both free and slave.[10] Less than 700 miles away from Southampton, and only two years following Turner's infamous showing, Sumner founded his Nashville school for free black children on March 4, 1833, the very same day Nashville's Andrew Jackson was sworn in for his second term as the nation's seventh president.

It is plausible that the uneasiness caused by the Southampton affair was felt locally. Given those realities, Sumner was likely to have "gauged their [white customers] sentiment about blacks in general" and concluded that "if things were done quietly, most elite whites would not oppose free Negro classes."[11] Elite men of color like Sumner depended on their privileged place as leading blacks, as well as the paternalistic sympathies of white Nashvillians, in order to anticipate that they would turn a blind eye to a school for black children, a venture that was provocative anywhere in the South. Such "understandings" were however, not made without restriction. Sumner's school was no exception, as whites allowed it to operate with "the understanding that none but free children should attend."[12]

James P. Thomas was among the first students of Sumner's school. The son of white judge John Catron and Sally Thomas, a slave woman turned self-employed laundress, he recalled that "the authorities allowed [the] school to be kept for teaching the children of Free persons."[13] Even so, there is evidence that there was at least a small number of slave children among Sumner's earliest pupils and some even had the permission of their owners. Sumner began as the school's sole teacher but his professional commitment soon led to the hiring of other free blacks as teachers, including Daniel Wadkins, whose role in black education is Nashville would eclipse Sumner's in the coming years. By 1836, the school's student population rose from twenty to about 200 under Sumner and Wadkins's leadership, a number that was achieved in spite of dangerous outbreaks of cholera and smallpox that temporarily forced the closure of the months at a time each year.[14]

That year, an even more formidable challenge to the school's operation emerged when Sumner was accused of writing and sending two letters "containing important information to two fugitives" living in Detroit, Michigan.[15] While there is no evidence of Sumner's involvement either as a way to supplement his income or even as an act of goodwill, Wadkins recalled that the intercepted letters were used as proof of Sumner's involvement and "in consequence…Sumner was nearly whipped to death, and compelled to leave the State never to return."[16] Thomas, who also recollected the incident, characterized Sumner as a "fine scollar," [sic] who was "taken out by what was termed the slicks and whipped pretty near to death. The leader of the gang," Thomas remembered, "was a son of the most distinguished Jurist in the state."¹⁷ Whether or not Sumner was guilty, the whipping he received at the hands of the white vigilante group was bad enough to convince him to flee Nashville for Cincinnati, where he established a new life of community activism.

Nashville's connection to black Cincinnati can be traced back to the earliest days of the secret, loosely organized network of people and the hiding spaces they used to guide slaves to freedom through the Underground Railroad. Hundreds of black slaves escaped overland from Tennessee. The waterways of the Cumberland and Tennessee rivers, which had brought Nashville's founders to the region, similarly provided a means for slaves to escape to Cincinnati. Once in Cincinnati, Sumner joined ongoing education, antislavery, and social reform efforts of the black community and soon became an important leader.¹⁸

If Sumner's hasty departure is not evidence enough of the threats and challenges facing free black education in antebellum Nashville, consider the fact that Amos Dresser, a white missionary who was at the time a theological student, had suffered a similar fate just one year before Sumner. When Dresser stopped in Nashville to sell Bibles in 1832, a vigilante committee arrested him for possessing anti-slavery tracts. His prosecutors contended that he had distributed some of the abolitionist literature in the state, for which he was stripped naked and received twenty lashes on the public square before a "goodly" crowd.¹⁹ Dresser's treatment was legal due to a new 1831 state law that gave local courts the "discretion" to punish abolition agitators by "jailing, whipping, standing in the pillory, death—and [for which] no appeal was to be allowed."²⁰ Ordered to leave the city within twenty-hours, Dresser "shook the dust of Nashville from his feet," fleeing Nashville in fear of losing his life.²¹

These incidents not only resulted in nearly fatal consequences for Sumner and Dresser, they demonstrated the violent lengths to which Nashville whites could go when they perceived a threat to their authority and way of life, despite their paternalistic tendencies.²² The beatings also signaled the beginning of increasingly difficult times for black education in Nashville. Sumner's school closed for two years in the aftermath of his exile. In 1837, voters defeated an attempt by the mayor to consider the possibility of a black school. The city's free black population felt so much white opposition to the idea, that they "were intimidated [and] thought if best to wait 'until the storm blew over.'"²³

> Mr. [Wadkins] gave out each word with such an explosive jerk of the
> head and spring around the body, that it commanded our profound
> respect. His eyes seemed to see every one in the room, and woe be to

the one who giggled or was inattentive, whether pupil or visitor, for such a one constantly felt a whack from his long rattan.—Ella Sheppard Moore, in *Beyond Emancipation*[24]

Hailed as "the father of Negro education" in Nashville, Daniel Wadkins was one of only two blacks to continuously teach in the year's following Sumner's forced departure. As native school owners and operators, Wadkins and Sarah Porter Player somehow educated both free and slave Nashville blacks, effectively managing along the way their relationship with white Nashville elites, securing additional teachers, locations, and supplies as well as avoiding white violence.[25]

The next period of free black education in Nashville began in 1838, a year after the mayor's failure to gain public support for free black schools. "There were no more schools until January 1838," recalled Wadkins, "when the most energetic free colored citizens got up a petition, which was signed by a number of leading citizens, asking permission to have a school for free children only, and to be taught by a white man."[26] The proposal's intentional proscriptions of slave pupils and black teachers made it easier for whites to support. Soon thereafter, a free black man hired and paid John Yandle, a white man of Wilson County, to be the teacher.

Yandle operated the school for about a year on McLemore Street (now Ninth Avenue), near Line Street (now Jo Johnston), before operating for the same period of time on North High Street (Sixth Avenue), again near Line Street. The school had an average of thirty students "who learned to read and write, and something of arithmetic and geography." While he received the assistance of Daniel Wadkins and eventually quit teaching to pursue better paying work, Yandle's initial decision to teach free blacks was a courageous and possibly dangerous one, which Wadkins noted, drew threats of violence "more than once."[27]

Wadkins, who had served as a substitute teacher to Sumner before assisting Yandle, similarly served Sarah Porter Player, who had opened a school in her Broad Street home in 1841. Player was free but her husband was a slave who belonged to "an excellent family of white people, whose slaves enjoyed every privilege that free people enjoyed." A "woman of some education," Porter relocated the school the following year to the home of a supporter, hiring Wadkins as her assistant.[28]

After serving the school for about a year, during which time the school's enrollment noticeably increased, Wadkins founded his own school in 1842 in the house of a supporter on Front Street (then called Water Street and now First Avenue) near to the city jail.[29] In doing so, Wadkins assumed the mantle of leading the educational efforts of black Nashville over the course of the next decade. As someone who had long been in the trenches of the struggle for black education, Wadkins knew the undertaking was a dangerous one; he responded to the challenges cautiously so he would not meet a fate similar or worse than met by Sumner.

Described by Ella Sheppard Moore, who later became a Fisk Jubilee Singer, educator, and community leader, as "a typical 'John Bull' in appearance and an 'Uncle Sam' in vivacity," Wadkins was already an old man by the time Sheppard was his student. Still, her choice of these two distinct caricatures, recreate an image of Wadkins as a white-bearded short and stout man whose liveliness was apparent to his students.[30] Lovett assuredly characterized him as "an unskilled free Negro laborer, [who] was known as a man who readily accommodated the [white] ruling-class members' conservative racial attitudes."[31] But Wadkins's conciliatory approach may have been wise given his struggle to keep his school open amid the tenuous nature of black and white power relationships in Nashville. He kept his school in operation despite moving six times between the years of 1842 and 1856. "He taught a large day and night or evening school," aided sometimes by bakery owner Joseph Manly and barber shop owner George Barber.[32] A move to a residence on High and Crawford streets in 1853 signaled the beginning of increasingly intermittent stays for Wadkins's school as he moved once each subsequent year, operating next at the Second Colored Baptist Church, and then in private homes on the corner of Line and McLemore and in another residence on College Street (now Third Avenue).[33]

Two plausible reasons may account for Wadkins's frequent moves. First, demand for his services steadily increased. His school's enrollment steadily grew from thirty-five students at the time of the school's founding to fifty students in 1844 to sixty students by 1855. Second, Wadkins wisely moved to "avoid public scrutiny" of his school.[34] Hence, Wadkins probably had mixed feelings when an 1850 editorial in the *Nashville Union* proclaimed, "Until yesterday we were not aware that there were several schools for free negroes in the city and all of them in a flourishing condition." In as much as the editor's "genial notice" of the schools reflected the sentiments of paternalistic whites who were sympathetic to the cause of black education, it must have also attracted the attention of white opponents.[35] Therefore, it is very probable that Wadkins (and other black teachers) also instructed native school students and their families to be discreet about details of the school's operation and even its sheer existence. Students, for example, may have been advised to keep a low profile on Nashville streets by concealing their writing tablets, papers, and books and warned not to bring undue attention to themselves by walking in groups through city streets."[36]

Despite Wadkins's efforts, serious challenges to his school as well as his personal safety emerged in 1855. "A number of citizens, about a dozen in all," he recalled, came to his home and told him "not to teach that negro school another day; if negro schools are taught, it must be done in Illinois, Indiana, or some other free state, and not here among the slaves....Able lawyers had been consulted," claimed Wadkins, who said the school was legal. They responded that "the neighborhood objected" and warned that if Wadkins continued to operate the school, he "must look out for the consequences."[37]

Wadkins closed his school and it remained closed until 1856 when he briefly reopened it on College Street. Only seven months later, the city's police captain told Wadkins that "he was ordered by the City Council to close the negro school, and it must not be taught another day [because] they were in possession of a great many facts that convinced them that the negroes contemplated a general insurrection, and there was great excitement, not only in Nashville and Tennessee, but throughout the South."[38] This order effectively closed free black schools in Nashville until, as Wadkins observed, "the Federal troops took possession of the city" during the Civil War.[39]

The "great excitement" of whites in Nashville, across the state, and through the South to which the police captain referred, was the insurrection panic of 1856. Fueled by the nagging fears of whites that remained as vestiges of the slave uprisings of Gabriel Prosser, Denmark Vessey and especially Nat Turner, "wild rumors of an all-embracing slave plot extending from Delaware to Texas, with the execution set for Christmas Day, spread throughout the South."[40] Despite acknowledging these rumors as "exaggerated reports of excitement in Tennessee," the December 20, 1856, issue of the *Nashville Union and American* acknowledged, "There is no doubt that the negroes had talked of insurrection, and of fighting their way to a free state."[41]

While some historians including Charles Drew have since concluded that "the fright of the white community was probably groundless," many whites were convinced of the rumors' truth.[42] The racial climate in Nashville that was tenuous at best soon turned ugly. Nashville blacks were increasingly subjected to the "violence and the gratuitous meanness of poor whites and of the city's watchmen." They must have known that they could never expect white men, no matter how patrician their nature, "to become their public champions."[43] Consequently, white supporters of black education stood by while white gangs intimidated local blacks, including Wadkins and Player, who was also forced to close in 1856, probably as a result of white harassment.[44]

The events surrounding the scare signaled the beginning of a wave of dramatic changes in Nashville's race relations. Soon after, the city council instituted a series of severe restrictions on black life. The new codes ordered that "there shall be no school for Negroes," prohibiting their instruction by either blacks or whites. The ordinances also included a $50 fine for "any white man found teaching blacks" and ordered that "there shall be no assemblage of Negroes after sundown for the purpose of preaching; and no colored man shall be allowed to preach to colored people, and no white man after night."[45]

Officials hoped the new codes would derail two decades of work begun by black educators in Nashville. "The fear of the North and its antislavery leaders only heightened Negrophobia in Nashville," observed Lovett, "thereby placing the privileged Negroes under suspicion and forcing the elite whites to tighten the controls on any privileged blacks rather than run the risk of alienating the white masses in times of crisis."[46] While the frenzy characterizing the period presented challenges in Nashville and across the South, it was the yet untold conflict between the North and South that would produce the most salutary changes for black education in Nashville.

> The free Negro population of this country, although it may contain meritorious individuals, is a class, corrupt, vicious and degraded.
> —*Daily Nashville Patriot*, December 18, 1856

Despite the caustic comments of the *Daily Nashville Patriot*, the door for free black education slowly reopened between 1859 and 1861. In 1859, William Carroll and his wife, who were the parents of James C. Napier, a former Wadkins student who would later become black Nashville's "most powerful politician and its most influential citizen,"[47] hired Rufus Conrad of Cincinnati to start a new school for blacks. It is likely that Conrad knew Alphonso Sumner, since they both resided in the same community near Cincinnati's Harrison Street and it is possible that Conrad was hired on Sumner's recommendation.[48]

Napier recalled that the school had only been open for two or three months when a white official suddenly arrived and told Conrad, "I have been authorized by the powers that be in Nashville to send these children home, to close the doors of this school and give you just 24 hours to leave this town."[49] The school never reopened.[50]

As did Dresser and Sumner before him, Conrad left Nashville for Cincinnati. Additional free Nashville blacks, including the family of William Carroll, moved to Cincinnati soon after, where their children became students of Conrad again. Conrad reemerged as a leading figure in black Cincinnati, where he later served as president of the Colored Orphan Asylum before later serving as a member of the board of directors for the city's school and by the 1870s as pastor of Harrison Street's The Disciple Church.[51]

Nashville's black schools remained closed until after Federal troops occupied the city in 1862. That same year, assisted by J.M. Shelton and his wife, Daniel Wadkins was able to re-start his black educational efforts. He opened a school in the First Colored Baptist Church, successfully operating there for eighteen months, before moving to High Street. There, Wadkins, "assisted from time to time by Miss Ode Barber, Mrs. Mariah Patterson and Miss Selina Walker" taught about one hundred and fifty students. Despite the school's success, it, as well as eight other Nashville schools owned and operated by black teachers, was closed upon the opening of the Fisk Free School in 1865.[52]

The closure of all of Nashville's independently owned and operated black schools had to be a tremendous blow to the countless black teachers who sacrificed to keep them open from 1833 to 1865, the thirty-two year span of their on-again-off-again history. Their existence represented a "considerable achievement of the antebellum decades," observed Anita Shafer Goodstein, "especially when their existence and dogged maintenance are contrasted with the skimpy provision made for poor white children."[53] Goodstein's assessment is especially telling given the narrative of white education during the same period. While there had been a longstanding history of private tutorials to those that could afford it, educational opportunities for Nashville's poor whites remained restricted until the mid-nineteenth century despite the passage of laws regarding public education for whites in Nashville as early as 1829. Slow to support public education, local whites generally reproached public schools as "poor" and rendered laws for their establishment as little more "salutatory exhortations."[54]

With little faith in public education's efficiency or economy, Nashville officials did not make their "first stride towards a more efficient system" of a public education system for white children until more than a decade after Alphonso Sumner first opened his native school.[55] Leading this effort was Professor J.H. Ingraham, who in 1848 reported that an "intelligent and highly respectable gentleman" was hired to operate a free school for whites. The school had as many as seventy students, yet Ingraham determined that there were as many as 1,500 school-aged children in the city, some of whom were enrolled in private schools, but the vast majority of which, "get along as they can, move away to other cities which are better provided with schools, or suffer their children to grow up in ignorance and vice."[56] Not until 1855 were plans for Nashville's first permanent public school realized when the Hume School was opened in at the corner of Eighth Avenue (then Spruce Street) and Broad.[57]

With the emergence of Nashville's public schools, white educational opportunities grew for both rich and poor whites alike well before the Civil War. But for many blacks in Nashville, it was the changes brought on by the Civil War that would most notably extend educational opportunities to them. It is ironic, though, that the coming of emancipation would spell the end of the earlier efforts at Nashville education by-and-for black people. While they were undoubtedly disappointed by the closure of their schools, black teachers were probably not surprised. By the height of the Civil War, the arrival of white Congregationalist minister Joseph G. McKee offered black teachers a glimpse of the looming threat white missionary education posed to Nashville's native schools and black teacher tradition.

As the first Northern missionary to offer free education to black children in Nashville, McKee was probably surprised to find that black Nashville had an already established tradition of education. Nashville's native schools, as a rule, required tuition. But McKee's missionary funding allowed him to offer his classes free of charge, offering the opportunity of an education to a number of black students who may not have been able to afford it otherwise. Viewed as an expansion of black educational opportunities, McKee's efforts were welcomed by the Reverend Nelson G. Merry, pastor of the First Baptist Colored Church, who permitted McKee to operate his free school on the church's ground floor. Shortly thereafter, Wadkins, who had previously operated his school in the church, reportedly vehemently objected to McKee's presence.[58] But Wadkins's history of black education in antebellum Nashville gives no record of it, leaving historians to offer conjecture on the extent of and the reasons for his opposition. It is not difficult to believe that he did attempt to thwart McKee's attempts to establish his school. Perhaps he took exception to the content of McKee's lessons or perceived McKee's attempts as patronizing or as an attempt by whites to take control of black education in Nashville.

What is certain, however, is that even with Wadkins's long and impressive record of teaching, he must have found it difficult to compete with the fact that McKee's classes were not only free, they were being offered in Nashville's oldest black church that called many of the city's most distinguished blacks its members. The matter sparked what has been characterized as "an unsightly brawl" between Wadkins and Merry, who was an advocate of McKee, but was probably more accurately a struggle for influence over the future of black education. Using his long-standing influence in the community, Wadkins was able to secure enough support among the church's membership to force the end of McKee's classes at the church.[59]

Wadkins's success however, was short-lived. While he and the city's other black teachers probably recognized that white missionary efforts presented a threat to the viability of their schools, jobs, and educational traditions, they were powerless to stop them. Led in part by McKee, the founding of the Fisk school spelled the end of the history of Nashville's native schools. Still, the history of black education in antebellum Nashville pointedly demonstrates the desire for black education among free blacks and enslaved persons alike. Nashville blacks, indeed, much like nineteenth century blacks held in bondage across the American South, actively sought educational opportunities to learn. Even in a state where slavery was deemed moderate, and in a community where paternalistic whites had a fairly liberal attitude towards privileged free and quasi-slave blacks, education for blacks was generally either nonexistent or was limited to the occasional sympathetic instruction of white owners. With little to no provision for black education, free blacks single-handedly created provisions for free and slave blacks by founding schools for local black children.

> Before the late Civil War, Virginia [Walker Broughton] attended a private school, taught by Professor Daniel [Wadkins], and was reading in the fourth reader when the new day of freedom dawned upon the race and brought with it the glorious light of education for all who would receive it.—Virginia Walker Broughton, *Twenty Year's Experience of a Missionary*[60]

Missionary, educator, and feminist Virginia Walker Broughton was only one of the many successful graduates produced by Nashville's antebellum black schools. Named after her father's home state, Broughton proudly declared that she was "born of honorable parents who had secured their freedom at great cost." Her father Nelson Walker "was an industrious, intelligent man, who, early in life, hired his time from his master and thereby was enabled to purchase his own freedom and also that of his wife." Together with his wife Eliza Smart Broughton, "they began to build up a home and rear children who could enjoy the privileges of education that only very few of our race could enjoy at that time." The training Broughton received in Wadkins's school was not only a privilege, it was an advantage that paid off when she attended the Fisk Free School in 1865 as an advanced student. Ten years later, after "consecutive years of faithful study" she graduated from the College Department of Fisk University in May 1875.[61]

There is little doubt that the success of antebellum black-owned and operated schools in Nashville was due to the sacrifice of the students' parents. Still, these schools also owed much of their success to the courage and dedication of black teachers who continuously tried to navigate the changing positions of local whites. With sympathetic whites vacillating between being supportive, seemingly indifferent, and/or oblivious to their existence, black schools were high-risk enterprises. It was dangerous to operate these schools amid a white community that was not at all hesitant to demonstrate its opposition through acts of violence. White hostility forced the schools to move often and to operate in secret. "Broken up time and again," wrote Anita Shafer Goodstein, "the schools' persistence is testimony to the stubborn determination of parents and teachers [as] …there is no evidence of financial or political support ever offered by the white community."[62]

As the principal source of stability for these schools, teachers like Wadkins and Porter constantly struggled to escape "the lynx-eyed vigilance" of those opposing black education.[63] In doing so, native schools not only represent black Nashville's earliest attempts of black self-determination, they point to the formative nature of these teachers in shaping the character of Black Athens. Long after she had been a student in Wadkins's school, Ella Sheppard Moore could still vividly remember her educational experiences. "He used the old Webster blue back spelling book. Each class stood up against the wall, head erect, hands down, toes straight. I recall only three classes: the Eb, Ib, Ob class; the Baker, Maker, Taker class; and the Replication, Replication class. They spelled in unison in a musical intonation, swaying their bodies from side to side, with perfect rhythmical precision on each syllable, which we thought grand."[64]

Moore's recollections of learning in Wadkins's school as "grand" were probably not unlike those of other former students in Nashville's native schools. In addition to helping students like Moore excel academically, Wadkins's instruction methods reflected early efforts of black teachers to incorporate discipline, deportment, and pride into their lessons. Wadkins's own carriage commanded the "profound respect" of his students—students who would increasingly assume positions of influence in Nashville and across the South during the post-Civil War period. Moore, for example, was a student in Wadkins's school up until 1856, before her father fled with her to Cincinnati. More than a decade later, she returned to Nashville where she attended Fisk and received international acclaim as a member of the world-famous Jubilee Singers. As the first black instructor at Fisk, her influence on several classes of Fiskites mirrored her national renown as a highly sought after public speaker, missionary, and woman's rights activist.[65]

Ella Sheppard Moore was only one of a host of former students in Nashville's native schools who achieved local, national, and even international prominence. Arguably black Nashville's most powerful politician and its most influential citizen from the 1870s up until the turn of the century, James C. Napier was also famously taught by Wadkins. Napier, who like Sheppard Moore had moved with his family to Cincinnati in the late 1850s, returned to the Nashville during the Civil War. He soon after became involved in Republican Party politics and was the mentee of slave-turned-Republican congressman John Mercer Langston. Napier graduated from Howard University Law School before returning to Nashville where he was a prominent figure in local and state politics. He along with his wife Nettie Langston, the daughter of his mentor, led black Nashville's elite circle for more than a half century. With his local influence secured through the passage of legislation that created opportunities for black professionals ranging from black teachers to black firemen, Napier used his personal savings to establish the Nashville One-Cent Savings Bank, one of the nation's first black-owned and operated banks, and helped lead the push for the founding of Tennessee Agricultural and Industrial Normal School for Negroes. Shortly after the turn of the century, Napier's influence reached national prominence when he served as Register of the United States Treasury from 1911–1913 under President Taft.[66]

Long before Napier entered the banking world, Nelson Walker, the father of Virginia Walker Broughton, another famous alumna of Nashville's native schools, served as chairman of the Freedman's Savings and Trust Company Bank. Organized in December 1865, it was the city's first black bank. The same year, Walker, a colored barber and businessman, persuaded the Tennessee General Assembly to incorporate the Nashville Barbers' Association and was among attendees at the first National Equal Rights League in Cleveland, Ohio.[67] The following year, he also helped to establish the Nashville Order of Sons of Relief Society as a benevolent organization and the Annual Agricultural and Mechanical Association to encourage freedman to draw on their occupational strengths as skilled craftsman and agricultural workers.[68]

Samuel Lowery was also among the alumni of Nashville's native schools. Like Walker, Lowery was also among attendees at the first National Equal Rights League in Cleveland in 1865.[69] His father Peter Lowery, who was a minister, ran a semi-independent black church on William G. Harding's Belle Meade plantation and is believed to have used his Sunday school for religious as well as academic instruction.[70] Together with his father, the younger Lowery, also a teacher and minister, founded Tennessee Manual Labor University, the only college in the state founded by and for blacks.[71] While he later became a noted silk culturist and successful businessman, Lowery was also a pioneering jurist. Admitted to the bar in Tennessee and then Alabama in the 1870s, Lowery, with the help of Belva V. Lockwood (the first woman admitted to the Supreme Court bar), became the fifth black American and first Southern black admitted to the Supreme Court bar in 1880.[72]

After establishing himself as a local barber and businessman in Nashville, James P. Thomas, youngest son of Sally Thomas and one of Alphonso Sumner's earliest students, moved to St. Louis, Missouri, where he became a leading real estate investor. By 1870, Thomas remarkably had become one of the richest men in the state, white or black. Over the course of the next two decades, Thomas and his heiress wife Antoinette Rutgers led St. Louis's elite black community. The famous family also included Sally Thomas's grandsons John H. Rapier, Jr., and James Rapier, also once students in Nashville's native schools. Born in Alabama, the Rapier brothers were reared in Nashville by their grandmother. Like their uncle James Thomas, their father John H. Rapier was a successful barber who had taught himself to write using a system of phonics. John Rapier, Jr., eventually became a surgeon with the Freedmen's Hospital in Washington, D.C., while his brother James was elected as a Republican to the Forty-third Congress (1873–1875), where he was one of seven black Representatives who fought for the passage of the major Civil Rights Bill of 1875.[73]

As successful teachers, lawyers, doctors, businessman, clergy and politicians, Broughton, Moore, Napier, Walker, Lowery, Thomas, and the Rapier brothers represent the generations of black children who were educated in Nashville's black antebellum schools. The school's primary function may have been to offer them the rudiments of an education. But in addition to offering their students the basics of reading, writing, and arithmetic, black teachers demanded the best of their students. They provided them with living models of black intelligence and achievement. They imbued them with self and race pride and instill in them a spirit of service to their communities. In doing so, black teachers nurtured a generation of "civic minded" black children who not only assumed influential positions in black Nashville, but assumed the mantle of civil rights through the creation of additional educational opportunities as well as economic and political empowerment for blacks.

The formative nature of these teachers in shaping the character of Black Athens would become more and more clear in the ensuing decades. Their importance was not only due to their continued educational activism or even chiefly due to their pupils' positions of influence. The most lasting contributions of these schools were the lofty expectations for black education (as well as for what one could and should do with it) they created in the minds of their students. Even so, the influence of these black schools and black teachers was not limited to its students. To be sure, those blacks who did not have the opportunity to attend Nashville's native schools were watching and waiting. When white missionaries arrived in Nashville, they would be surprised to find eager students as well as an existing black teacher tradition, which had set standards by which they would soon be measured.

⁂

1. Don H. Doyle, *New Men, New Cities, New South: Atlanta, Nashville, Charleston, Mobile, 1860–1910* (Chapel Hill, 1990), 30.

2. See Joyce Hollyday, *On the Heels of Freedom: The American Missionary Association's Bold Campaign to Educate Minds, Open Hearts, and Heal the Soul of a Divided Nation* (New York, 2005); William H. Watkins, *The White Architects of Black Education: Ideology and Power in America, 1865–1954*, (New York, 2001); Jacqueline Jones, *Soldiers of Light and Love: Northern Teachers and Georgia Blacks, 1865–1873*, (Chapel Hill, 1980).

3. James D. Anderson, *The Education of Blacks in the South, 1860–1935* (Chapel Hill, 1998), 5.

4. H. S. Bennett, "Fisk University," *A History of Colored School of Nashville, Tennessee* (Nashville, 1874), 21.

5. Census records as early as 1839 and 1840 list A.M. Sumner as "school teacher." See Greater Cincinnati connections, "Directory of Cincinnati Colored, 1839–40," http://www.cincytristate.com/1839-40%20Cincy%20Blacks.html (accessed 8 January 2009); The USGenWeb Project, "1840 Cincinnati City Directory For Colored Citizens," http://www.rootsweb.ancestry.com/~ohhamilt/dir1840cinticol.html (accessed 8 January 2009); Bobby L. Lovett, *African-American History of Nashville, Tennessee, 1780–1830: Elites and Dilemmas* (Fayetteville, Ark., 1999), 34.

6. Quincy T. Mills, "Razors, Rights, and Paradoxical Publics: Black Barber Shops and the Civil Rights Act of 1875," (Paper presented at the annual meeting of the Association for the Study of African American Life and History, Charlotte, N.C., 11 December 2008).

7. Janet Cornelius, *When I Read My Title Clear* (Columbia, S.C., 1991), 17, 19.

8. Barry Hankins, "The Second Great Awakening and African American Religion," *The Second Great Awakening and the Transcendentalists* (Westport, Conn., 2004), 68.

9. Cornelius, *When I Read My Title Clear*, 17, 19.

10. James Oliver Horton and Lois E. Horton, *Slavery and the Making of America* (New York, 2004), 115.

11. Lovett, *African-American History of Nashville, Tennessee*, 34.

12. Daniel Wadkins, "Origin and Progress before Emancipation," *A History of Colored School of Nashville, Tennessee*, 3.

13. See James Thomas, *From Tennessee Slave to St. Louis Entrepreneur: The Autobiography of James Thomas* (Columbia, Mo., 1984), 31, and John Hope Franklin and Loren Schweninger, *In Search of the Promised Land: A Slave Family in the Old South* (New York, 2006), 18.

14. Lovett, *African-American History of Nashville, Tennessee*, 34; Thomas, *From Tennessee Slave to St. Louis Entrepreneur*, 31.

15. Wadkins, "Origin and Progress before Emancipation," 4.

16. Ibid.

17. Thomas, *From Tennessee Slave to St. Louis Entrepreneur*, 32.

18. Nikki Marie Taylor, *Frontiers of Freedom: Cincinnati's Black Community, 1802–1868* (Athens, Ohio, 2005), 131; William Cheek and Aimee Cheek, *John Mercer Langston and the Fight for Black Freedom, 1829–65* (Urbana, Ill., 1996), 79, 46n.

19. For accounts of Dresser prosecution and punishment see Amos Dresser, *The Narrative of Amos Dresser* (New York, 1836); James Gillespie Birney, *The American Churches, The Bulwarks of American Slavery* (Concord, Mass.,1842), 9; Benjamin Lundy, *Life, Travels and Opinions of Benjamin Lundy* (New York, 1969 [1847]), 188; Will Thomas Hale and Dixon Lanier Merritt. *A History of Tennessee and Tennesseans: The Leaders and Representative Men in Commerce, Industry, and Modern Activities* (Chicago, 1913), II, 299; Chase C. Mooney, *Slavery in Tennessee* (Bloomington, 1957), 16–17.

20. Mooney, *Slavery in Tennessee*, 14.

21. Hale and Merritt, *A History of Tennessee and Tennesseans*, 299.

22. Benjamin Lundy, the famous Quaker and abolitionist, recalled that while visiting Nashville in the 1830s, only shortly before the attack on Dresser, he only narrowly escaped the same fate. See Lundy, *Life, Travels and Opinions of Benjamin Lundy*, 188.

23. Anita Shafer Goodstein, *Nashville 1780–1860: Frontier to City* (Gainesville, Fla., 1989), 51; Wadkins, "Origin and Progress before Emancipation," 5.

24. Ella Sheppard Moore, "Before Emancipation," American Missionary Association. n.d., 7–8

25. See Bobby L. Lovett, "Tennessee Manual Labor University," The Tennessee Encyclopedia of History and Culture, Carroll Van West, et al., eds., (Nashville, 1998), 938–939; Wadkins, "Origin and Progress before Emancipation," 4–6; Wadkins's own narrative demonstrates that Sarah Porter began teaching in her school in 1841, one year prior to him joining her as his assistant and that her school continued in various locations until it was forcibly closed in the same year as his. See Franklin and Schweninger, In Search of the Promised Land, 35.

26. Wadkins, "Origin and Progress before Emancipation," 5.

27. Ibid.

28. Carter G. Woodson, ed., "Documents: School for Free Negroes and Slaves," *Journal of Negro History*, 5 (January 1920): 117. Despite mistakenly referring to Player as "Sallie Player," Woodson's description is most likely of "Sarah" Porter Player.

29. Ibid.

30. Moore, "Before Emancipation," 7–8. As personifications of their respective nations, Uncle Sam and John Bull became popular during the nineteenth century. Portrayed as a stout, feisty man, John Bull is represented as "a bluff, kindhearted, bull-headed farmer," who is usually is shown in a suit made out of the British flag. See Ebenezer Cobham Brewer, *Dictionary of Phrase*

*and Fable: Giving the Derivation, Source, Or Origin of Commom Phrases, Allusions, and Words that Have a Tale to Tell* (London, 1870), 462, and E.D. Hirsch, Jr., Joseph F. Kett, and James Trefil Editors, *The New Dictionary of Cultural Literacy*, Third Edition, (New York, 2002), 318–19. Similarly, Uncle Sam is a figure who "stands for the government of the United States and for the United States itself." His initials are the abbreviation of United States and he is typically "portrayed as an old man with a gray goatee who sports a top hat and Stars and Stripes clothing." Hirsch, et. al., *New Dictionary of Cultural Literacy*, 354.

31. Lovett, *African-American History of Nashville, Tennessee*, 35.

32. Wadkins, "Origin and Progress before Emancipation," 5; Lovett. *African-American History of Nashville, Tennessee*, 35.

33. Wadkins, "Origin and Progress before Emancipation," 5.

34. Ibid.

35. *Nashville Union and American*, 20 September 1858, quoted in Anita Shafer Goodstein. *Nashville 1780–1860* , 152, and Franklin and Schweninger, *In Search of the Promised Land*, 35.

36. Lovett, *African-American History of Nashville, Tennessee*, 35.

37. Wadkins, "Origin and Progress before Emancipation," 5–6.

38. Ibid, 6.

39. Ibid.

40. For a more information on the 1856 scare, see Harvey Wish, "The Slave Insurrection Panic of 1856,"*Journal of Southern History*, 5 (May 1939): 206–222, and Charles B. Dew, "Black Ironworkers and the Slave Insurrection Panic of 1856." *Journal of Southern History*, 41 (August 1975): 321–338.

41. *Nashville Union and American*. December 20, 1856, quoted in Dew, "Black Ironworkers and the Slave Insurrection Panic of 1856," 321.

42. Ibid, 322.

43. Goodstein, *Nashville 1780–1860*, 156.

44. Wadkins, "Origin and Progress before Emancipation," 5–6.

45. See City of Nashville Ordinances, November 17, 1836–September 29, 1865.The ordinance also included the following provisions: "The mayor of the city has the authority to employ additional policemen, for day and night, and for the next thirty days," and "Free persons of color are prohibited from removing themselves from other counties and residing in this city."

46. Lovett, *African-American History of Nashville, Tennessee*, 37.

47. Herbert Clark, "James C. Napier (1845–1940)," *Profiles of African Americans in Tennessee History*, Bobby L. Lovett and Linda T. Wynn, eds. (Nashville, 1996), 94.

48. Lovett, *African-American History of Nashville, Tennessee*, 37.

49. Carter G. Woodson, "Documents: School for Free Negroes and Slaves," 116.

50. Ibid.

51. Nikki Marie Taylor, *Frontiers of Freedom*, 265, 53n; Rev. B. W. Arnett "The Benevolent

and Charitable Societies of Cincinnati, Ohio," Cincinnati: 1874. From online collection African American Perspectives: Pamphlets from the Daniel A. P. Murray Collection, 1818–1907, in American Memory, Library of Congress, http://memory.loc.gov/ammem/aap/aaphome.html (accessed 12 January 2009).

52. Wadkins, "Origin and Progress before Emancipation," 6.

53. Goodstein, *Nashville 1780–1860*, 150.

54. William Robertson Garrett and Albert Virgil Goodpasture, *History of Tennessee: Its People and Its Institutions from the Earliest Times to the Year 1903* (Nashville, 1903), 300.

55. Ibid.

56. "Report Upon A Proposed System of Public Education for the City of Nashville, Respectfully Addressed to its Citizens, by Prof. J.W. Ingraham, 1848," quoted in John Egerton, *Nashville: The Faces of Two Centuries, 1780–1980* (Nashville, 1980), 102.

57. Garrett and Goodpasture, *History of Tennessee*, 300.

58. J.W. Wait, "Mission in Nashville," *Historical Sketch of the Freedmen's Missions of the United Presbyterian Church, 1862–1904*, (Knoxville, 1904), 2–3; John Cimprich. *Slavery's End in Tennessee, 1861–1865* (Tuscaloosa, 1985), 77.

59. Ibid.

60. Virginia Walker Broughton, *Twenty Year's Experience of a Missionary* (Chicago, 1907), 7.

61. Ibid., 8; Jessie Carney Smith, "Virginia E. Walker Broughton," *Notable Black American Women*, Book II, (Detroit, 2003), 57–60; See Evelyn Brooks Higginbotham, "The Feminist Theology of the Black Baptist Church, 1880–1890," *Religion and American Culture: A Reader*, David G. Hackett, ed., (New York, 2003), 267–288.

62. Goodstein, *Nashville 1780–1860*, 150–151.

63. Henry Allen Bullock, *A History of Negro Education in the South: From 1619 to the Present*, (Cambridge, Mass., 1967), 25.

64. Moore, "Before Emancipation." 7.

65. Ibid; Jessie Carney Smith, "Ella Sheppard Moore (1851–1914),"*Notable Black American Women*, Book I, (Detroit, 1992), 1005–1010.

66. Lester C. Lamon, "James C. Napier (1845–1940)," *Dictionary of American Negro Biography*, Rayford W. Logan and Michael R. Winston, eds. (New York, 1982), 470–71; Linda T. Wynn, "James C. Napier (1845–1940)," *Notable Black American Men*, Jessie Carney Smith, ed. (Detroit, 1998), 868–71.

67. "Chapter XVI," *Acts of the State of Tennessee Passed at the General Assembly: Passed at the First Session of the Thirty-fourth General Assembly, for the Year 1865* (Nashville, 1865), 86.

68. "Chapter CLV," Acts of the State of Tennessee Passed at the General Assembly: Passed at the Second Session of the Thirty-fourth General Assembly, for the Years 1865–66 (Nashville, 1866), 391–393; Nina Mjagkij, "Nashville: Civic, Literary and Mutual Aid Associations," Organizing Black America: An Encyclopedia of African American Association (New York, 2001), 351–352.

69. *Proceedings of the First Annual Meeting of the National Equal Rights League, Held in Cleveland, Ohio October 19, 20 and 21, 1985* (Philadelphia, 1865).

70. Woodson, ed., "Documents: School for Free Negroes and Slaves," 116; Robert W. Hooper, *A Distinct People: A History of the Churches of Christ in the 20th Century* (West Monroe, La., 1993), 257.

71. Acts of the State of Tennessee Passed at the Second Adjourned Session of the Thirty-fourth General Assembly, for the years, 1866–1867 (Nashville, 1866), 45–48.

72. William J. Simmons and Henry McNeal Turner, *Men of Mark: Eminent, Progressive and Rising* (Cleveland, 1887), 144–148; "A Colored Lawyer's Mission: Samuel R. Lowery to Practice in the United States Supreme Court—His Plan for Educating His People," *New York Times*, 3 February 1880; Jill Norgren, *Belva Lockwood: The Woman Who Would Be President* (New York, 2007), 107–108.

73. See Franklin and Schweninger, *In Search of the Promised Land*; James Thomas, ed., Loren Schweninger, *From Tennessee Slave to St. Louis Entrepreneur: The Autobiography of James Thomas* (Columbia, Mo., 1984).

# FISK UNIVERSITY:

## The First Critical Years

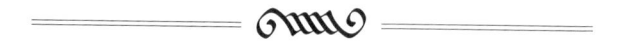

### Joe M. Richardson

The history of black Americans since their emancipation in the United States has been a dramatic struggle against social and economic adversity. Suddenly almost 4,000,000 ex-slaves were removed from a condition of total dependence, and "thrown upon their own resources to fight the battle for existence." They were forced to adjust themselves to a radically changed position, and make a place for themselves in a "kaleidoscopic civilization" that was growing more complicated with the passing of each year.[1] Life as a slave had provided little or no exposure to formal learning, and the newly liberated freedmen's responsibility for their own well-being and livelihood necessitated education. Fortunately, a majority were eager for knowledge. One historian has said that "the zeal with which the ex-slaves sought the benefits of literary education is unparalleled in history."[2]

A few Northerners, especially abolitionists, showed an interest in educating freedmen from the beginning of the Civil War. Sympathetic Union soldiers and chaplains taught slaves who congregated at their camps and their work was soon supplemented by representatives of various Northern aid societies. By 1865 approximately 75,000 black pupils were being trained by zealous teachers in areas occupied by Union armies. The crusade for emancipation was transformed into enthusiasm for education.[3] Among the scores who went South to assist the freedmen were three men, John Ogden, Erastus M. Cravath, and Edward P. Smith, who became prime movers in founding one of the outstanding black universities in the United States.

Ogden became concerned about the former slaves while serving as a lieutenant in the Second Wisconsin Cavalry. Because of his interest in the freedmen and his previous experience as principal of the Minnesota State Normal School he was appointed superintendent of education for the Freedmen's Bureau in Tennessee. In 1865 he took office with headquarters in Nashville.[4]

Cravath also had the proper background for his important work in education. Born to an abolitionist family in Homer, New York, he was sent to New York Central College, founded by abolitionists. He came in contact with slaves and slavery at his father's house, which was an underground railroad station for escaping fugitives. In 1851 the Cravath family moved to Oberlin, Ohio, where young Cravath entered Oberlin College, a hotbed of anti-slavery agitation. In December, 1863, he resigned as pastor of the Berlin Heights, Ohio, Congregational Church to become chaplain of the 101st Regiment of Ohio Volunteers. Impressed with the needs of the former bondsmen during the war, he decided to devote his life to educational work in the South. When he was mustered out in Nashville in June, 1865, Cravath accepted the position of field secretary of the American Missionary Association, one of the most important benevolent societies engaged in teaching Negroes.[5]

In 1865 the Reverend E. P. Smith assumed the work of district secretary of the newly created Middle West Department of the American Missionary Association at Cincinnati. He and Cravath were directed by the association to establish a school for freedmen in Nashville. After a brief survey of the area they decided the city was a focal point warranting more than the mere anticipated elementary school. Nashville in 1860 was a town with a population of 16,988 of which only 3,945 were blacks, but Cravath and Smith were convinced that its central location would enable a school to serve both the border states and the deep South.

From the beginning the three men encountered difficulty. Suitable plots of land for sale suddenly became unavailable when owners discovered the land would be utilized to educate freedmen. Land that could be bought was in the wrong location or too expensive. Previous enthusiasm was turning into discouragement when Smith and Cravath discovered that the Union hospital west of the Chattanooga Depot was to be given up by the government. The hospital complex was located on a block of land about 310 feet by 320 feet and held almost twenty buildings in the midst of the heaviest concentration of Negroes in the city. It seemed perfect for their needs. However, optimism was soon slightly dampened. Officers of the AMA favored the plan to establish a school of higher instruction for freedmen but there were no funds for acquiring the privately owned land on which the hospital buildings were located. The purchase price was $16,000, with one-fourth down and the remainder to be paid in three annual installments. Ogden, Cravath, and Smith, refusing to be thwarted by lack of funds, pledged personal notes to raise $4,000 and a black university was born. The American Missionary Association and the Western Freedmen's Aid Commission paid the second and fourth install-ments and eventually reimbursed the original buyers.[6] The third payment of $4,000 was made by the Freedmen's Bureau.[7]

The land had been purchased but the hospital buildings still belonged to the government. With the active assistance of General Clinton B. Fisk, Assistant Commissioner of the Freedmen's Bureau for Tennessee and Kentucky, the buildings were acquired for the school. The hospital was quickly transformed into school facilities. Officers' quarters were turned into homes for an earnest band of teachers, the sick wards became schoolrooms, and the death house was converted into a storeroom for needy and hungry pupils. Because of Fisk's assistance in securing the buildings and his continued interest—he eventually gave Fisk approximately $30,000—the school was named for the general.

The aims of the Fisk School, sometimes known as Fisk "Free Colored School," were commendable and lofty—some thought impractical. The founders proposed to provide a free school of grades from primary to normal based upon a "broad Christian foundation." Fisk was also intended to supply the desperate need for properly qualified black teachers. But the founders had no intention of stopping with a normal school. They hoped that Fisk would ultimately become a first-class college that would give black youth the same opportunities and advantages of education enjoyed by whites. The aim in founding Fisk and similar schools, a famous Fisk alumnus, W. E. B. DuBois, said, was to maintain the standards of lower school training by giving leaders and teachers the best possible instruction, and more important, to furnish them with "adequate standards of human culture and lofty ideals of life." It was not sufficient, DuBois stated, to train black teachers in technical normal methods; they must also, so far as possible, be broadminded, cultured men and women, who would scatter civilization among a people whose ignorance was not simply of the alphabet, but of life itself.[8]

Fisk School was opened January 9, 1866, with appropriate ceremonies. Distinguished visitors, including Governor W. G. Brownlow and General Fisk, spoke to a large crowd of teachers and pupils from local schools. Brownlow advised freedmen to be "mild and temperate" in habits, spirit, and conduct toward white people. As a friend of the institution and desiring its prosperity he counseled teachers to be "exceedingly prudent and cautious" to avoid giving offense to the white majority. Without federal troops, Brownlow stated, black pupils would not be permitted to occupy the school room "a week, not a week."[9]

The founders of Fisk were seemingly unconcerned about white hostility. They could see no reason for apprehension of any serious disturbances in judiciously managed Negro schools, but events soon proved them wrong. Many whites simply opposed black education. In central Tennessee a man was tied to a stake and whipped with forty lashes for teaching eight boys to read. Two school houses were burned in Gallatin in 1865. When a school was opened in Springfield, "fellows of the baser sort" broke up the benches, knocked down the door, and gave the instructor "such broad hints of visiting him with their wrath, that he shook off the dust of his feet against them and left." In 1868 a Fisk student who went to Woodbury to organize a school left after local blacks warned him he would be "Kukluxed" if he remained. Two Fisk students teaching for the summer were whipped and driven from their schools in 1869. During the Memphis race riot in May, 1866, twelve school houses were burned. One hundred Klansmen rode down Church Street in Nashville on March 5, 1868, to terrify Negroes and Republicans.[10] It was under these conditions that Fisk School opened. The immediate postwar years were bitter and fearful ones for the ex-slaves—a time of intimidation, bigotry, lynchings, and murders, but both the teachers and students were optimistic. It was also a time full of hope.

When Fisk opened, students came by the hundreds. Almost 200 were enrolled immediately and by February there were 500 scholars in day school and 100 in a night class. On May 1 there was an enrollment of 900 pupils and the number increased to an average daily attendance of 1,000 for 1866. In the words of Booker T. Washington, "those were wonderful days, directly after the war! Suddenly, as if at the sound of a trumpet, a whole race that had been slumbering for centuries... awoke and started off one morning to school."[11]

Not all the pupils were children. One teacher had a class ranging in age from seven to seventy, reading on the same page. Parents and children, husbands and wives, were all trying to learn. One student over seventy was just learning his letters. His ambition was to read the Bible for himself. Although his eyes were dim he made commendable progress because his zeal was great. A drayman while out of class, the old gentleman carried his books with him to study during odd moments of leisure time. A former slave of over fifty, Lizzie Wilson, had made such progress in reading as to surprise one unaccustomed to the intense desire of "these poor people," a teacher reported. The adults usually attended night school after working all day.[12]

Naturally most of the 1,000 students were in primary work, learning the alphabet or struggling to master the most elementary words in the First Reader, but even in the first month at least 106 of the 190 could read. Forty were doing mental arithmetic, nine written arithmetic, twenty-eight were studying geography, and fifty were writing. Progress was rapid. The monthly school report for April listed only 100 still working with the alphabet. More than 600 were spelling, 655 were reading, 198 were writing, 226 were in arithmetic class, 104 were studying geography, and twenty were doing battle with English grammar.[13]

The astonishing improvement of Fisk pupils can be understood only if their extraordinary thirst for knowledge is recognized. Many observers falsely thought the intense desire to learn would decrease after a short time, but teachers reported that the sometimes frantic pursuit of learning continued unabated. Dedicated instructors were another reason why Fisk students surged ahead in education. Most of the teachers were on a crusade, sacrificing a more pleasant life, sometimes better paying jobs, and frequently health to work with the ex-slaves. It was the missionary impulse that sent them forth. Inspired with enthusiasm and high purpose, they performed an incalculable service to the South and the Negro. Having faith in the possibilities of the freedmen, they believed opportunities for the highest human development should be open to them. Their dedication and belief in the future of the Negro spurred their pupils on.[14]

The early teachers at Fisk were sent by the American Missionary Association. The AMA was not organized primarily for freedmen's aid, but was in a position to answer the needs of destitute blacks on the outbreak of the Civil War.[15] Organized September 3, 1846, as a protest against the relative silence of other missionary societies concerning slavery, the association had carried on a nondenominational work attempting to convince Southerners of the evils of slavery. When the first slaves escaped to Union lines, the AMA led the way in systematic relief and education. It sent missionaries to Fortress Monroe, Virginia, as early as September, 1861, and the number increased until by 1866 it employed over 350 persons in school and church work among freedmen. The AMA was the first and most notable of the great missionary societies for the training of former slaves. It established, in addition to Fisk, Hampton Institute, Berea College, Atlanta University, Talladega College, Tougaloo University, and Straight University. The history of the association is one of the patient and persevering efforts of hundreds of persons who gave themselves and their means to aid a people struggling upward from slavery.

The man selected to supervise the AMA's missionary teachers at Fisk was John Ogden, who resigned as superintendent of education of the Freedmen's Bureau to accept the position of principal. Ogden was primarily interested in training teachers who could go out and instruct thousands of others. Most of the other early teachers, remaining at Fisk only a short time, left no lasting impression, but did commendable work while there. In April, 1866, there were ten instructors assisting Principal Ogden.

Nearly all the instructors had duties besides teaching. To provide a free school for the recently emancipated was not enough. Numerous people still needed food and clothing. Teachers visited throughout the city trying to determine those most in need of relief. Food packages and especially clothing were distributed. Mrs. Charles Crosby dispensed eighty-four packages of clothing to the destitute in one day in May. Multitudes came to the doors of the teacher-missionaries for help. In one April, 1866, shipment, Ogden received clothing valued at $3,000 from various aid societies. On another occasion twenty boxes and three barrels of clothing arrived from England but the gifts were never sufficient. The clothing was sold to those who had some money, and given to the impoverished.[16] Some books were sent to Fisk by charitable associations but not enough. Fisk students reputedly gathered and sold as scrap metal rusty handcuffs from the city's former slave mart to purchase books.

Religious work was even more important to the faculty than relief. In the words of Cravath, "It is better that some suffer for food and clothing than that so many suffer for light and truth." The missionaries who went South to teach were imbued with the puritan tradition. They were men and women of religion first and teachers second. They maintained strict rules for the student and endeavored to prevent any immoral or even frivolous conduct. To many of the teachers, there was no division between religion and education. One of the primary objects of the school, according to Principal Ogden, was to illustrate that conversion was the proper door into both the kingdom of science and the kingdom of heaven. Science and religion were made to go hand in hand, he said, and the two joined were the heaven-appointed means of "uplifting humanity to its proper standing and dignity."[17]

The AMA not only approved Fisk's missionary activities but at its 1867 annual meeting resolved that education should be thoroughly religious and none but evangelical teachers should be sent South. For many years Fisk remained religiously oriented. Faculty meetings were always opened with a prayer. Services were held daily. In 1869 the faculty voted to hold short prayer meetings after the usual prayers at night.[18] The religious work was non-sectarian.

Fisk's benevolent activities and religious emphasis did not allay white suspicion. Schools in Tennessee and throughout the South continued to be destroyed and white teachers ostracized and abused. Fisk experienced less difficulty than many schools. Though the faculty was not accepted by local white society there was seldom physical mistreatment. The same could not be said for students. Children were often abused on the way to school. Miss E. A. Easter sometimes acted as guard to protect her students from stoning. One teacher applied to the city for a guard to defend pupils to and from home. In March, 1866, Ogden requested the Freedmen's Bureau to restrain the mobs of boys, black and white, who collected near the school throwing rocks and other missiles at each other to the danger of peaceful citizens. Fisk pupils, complained Ogden, were almost daily assailed on their way to and from campus, and were cut and bruised to an alarming degree.[19] General Fisk gave orders to arrest and punish such offenders independent of color. These outbreaks were symptomatic of conditions in most of the South and Tennessee. Governor Brownlow seemed to think little could be done. If Christ came to Davidson County, Tennessee, Brownlow stated, with shoulder straps and stars on his shoulders, with a military staff of apostles, he could not give satisfaction to rebels of the area.[20] Fisk students would continue to be subjected to discrimination and sometimes abuse by white people.

Despite difficulties, 1866 proved to be a good year for Fisk. Though there was considerable hostility some whites had grudgingly accepted the idea of black education and were beginning to recognize the freedmen's ability. Moreover, the first demand of Fisk School was to provide its pupils with enough learning to enable them to teach. Several students acquired sufficient knowledge to instruct pupils throughout the state in the summer of 1866. When classes ended on June 15, Cravath was convinced the school had been successful and had made a favorable impression not only in Nashville but throughout the state.[21]

During 1866 only the most elementary subjects were taught, but the dream of a normal school and college was not lost. Since its inception Ogden had argued that Fisk should be in the "business of making teachers," leaving elementary education to others. Then in the spring of 1867 a Tennessee school law provided for free, segregated, common schools. Although this separation of races was vigorously attacked by Ogden as an attempt to "pander to wicked prejudices," it made the training of black teachers even more imperative.[22] When in the fall of 1867 Nashville opened free public schools for all races, relieving Fisk of many of its elementary pupils, it advanced the goal of normal and higher education.

In keeping with Ogden's desire for a Negro college in Nashville, Fisk was incorporated August 22, 1867, as Fisk University. Ogden, Joseph H. Barnum, W. W. Mallory, John Lawrence, and John Ruhm were the incorporators.[23] The purpose of the corporation as stated in the charter was the education and training of young men and women of all races. Trustees were authorized to confer all such degrees and honors as were granted by universities in the United States. This was a masterly statement of human expectation and optimism, since Fisk did not yet have students even of normal grade. A board of trustees of not less than three or more than nine members was to be organized. The school would remain under AMA control.

College work could not be immediately offered but a normal department was organized at the beginning of the 1867 school term. The first class of twelve was accepted in November, 1867, and a second one was enrolled in January, 1868. A month later Ogden, a normal school expert, claimed that the original class was doing as well or better than any class he had ever seen. The second group was doing nearly as well. Dr. Barnas Sears, general agent for the Peabody Fund, and former president of Brown University, was sufficiently impressed after visiting Fisk to appropriate $800 in scholarships for sixteen of the most promising students.[24] Two years later Sears declared that Fisk was the best normal school he had seen in the South.

The course of study in the normal class did not, as white opponents charged, consist entirely of Latin and Greek. Reading, arithmetic, geography, and penmanship were studied the first two terms of the beginning year. The third term students worked with reading and sentence analysis, arithmetic, English grammar and composition, and elementary algebra. The second year included the previous subjects plus botany and natural history. Geometry, history of the United States, teaching theory, natural philosophy, chemistry, physiology, and natural science were taught in the final year. In addition to "the most rigid and searching class drills" in the above subjects, there was a daily study of the science of education and the art of teaching. Furthermore, normal students, to acquire skill in teaching and managing schools of various grades, taught one-half hour each day in the model school under the principal's direction. The model school, organized for this specific purpose, contained about sixty pupils studying reading, arithmetic, and geography.

In 1869 the Tennessee superintendent of public instruction, John Eaton, Jr., was inspired by a Fisk visit. "The proficiency of those examined was gratifying," Eaton stated, and indicated the wisdom of efforts made to prepare competent teachers. John M. Langston, the general inspector for Freedmen's Bureau schools, was no less pleased after spring examinations. Classes in the model school were examined by students in the normal department. These teacher-pupils exhibited good teaching talent, Langston thought, and the scholars showed "much capacity" and gave evidence of having been "well drilled... with great advantage." Examinations in the high and normal school were conducted by teachers of the university and were "in every way highly satisfactory and creditable to the scholars as well as their instructors." Langston was especially impressed with the "remarkable degree of proficiency" exhibited in algebra, bookkeeping, arithmetic, English grammar, and Latin.[25]

By 1869 twelve students had gone out from the normal school to teach and were doing splendidly. These teachers, the AMA thought, were more effective than white instructors from the North. They had "the readiest access to their own race," and could "do a work for them" no other teachers could accomplish.[26] Of course the normal school students were only a small portion of those from Fisk who taught. Numerous students operated schools in the spring and summer. The number of pupils taught by Fiskites in the first few summers after the university's opening has been estimated at 10,000. Some estimates indicate 10,000 in one year. Fisk teachers could be found in almost every Southern state.

The establishment of the normal department was accompanied by a reorganization of the entire school. In 1869 Fisk consisted of a normal and high school, model school, theology department, a very practical commercial department, and the college. In addition, special courses in vocal and instrumental music were offered. The normal and high school had about 120 pupils, three-fourths of whom were preparing to teach. The model school included three grades and served as a training laboratory for older pupils. Although it was never large, the theology department was organized to accommodate those who expected to enter the ministry of any evangelical denomination.

The college department, including a three-year preparatory course, was fully organized in 1869, but there were no students until four were accepted in 1871. The number increased to eight in 1872 and nine in 1873. For years the college was the smallest department at Fisk. The number of students was small, but their program of studies was rigid. A skeptical visitor who witnessed an examination of the college students in 1875 concluded that blacks were capable of mastering the most difficult studies in the best colleges. The freshmen were tested on Virgil's *Aeneid*, geometry, and botany. Sophomores stood an examination on Latin, Greek, and botany.[27]

The curriculum in the college and college preparatory classes was similar to that in a majority of the contemporary liberal arts schools. The freshmen studied Latin, Greek, and mathematics. Greek, Latin, French, mathematics, and natural science were taught to the sophomores. The juniors labored over the same courses with additional work in German, natural philosophy, history, English, and astronomy. Mental and moral science and political science were added for the seniors. The college prep pupils studied Latin, Greek, English, arithmetic, world history, and algebra. All students received a lesson in the Bible once a week.[28]

Most of the Fisk college students received their earlier training at Fisk since there were few schools for blacks above the most elementary level. Some localities in Tennessee were reluctant to pay school taxes. By 1872 only twenty-nine counties had levied a special tax for schools. One Fisk student attended school in a log cabin so well ventilated, he said, one could throw a cat between the logs and never touch a hair. It was admirably suited for the study of astronomy, he thought, for one could see "the glory of God reflected in the heavens" through the roof, but the instructors and facilities were inadequate to prepare students for further training. Such schools generally operated only about three months out of twelve. For this reason Fisk continued to maintain lower departments. In 1872 there were ninety-four pupils in primary grades, eighty-seven in intermediate, thirty-five in the normal school, thirty-three in the college preparatory course, and only eight in college.[29]

The reorganization of the school mentioned above included the establishment of a boarding department or the "home." Since most of the pupils were in primary grades and quite young and many students were from outside the city some kind of boarding arrangement was needed. In early 1867 a building was set aside to accommodate thirty young women. Two lady teachers lived with the girls and helped them with their studies after school hours. Dining and living in common with the teachers seemed to have such a good influence on the pupils the idea of a "home" began to be considered. A majority of instructors favored a common dining hall where the influence of the faculty could be brought to bear on pupils.[30]

Teachers and students boarding on campus were organized into a family or home. A system of detailed labor was arranged, each pupil having certain duties in the home each day. This work was intended to help pay expenses and also to train students in matters of housekeeping and economy. Students were charged $2.75 per week for living in the home. This sum paid for room rent and all other necessities, which seemed to be cheap. Still a majority of students were unable to pay; consequently the strictest economy had to be observed. Students believed that money was saved on food. In later years an alumnus said the thing that most impressed him upon going to Fisk was the "scarcity of the supper."[31]

A major reason for organizing the home was to improve morals and manners as well as the mind; therefore rigid regulations were uncompromisingly enforced. Most students had neither the time nor inclination to violate many of the regulations. A number of them were in their late teens or older and to them education was a serious business. It was a fortunate student who was enabled to attend Fisk and most of them attempted to take advantage of the opportunity. The privations that students would inflict upon themselves in order to remain in school were incredible to observers. Board and room were less than three dollars a week and tuition for primary students was only one dollar per month. Tuition in the high and normal school and college was only twelve dollars a year but even that was high when the average wage for a farm laborer was from eight to fifteen dollars a month. Some of the city pupils in the winter of 1868 were forced to miss school because it was too cold to walk barefooted. Staying in school was a desperate struggle. Numerous Fisk students taught through the year to pay their expenses, but frequently at the end of the session they discovered they could not collect their wages for months, if at all. In 1873 almost one-half of the student body, 110 of 256, taught from five to six months. Pitiful letters were written by parents begging officials to wait while they struggled to scrape up enough money for their children's board and tuition. Sterling Brown's struggle is but one example of their difficulty in staying in school. Brown was born a slave at Post Oak Springs, Tennessee, in 1856. After emancipation he worked on a farm until 1867 when he entered Fisk, attending for a short time, then dropping out to earn enough money to return. Ten years after his first enrollment he was still a student. In the ten years he had managed to be in school about twenty-six months.[32]

The school gave financial aid to as many students as possible. Teachers raised money from their friends, home communities, and churches. The Freedmen's Bureau seldom provided aid for individuals but in 1868 it furnished transportation to the university for twenty normal school students. Black churches frequently sponsored a local student, sometimes several if possible. More important was the Peabody Fund, which assisted both black and white throughout the South. It provided $800 for normal students in 1868 and renewed the sum annually for several years. Peabody aid was granted to students in their last year of the normal course. Recipients obligated themselves to teach at least two years. No one was to be aided more than fifty dollars, or more than one year.[33]

Financial problems were not the only ones encountered by Fisk students. They were never able to forget for long that many Southerners considered them second-class citizens. Each wave of violence affected the school and the morale of pupils. Klan activity in the vicinity of Nashville in 1869 kept some students out of school. "School will probably begin small," a Fisk instructor wrote in late 1874. There was great excitement, he mentioned, over the question of civil rights that had resulted in much bloodshed.[34]

Despite numerous difficulties Fisk students continued to advance. Examinations in 1871 showed that standards of scholarship were rapidly improving. Even skeptical local whites were convinced. Fisk's reputation for well trained students resulted in its graduates usually securing good positions as teachers. Superintendents of education in several states were so impressed with Fiskites that they virtually monopolized several school systems. The demand was greater than Fisk was able to supply. A few white children even availed themselves of the opportunity to attend Fisk, at least one of whom taught with "marked distinction."[35]

While the number of students declined after 1867, the addition of a normal school and college department necessitated a faculty increase. By 1869 thirteen were associated with Fisk, all of them missionary-type teachers. Dedication was necessary to tolerate their living conditions. The furnishings and equipment were Spartan-like in their plainness. A teacher who arrived in 1869 was shocked to see her room. Furnishings consisted of a hospital cot, a wash-stand, table, a small wardrobe, and "a very small, very unmanageable stove." Of all the missionary beds she had slept in, another instructor said, the one in Nashville was the hardest. In addition to classroom work teachers had to do considerable housework. It was not until 1870 that the faculty voted to exempt ladies from splitting kindling and carrying coal to build fires in the public sitting room.[36]

Salaries were poor, and commonly in arrears. Poor health, caused in part by overwork and poor food, was a common complaint of the faculty. All of the staff ate at a common mess that was generally judged to be poor. Although the teachers undoubtedly exaggerated about the food, health was a constant problem. It was necessary to be physically as well as spiritually strong to teach at Fisk. When an AMA official recommended a teacher for Fisk who was good but "always weakly," the steward asked that she not be sent. "We have too many weak lungs and sour stomachs now for the good of the cause," he said. From 1866 through 1875 letter after letter told of someone who was ill with chills and fever, nervous exhaustion, or simply suffering from overwork." These hardy souls could seemingly tolerate almost anything except each other. The sacrifice, constant privations, overwork, and social ostracism, perhaps, made necessary some method of emotional release. The method seemed to be fighting with each other. Quarrelling was common, and in 1868–1869 it threatened to disrupt the school.

Much of the resentment was directed at Principal Ogden and his wife. Mrs. Ogden was matron of the boarding department without pay. She and Ogden considered her work satisfactory, but other teachers complained. The faculty squabble was ended when Ogden resigned in 1870 to accept a similar post at the Ohio State Normal School. While at Fisk Ogden did good work and most of the credit for the school's early success is due him. The confidence of the community was temporarily shaken by his departure. He was not particularly popular with local whites—no one who taught black students was—but they respected his ability and sincerity.

Ogden was replaced by Adam K. Spence who gave up a professorship of foreign languages at the University of Michigan to come to Fisk. Born in Aberdeenshire, Scotland, in 1831, and brought to the United States in 1833, Spence attended Olivet College, Oberlin, and the University of Michigan, receiving the B.A. degree from the latter in 1858. He was immediately made instructor in Greek at his alma mater and remained there until 1870. He was brought to Fisk to build the college department and is properly credited with the initiation of collegiate work. At first Spence was not convinced that Negroes were equal in ability to whites, but he believed they should be given a chance to prove themselves. He frequently told local citizens that if the Negro is inferior to whites, give him a superior training, and if he is superior give him inferior training, but if equal, give him the same. A strong advocate of civil rights, he sometimes sat in the galleries at Nashville theaters because the management refused to seat Fisk students elsewhere. He retained the position of principal until 1875 when

Erastus Milo Cravath became president of Fisk. Spence continued to serve as professor of Greek until 1900.[38]

Spence's appointment solved some of the personnel problems, but he could do nothing about Fisk's precarious financial condition. From the beginning the institution verged on bankruptcy. The AMA had many schools to support beside Fisk. Tuition was supposed to pay part of the expenses, but hard times and poor jobs available to Negroes made it difficult to collect. Conditions were so critical in 1869 that the faculty voted to dispense with dessert in the dinning room except once a week. Teachers preserved blackberries, huckleberries, apples, peaches, and vegetables through the summer to feed boarders during the year. There was some outside aid, but not nearly enough. The Peabody fund, as mentioned previously, applied to only sixteen students. Generous donations received from the Freedmen's Bureau were primarily for construction.

By 1871 circumstances were so critical it seemed the school would fold. The boarding department matron gloomily predicted the institution's downfall. Not even local debts for food and fuel could be paid. Total indebtedness was about $2,000, and creditors were pressing for payment. The good name of the institution was at stake. The decaying old barracks were virtually beyond repair, making obvious the need for new buildings and a larger campus.[39] It was at this juncture that one of the most dramatic stories in the history of education began—a trial tour by the Fisk Jubilee Singers to secure funds for the university.[40]

The singers left for the North in early 1871 and within a few months had earned $20,000 for the school. By 1874 they had raised nearly $50,000, thereby helping to guarantee the permanence of the young university. More important, perhaps, the Jubilee Singers' amazing success and popularity made Fisk the best-known black university in the country.

Like most private schools, Fisk continued to struggle annually to balance the budget. But its existence was never again seriously threatened. During the next several years Fisk experienced constant growth in the faculty, college department, facilities, physical plant, and its reputation as an outstanding school for black youth.

*This article first appeared in the Spring 1970 issue of the* Tennessee Historical Quarterly.

1. U.S. Department of Interior, Bureau of Education, *Survey of Negro Colleges and Universities,* Bulletin No. 7 (Washington, D.C., 1929), l.

2. Francis B. Simkins, "New Viewpoints of Southern Reconstruction," *Journal of Southern History,* V (1939), 59.

3. George R. Bentley, *A History of the Freedmen's Bureau* (Philadelphia, 1955), 70. For reaction of abolitionists to freedmen's education see: James M. McPherson, *The Struggle for Equality: Abolitionists and the Negro in the Civil War and Reconstruction* (Princeton, 1964) and Willie Lee Rose, *Rehearsal for Reconstruction: The Port Royal Experiment* (New York, 1964).

4. E. E. White to John Ogden, 30 April 1864, L. H. S. Dewey to Ogden, 16 June 1865, Fiskiana Collection, Fisk University Library, Nashville, Tennessee.

5. Allan Johnson and Dumas Malone, eds,, *Dictionary of American Biography* (20 vols., New York, 1930), IV, 516; Minutes of the Board of Trustees of Fisk University, 18 April 1940, in Fiskiana Collection; *Nashville Banner*, 5 September 1900; "Erastus Milo Cravath," pamphlet in Fisk University Library.

6. The Western Freedmen's Aid Commission had been organized on 18 January 1863, to work "for the physical relief and the mental and moral elevation" of the recently emancipated Negro. *Second Annual Report of the Western Freedmen's Aid Commission* (Cincinnati, 1865), 5.

7. E. P. Smith to M. E. Strieby, 11 October 1865, in American Missionary Association Archives; Ullin W. Leavell, *Philanthropy in Negro Education* (Nashville, 1930), 35–36; J. B. T. Marsh, *The Story of the Jubilee Singers with their Songs* (3rd ed., London, 1876), 10–11; Report of a sub-committee of the Board of Trustees of Fisk University, 27 December 1898, MS. in Fiskiana Collection.

8. W. E. B. DuBois, "Of the Training of Black Men," *Atlantic Monthly*, XC (1902), 292–93; Ullin, *Philanthropy in Negro Education*, 36; *American Missionary*, X (February, 1866), 41.

9. *American Missionary*, X (March, 1866), 59–60; *Nashville Daily Union and American*, 10 January 1866.

10. F. Ayers to G. Whipple, 28 October 1865, Ayers to M. E. Strieby, 2 October 1865, E. P. Smith to Strieby, 11 October 1865, in American Missionary Association Archives; *American Missionary*, X (March, 1866) 61, XXXI (October, 1869), 229; James W. Patton, *Unionism and Reconstruction in Tennessee* (Chapel Hill, 1934), 130.

11. Booker T. Washington, "A University Education for Negroes," *The Independent*, LXVIII (24 March 1910), 613.

12. Mrs. C. S. Crosby to M. E. Strieby, 1 May 1866, Miss E. A. Easter to Strieby, 12 February 1866, in American Missionary Association Archives.

13. E. M. Cravath to G. Whipple, 13 February 1865, C. A. Crosby to M. E. Strieby, 1 May 1866. Monthly School Reports, January, February, April, 1866, in American Missionary Association Archives.

14. F. Q. Blanchard, "A Quarter Century in the American Missionary Association,'" *Journal of Negro Education*, VI (April, 1937), 155; Washington, "University Education for Negroes," *The Independent*, LXVIII (24 March 1910), 614.

15. For background of the American Missionary Association see Clifton H. Johnson, "The American Missionary Association, 1846–1861: A Study of Christian Abolitionism," (PhD dissertation, University of North Carolina, 1959).

16. Mrs. C. S. Crosby to M. E. Strieby, 1 May 1866, T. Kennedy to J. Ogden, 17 January, 21 April 1866, in American Missionary Association Archives.

17. J. Ogden to G. Whipple, 29 February 1868, E. M. Cravath to M. E. Strieby, 12 February 1866, in American Missionary Association Archives; *Nashville Tennessean*, 20 August 1930; Marsh, *Jubilee Singers*, 13.

18. Minutes of the General Faculty of Fisk University, 8 November 1869, MS. in Fisk University Library; *Twenty-First Annual Report of the American Missionary Association and the Proceedings at the Annual Meeting... October 17 and 18, 1867* (New York, 1867), 4.

19. Miss E. A. Easter to .M. E. Strieby, 12 February 1866, in American Missionary Association Archives; J. Ogden to C. B. Fisk, 8 March 1866, in Fiskiana Collection.

20. *Nashville Daily Union and American*, 3 and 10 January 1866.

21. E. M. Cravath to G. Whipple, 19 June 1866, in American Missionary Association Archives; *Nashville Tennessean*, 20 August 1930.

22. In attacking the school law, Ogden claimed that legislating for prejudice would make it respectable and provide for its continuation. If it hurt "somebody," Ogden suggested, "let somebody get out of the way." *Nashville Daily Press and Times*, 15 November 1867; Patton, *Unionism and Reconstruction in Tennessee*, 161–62.

23. Original articles of incorporation are in Register's Office, Davidson County, Tennessee, Book 38, page 339.

24. J. Ogden to G. Whipple, 29 February 1868, in American Missionary Association Archives.

25. Report of John M. Langston, General Inspector of Schools, Bureau of Freedmen and Abandoned Lands, n.d., 1869, MS. in American Missionary Association Archives.

26. J. Ogden to E. P. Smith, 15 February 1869, in American Missionary Association Archives; *Twenty-Fourth Annual Report of the American Missumary Association and the Proceedings at the Annual Meeting... November 9 and 10, 1870* (New York, 1870), 4.

27. Edward King, *The Southern States of North America* (London, 875), 604–605: A. K. Spence to E. Spence, 28 March 1891, in Mary E. Spence Collection, Fisk University Library; Report of Fisk University, November, 1872, MS. in American Missionary Association Archives.

28. *Fisk University Catalog, 1868–1870*, 20–21, 1871–1872, 18–20.

29. Henry Hugh Proctor, *Between Black and White: Autobiographical Sketches* (Boston, 1925), 7; Report of Fisk University, November, 1872, MS. in American Missionary Association Archives.

30. C. Crosby to E. P. Smith, 12 January 1867, E. M. Cravath to G. L. White, 6 January 1868, in American Missionary Association Archives; *Twenty-second Annual Report of the American Missionary Association and the proceedings at the annual meeting... 1868* (New York, 1868), 55.

31. *Fisk Herald*, I (June, 1884 ), 3; L. A. Roberts to G. L. White, 5 October 1870, in Fiskiana Collection.

32. Mrs. C. A. Crosby to E. P. Smith, 31 January 1868, M. T. Weir to E. M. Cravath, 27 April 1874, in American Missionary Association Archives; S. L. Grant to G. L. White, 8 December 1870, Mrs. E. Cole to J. Ogden, 16 November 1868, J. Coffey to G. L. White, 7 March 1871, J. Tillman to White, 13 April 1871, in Fiskiana Collection; S. Brown to Mrs. A. K. Spence, 25 February 1877, in Mary E. Spence Collection.

33. W. H. Bower to J. Ogden, 15 September 1868, E. M. Cravath to Ogden, 20 February 1868, E. O. Tade to G. L. White, 3 January 1871, in Fiskiana Collection; B. Sears to A. K. Spence, 26 December 1870, 4 March 1871, in Mary E. Spence Collection.

34. E. H. Freeman to M. E. Strieby, 3 August 1868, H. S. Bennett to M. E. Strieby, 30 August 1869, A. K. Spence to Miss D. E. Emerson, 5 September 1874, in American Missionary Association Archives.

35. J. Ogden to G. Whipple, 29 February 1868, Miss H. C. Morgan to E. M. Cravath, 28 March 1871, in American Missionary Association Archives; U. S. Commissioner of Education, *Report for the Year 1872* (Washington, D.C., 1873), 324.

36. Miss Nellie M. Horton to G. D. Pike, 23 October 1870, in American Missionary Association Archives; Fisk University News, II (October, 1911), 14–15.

37. Miss L. M. Stratton to E. M. Cravath, 29 October 1870, J. E. Benedict to Respected Sirs, 17 March 1871, G. L. White to E. M. Cravath, 21 August 1871, Miss A. E. Alden to E. M. Cravath, 7 December 1874 in American Missionary Association Archives.

38. Proctor, Between Black and White, 32–33; Fisk Herald, XVII (May, 1900 ), 3–.5; Greater Fisk Herald, II (June, 1927), 24–26; Fisk University News, XIV (January, 1924), 4.

39. Minutes of the General Faculty of Fisk University; P. Pearle to G. L. White, 24 August 1871, in Fiskiana Collection; M. E. Strieby to G. Whipple, 17 April 1869, A. K. Spence to E. M. Cravath, 24 November, 13 December 1871, in American Missionary Association Archives.

40. Probably the AMA would not have allowed Fisk to close but many of the teachers thought it would. The AMA was overextended. The end of the Freedmen's Bureau resulted in a loss of approximately $30,000 per year to the association. Then the Chicago fire of 1871 almost dried up Northwestern charity. The association began the 1870s with a retrenchment policy—a policy which included closing some of the schools. Since Fisk was one of the associations outstanding institutions it would, of course, have been last to close.

# E.O. TADE, FREEDMEN'S EDUCATION, AND THE FAILURE OF RECONSTRUCTION IN TENNESSEE

## C. Stuart McGehee

I feel that my ten years in the South has not been in vain," wrote the Rev. Ewing O. Tade in 1875 as he prepared to leave Tennessee for the West. Despite years of frustration and labor, Tade had helped to facilitate the difficult transition from slavery to freedom for many freedmen in Tennessee, established the first public school in Chattanooga, and helped to usher into existence the black community in the rapidly evolving East Tennessee industrial city. Missionary, teacher, minister, banker, real estate agent, and pioneer Tennessee educational administrator, Tade perfectly symbolizes the fervent zeal with which many Northern evangelicals approached the post-Civil War South, a zeal often criticized by historians for its supposed lack of awareness of the economic realities of Reconstruction. Although the disorganization and factional infighting of the Tennessee Republican party and the intransigence of Southern whites eventually combined to foil Tade's radical vision of the freedmen's place in postbellum Tennessee, the failure of his dream cannot be blamed upon insensitivity to the economic necessities of the ex-slaves. In Tade's bitter experiences in Chattanooga, however, may be clearly seen the rocks upon which radical Reconstruction in Tennessee foundered and ultimately collapsed, leaving only the vestiges of his farsighted plans and arduous labor.[1]

Chattanooga, Tennessee, was a fertile field for missionary endeavors in the immediate aftermath of civil war. Fought over and occupied by both Union and Confederate armies, the city had been converted by the Federal Quartermaster Corps into a strategic supply base for Sherman's victorious march through Georgia. Emancipated by Northern troops, thousands of blacks flocked to Southern cities like Chattanooga, hoping to find employment, news of estranged relatives, or respite from recalcitrant Southerners not yet reconciled to the approach of a new order. By early 1865, "Contraband," a freedman's camp, sprang to life across the Tennessee River from the small commercial city. "Contraband" was inhabited by several thousand refugee freedpeople, United States Colored Troops soldiers and their families, and a scattering of pre-war free blacks who helped to organize a rudimentary governmental structure amidst the chaos of the post-war South. Wracked by disease and poverty and kept under tight control by the Federal Quartermaster Corps that then ruled Chattanooga, "Contraband" nonetheless constituted the beginning of a community for the blacks as they sought to find their place in the rapidly evolving post-war social and economic structure.[2]

Early in 1865, Union artillery lieutenant Lyman W. Ayer wrote to the Rev. E. M. Strieby at the New York headquarters of the American Missionary Association, urging immediate assistance for the citizens of "Contraband." The AMA, the largest of the many Northern evangelical organizations founded to promote abolition and solve what was referred to as the "Negro Question," sent teachers and missionaries throughout the South on the heels of the Federal armies, seeking to minister to the newly emancipated slaves. Lt. Ayer was appalled by what he had seen at the camp, which he described as "damp, unhealthy, without good water and filthy in the extreme." The several thousand freedpeople at Chattanooga, he wrote, wanted only a "fair show," for, as he saw the situation, "it may well be doubted that their condition is much improved by obtaining their freedom." The mortality rate, wrote Lt. Ayer, was dangerously high, and moreover, there was no work for the able-bodied men. "They certainly need someone to look after their interests who has will, energy, and ability to do something for them," concluded the officer.[3]

Ewing Ogden Tade, perfectly suited to the formidable task of helping to establish a new society, possessed these qualities and more. Born in Illinois in the summer of 1828, Tade became interested in the work of the AMA while a student at Grinnell College in Davenport, Iowa, where he received his bachelor's degree in 1858. Ordained a Congregationalist minister in 1862 at Loda, Illinois, after study at Chicago Theological Seminary, Tade preached that "slavery is a sin," as well as that intemperance and "the abominable use of tobacco" were not proper Christian behavior. Tade's evangelical zeal soon led him to the AMA, to which he had earlier contributed money from his sparse salary as a preacher, believing the missionary organization to be "the pioneers in this work of benevolence."[4]

By 1865 Tade was in Memphis preaching to the emancipated slaves at Lincoln Chapel while his Pennsylvania-born wife, Amanda Loise, and his brother James A. Tade, taught in a freedmen's school. Tade was greatly inspired by what he called "this great and glorious work" and apparently he was quite successful in the river city on the Mississippi. F.E. Ensign, local AMA field agent in Memphis, wrote his superiors that "among all the Christian workers... I think none better adapted to the work of mission with freedmen than Rev. Tade." Indeed, Tade loved preaching to the "poor, degraded, and despised," as he termed the refugees, and contributed his wages to the efforts of Memphis freedmen to buy land upon which to build a church. "I think I am slowly gaining ground," he wrote, shortly before leaving Memphis for Chattanooga, where he had been promoted to field agent. "The horizon begins to brighten and the clouds to break."[5]

Tade arrived in Chattanooga shortly before Christmas of 1866 and immediately employed his considerable energies in the service of the freedmen at Contraband. Organizing rudimentary schools and quickly establishing a crude place of worship, Tade began to familiarize himself with the problems of the local freedmen. Although, as he reported to his superior, E.P. Smith, in New York, "there is no work or next to none for them," he was optimistic as always. The blacks, wrote Tade, were "energetic, and are beginning to learn about economy measures, so I know they will prosper." Tade urged the home office of the AMA to send more food, books, and clothing, while he formulated his plans. Believing that the freedman's best hopes for the future lay in a concerted policy, he hoped to build relig- ious, economic, and educational instructions, a tripartite strategy which he would follow for nearly ten years.[6]

The problems Tade encountered upon his arrival were foreboding of difficult times to come. The disparate social and economic classes in the city had little use for Northern missionaries who preached to the freedmen. The local Unionists and ex-Federal Quartermaster Corps officers who had settled in Chattanooga after Appomattox were not kindly disposed toward the blacks, many of whom themselves "fear[ed] some Yankee trick." The local Freedmen's Bureau officials and Union officers who had upheld martial law in the city urged blacks to sign binding labor contracts, passed laws restricting them to the northern bank of the Tennessee River, prohibited firearm possession, and banned alcoholic consumption. "This place seems to be gowing downhill," wrote Tade several months after his arrival in Chattanooga.[7]

Yet as events would prove, adversity only motivated Tade. His principal mandate was to establish schools for the ex-slaves, and indeed his lasting contribution to the foundations of the black community in Chattanooga was the organization of Howard

School, named for Oliver Otis Howard, Union general and national commissioner of the Freedmen's Bureau, the federal institution empowered to assist the blacks in the immediate post-war period. Howard, ironically located at the corner of 6th and Pine in Bragg Hospital, a former Confederate medical facility, was staffed by northern teachers supplied by the AMA and the Western Freedmen's Aid Commission. The building, a wooden structure roughly fifty feet square, was maintained by the local Freedmen's Bureau office, and hopeful blacks flocked to the new whitewashed school. Tade sought textbooks from sympathetic Northern publishers and fire protection from the local municipal authorities.[8]

Tade's efforts paid off quickly, for in May of 1867 he was named city school commissioner by the reconstituted Unionist local government. In September, less than a year after Tade's arrival in the city, Chattanooga's Board of Aldermen selected Howard as the official city school for freedmen, which made the black school the city's first public educational institution. Tade was elated over the unexpected financial assistance and immediately wrote his AMA superiors to send more teachers. Several months later a deal was struck between the city, county, and state boards of education to segregate the schools and entrust separately to Tade the state funds voted for black education. Gradually Tade phased in more and more black teachers, proof of the success of his policies, and Howard prospered under his tutelage. Between 1869 and 1870 the property, ominously deeded from abandoned lands acquired by the Freedmen's Bureau, doubled in value from three to six thousand dollars, while the staff grew to fifteen teachers. The northern missionary was gratified by the progress he saw around him and was optimistic about the future, planning to construct a larger building of brick. He found the blacks in Chattanooga to be thrifty, industrious, and religious, qualities he obviously approved of greatly. "To them," he wrote, "this nation is a very great debtor, and God cannot smile upon, nor bless us, till we show a willing spirit to refund the millions extorted by oppression and cruelty."[9]

Yet despite the success of Tade and other missionaries, the influence of Northern leadership should not be exaggerated, for the principal impetus behind the origins of public education in Chattanooga came from the freedmen themselves. A bureau official had written several years before that "schools exert a great influence in keeping them here. They wish to educate their children, and think it impossible to accomplish this object if they go to the country." A Northern traveler saw the same fervent desire for knowledge in the ex-slaves. "The colored people," he wrote, "are far more zealous in the cause of education than the whites. They will starve themselves and go without clothes, in order to send their children to school." Indeed, Tade and other

Northern white teachers had merely helped to facilitate the emancipated blacks' desires for training and literacy.[10]

Tade's plans for the future of Chattanooga's black community included spiritual sustenance as well as education, and early in 1867 he petitioned for land upon which to build a church. Organized in June, at Ninth and Lindsay, Pilgrim Church, or "Union Chapel," as Tade originally termed his church, began with a mere fifteen parishioners. Although Tade originally had intended his integrated church to be nondenominational, by 1868 the institution was more correctly known as the First Congregationalist Church of Chattanooga; it catered more to white Northerners than to local blacks, who often preferred their own houses of worship on the outskirts of the city. True to his evangelical ideals, Tade also founded a temperance committee, and sought to curb the use of tobacco among the freedpeople. Although he noted that the blacks favored their own more emotional preachers, nonetheless Pilgrim Church grew and prospered. The religious institutions that blacks and sympathetic whites like Tade founded would prove the most durable social structures of Chattanooga's black community in the dark years to come.[11]

Although Tade's principal efforts to assist the freedmen involved religion and education, nonetheless he understood that without economic and financial support his work would be in vain. Realizing that religion would not feed families, Tade purchased land in the northeastern portion of the city near Federal fortifications on which to settle, he wrote, "say, from 50 to 100 families to do them good physically, mentally, and spiritually." Eventually Fort Wood would be called "Tadetown" by grateful blacks. "With a little ready money," he had written his New York office, "I can help them to homes—a very important thing in this great work of reconstruction."[12]

In order to facilitate more easily the economic independence of the blacks, Tade organized a Chattanooga branch of the National Freedmen's Savings and Trust Bank, and could proudly report that by July, 1868, "the savings bank is doing well, over $2000 in interest." By 1870 the local office reported a balance of nearly twenty thousand dollars. Moreover, Tade possessed business connections with other local northerners in the banking industry, and was a director of the 2nd National of Chattanooga as well. He used his own rapidly growing bank account to help the freedmen acquire more property. "I can sell lots faster than all the real estate men put together," he wrote, noting later that his "real estate has nearly doubled in value in one year." Such financial success emboldened Tade to purchase two lots for himself on Chesnut Street in downtown Chattanooga from the AMA, which had received title from the Freedmen's Bureau. Later he was even able to donate his entire salary to the missionary organization, and the 1870 census reported Tade's personal wealth at over fifty-five hundred dollars, placing his among the top 10 percent of wealth holdings in the city. The financial gains accrued during his tenure in Chattanooga would later come back to haunt him.[13]

Active in a staggering number of community affairs, Tade officiated at statewide teachers' conventions, solicited funds from northern philanthropic institutions, and presided over local gatherings ranging from black protest meetings to the consecration of the new government cemetery. Moreover, the missionary was even nominated for mayor by one wing of Chattanooga's faction-ridden Republican Party. By the first of January, 1868, just one year after his arrival in Chattanooga, Tade was selected as Hamilton County's first Superintendent of Education. In addition to his work as banker, teacher, and minister, he now administered the educational policy of the Brownlow regime, which proved to be a strenuous task. By early 1869, when he submitted his first annual report to John Eaton, state superintendent, he could report that Hamilton County possessed eighty-two public schools, twenty-eight of them for blacks, and employed nearly fifty teachers to minister to almost three thousand students, a full third of whom were black. Considering Tennessee's antebellum prejudice against public schools, he had reason to be proud of his work.[14]

Energetic and industrious as he was, Tade was nearly overburdened by his varied labors. He described a typical day to his close friend Eaton:

> Up at 3:.30 a.m., traveled fifteen miles on the RR; walked six miles; made up Civil District Clerk's report; visited three schools; examined one teacher: traveled nine miles further; and reached home by cars at 8 p.m., eating one meal.

Tade's house on Chesnut Street in downtown Chattanooga was home to Ewing and Amanda Tade, their two adopted children, occasional relatives and boarders, visiting AMA and Freedmen's Bureau officials, and local transplanted northerners. Despite his herculean efforts on the behalf of the black community and the county school system, Tade still found time for his congregation, friends, and family.[15]

But the seeds of defeat for Tade's "great work of reconstruction" lay planted and approached maturity. The troubles lay in the clash of ideologies, cultures, and interest groups that characterized Reconstruction. The disparate racial and social classes of the population of Chattanooga—blacks, transplanted Northerners, and Southern whites—envisioned conflicting goals. The local Republican Party, Tade's only ally, was composed of Northern ex-Federal officers, Freedmen's Bureau officials, and local Unionists who quarreled bitterly over the city's political future. Interested primarily in establishing Chattanooga as an urban industrial center, most local Republicans saw the blacks as a ready source of labor for the mines and factories they hoped to build there. Tade had quickly realized that Brownlow's Tennessee Republican Party had little interest in the blacks except as votes to use against the resurgent Democrats. Moreover, Brownlow's interest in education was suspect as well, because the state law made no provision whatsoever for the erection of school facilities. The state school funds were used for "any and every purpose other than schools," wrote Tade, later calling misuse of Tennessee appropriations for education "a sham and a disgrace." The native Southern-sympathizing whites were bitter at the outcome of the war, and wanted no part of Yankee evangelical zeal, terming the AMA "foreign." "Here I must live a sort of dog's life—hated, shunned, and despised because I am a 'nigger preacher!'" wrote Tade bitterly. The blacks themselves were unsure of the future and wanted to be able to locate their place in the post-war society without white supervision, of which they had surely had enough. "I thought when we got free we should do our own business," a black leader told Tade. In the face of such centrifugal conflicts and pressures, it was no wonder that Tade's mission was doomed.[16]

Tade himself and other Northern missionaries like him must also share some of the burden for the eventual failure of radical Reconstruction. The rigid ideological and cultural beliefs that he brought to Tennessee were often out of place in the disorganized period immediately following the war. Tade's priorities seemed odd at times. He fretted and fumed over the lack of a silver communion service while blacks starved in Contraband, and he decried the number of illegitimate children while smallpox raged through the city. Tade bickered incessantly with his fellow missionaries and the black clergymen, accusing them of smoking and intemperance, vices which may or may not have hindered their effectiveness but were nonetheless odious to the puritanical Tade. S.A. Gaylor, an AMA field worker, wrote Tade, was "a rascal, liar and a thief—I am certain beyond a doubt." Worse still, "Superintendent Ogden [of Fisk University] in the first place is not a real gentleman, and in the second place has a poor moral reputation." "How is it," Tade fumed, "that a man is commissioned as an agent of the AMA who chews and smokes tobacco?" Tade's unyielding moral code prevented him from forming alliances with potential allies, and exacerbated factional squabbles within the local Republican camp.[17]

Moreover, Tade's radical politics placed him in poor stead with the local power structure, which soon became accommodated to the freedmen as industrial workers but not as political, social, or economic equals. Chattanooga's Republicans were not radical enough for Tade. Their "rose water policies will soon play out," he wrote.

Tade committed a mortal sin by praying for Parson Brownlow in Pilgrim Chapel, suffered in the local press as a result, and was forced to exonerate himself publicly from trumped-up charges of graft. Tade was furious. "What these conservatives need," he roared, "is what they ask, their constitutional rights—confiscation of property and to hang by the neck—say some five hundred." Such revolutionary outbursts quickly located Tade as an outsider among the emerging local power structure of Republican businessmen and "New South" Democrats.[18]

This local Republican factionalism was mirrored by events at the state level. Brownlow's abdication as governor for the United States Senate and DeWitt Senter's subsequent apostasy crushed the patchwork Tennessee Republican party for nearly a decade. Early in 1870 the victorious Democrats convened a constitutional convention and promptly repealed much of the Reconstruction legislation, including the state public school law, enacting instead a "local option" plan that allowed counties to make their own educational arrangements without state aid. Moreover, the legislature enacted the country's first poll tax. These events were paralleled nationwide as Northern Republicans began to retreat from the policies of Reconstruction, eventually agreeing to a reconciliation which would not require a commitment to racial equality on the part of the South.[19]

Tade saw the future clearly. "Things are in a bad state here," he wrote to Eaton. "Rebels rule and are trying to crush and kill out the 'nigger,'" he wrote early in 1870, scant months after Tennessee's redemption. All three of Tade's interlocking institutions were threatened. Howard School, founded upon land confiscated by the Freedmen's Bureau from former Confederates, would soon be evicted and forced to move. "We expect soon to be turned out of house and home," he wrote in despair. "Our tax title will not hold in this state and a 'reb' lawyer is trying to make out that the buildings are 'fixtures'—a law expression—and therefore cannot be moved." Howard School was not alone, for many of the county's public schools suffered a similar fate. John Alvord, national Freedmen's Bureau Superintendent of Schools, reported sadly that Tennessee's redemption "shows what may become true in any Southern State where a political element, prejudiced against the education of the colored race, is in the majority." Tade noted that "the whole school interest is dead in this state." Although Republican Hamilton County voted to continue aid to public education under the new state law, Tade saw quickly that the "white schools" were much better funded. The Chattanooga Board of Education gave black schools less money in general and at least once none at all for fuel. Tade noted that the still-zealous scholars shivered as they studied.[20]

The other two legs of Tade's tripartite plan for reconstruction fared even worse. He feared for his church as well as his school. "Cannot the AMA, before you entirely lose sight of us, help our Pilgrim Church amid the hills?" he pleaded. The last hope for Tade's vision collapsed in the summer of 1871, when the Chattanooga office of the National Freedman's Savings Bank closed, a victim of mismanagement at the national level. Thousands of dollars in hard-earned wages were lost. Still more crushing, the lots Tade had purchased for the freedmen in Fort Wood were returned to their owners, as the lands confiscated by the Freedmen's Bureau reverted to their antebellum owners. Despite all of Tade's prescient awareness of the economic realities of reconstruction, there was nothing he could do.[21]

Tade was despondent. "My seven years of labor here begin to wear and I think makes it rather necessary to have a change," he wrote in 1873 to the field office of the AMA, with which he had had little recent contact. Defeated, Ewing Tade left Chattanooga and accepted a professorship at Tusculum College in Greenville, Tennessee, where he taught mathematics and his daughter Mary secured a position in the music department. A year later Tade was also selected as "financial agent" for the college, yet he was not happy. "My heart is not fixed to here," he wrote. In 1875 a "college friend" in Reno, Nevada, offered Tade his pulpit and salary for several months, and Tade and his family prepared to leave the South, feeling that the children required educational opportunities he knew better than most they could never receive in the region. "I feel, too," he wrote sadly, "that mine has been no small sacrifice."[22]

E.O. Tade's sacrifices in the name of reconstruction, however, were far from over when he left the South. Eventually settling in California, he was unhappy there as well, terming the inhabitants "rough and reckless." In 1877, Tade's title to the two lots on Chesnut Street in downtown Chattanooga was challenged in court. He lost the suit and with it what money he had saved through the years. In 1869, by order of AMA field secretary Erastus M. Cravath, Tade had bought the two lots for the organization. Months later he purchased them in turn from the AMA for four thousand dollars, a thousand down, and the rest in notes. When the costly suit revealed that the AMA had never possessed clear title to the land, the lots reverted to their previous owner, but Tade still owed nearly a thousand dollars on his notes to the AMA. Despite Tade's years of selfless service and salary contributions, the organization would not absolve the debt, so he slowly paid the notes off from his meager salary as a missionary to the Indians and Chinese in California.[23]

Tade never returned to the South, the scene of his almost Biblical trials. He built Congregationalist churches in Antioch and San Mateo, California, and returned east several times, once to receive a doctorate in divinity from his alma mater, Grinnell. Eventually he managed to recover his financial losses, and settled in Los Angeles, where his wife and children taught school for many years. His health slowly fading, Tade died in "The City of the Angels" in 1919.[24]

Not possessed of Tade's longevity, Chattanooga's black community health was fading as well. It is impossible to over stress the adverse effects of redemption and sectional reconciliation upon the freedman's society. By 1875, the *Atlanta Constitution* reported, local blacks could only enter the Read House hotel "fearful of the consequences." Tade's successors lacked his energy and zeal, and finally the city's black leaders signed a petition protesting the policies of one. Local authorities quickly separated the educational administration of the county from the evangelical religious missionaries sent by the AMA.[25]

Chattanooga's mills and mines proved unprofitable and unhealthy, and Northern investors moved south to Birmingham, leaving the freedmen locked into the lowest levels of the city's declining occupational structure. When what little political power they had possessed during Reconstruction was removed by eventual disfranchisement and gerrymandering by the "New South" local government, the blacks retreated into a separate and markedly inferior existence in the new industrial city. U.S. Grant University, later the University of Chattanooga, was built on land donated by the Western Freedman's Aid Commission, but blacks were refused admission. A relic of earlier but better intentions, Howard School continued as the principal "colored" educational institution in Chattanooga, supplying generations of hopeful black Tennesseans with a manifestly inferior education. When blacks rose up in another reconstruction following the Second World War, Howard was bombed by "unknown parties" in January, 1958.[26]

What had gone wrong? In the face of conflicting goals and contending class interests, Tade's radical vision of blacks' place in the new order had proven impossible to fulfill, despite his clear understanding of the freedmen's requirements for something other than freedom with which to begin life as American citizens. White Southern resistance and northern apathy over the plight of the blacks combined to make Tade's missionary spirit almost as much a casualty as the hopes and dreams of thousands of American freedmen. Reconstruction in Tennessee failed because too few cared as much for them as did Ewing Tade.

Even in his despair, Tade had seen hopeful signs amidst the dark clouds gathering above. "The foundation is laid—no bad mortar used I think," he had written optimistically, and events would prove him correct. Despite years of frustration, the institutions of the black community, particularly the churches and Howard School, would constitute a firm base from which a later generation of black Chattanooga could begin to assail the segregated power structure of the city. Ewing Tade's ten years in the South had indeed not been in vain.[27]

*This article first appeared in the Winter 1984 issue of the* Tennessee Historical Quarterly.

1. E.O. Tade to M.E. Strieby, 14 September 1875, American Missionary Association Archives, Amistad Research Center, Fisk University, Nashville, Tennessee (Microfilm), hereinafter referred to as "AMA Archives"; Recent criticism may be found in Ronald E. Butchart, *Northern Schools, Southern Blacks, and Reconstruction* (Westport, Conn., 1980), Donald Spivey, *Schooling for the New Slavery: Black Industrial Education, 1868–1915* (Westport, 1978). A more balanced view is that of Robert C. Morris, *Reading, Riting, and Reconstruction: The Education of Freedmen in the South, 1861–1870* (Chicago, 1976). Dated but still valuable in Henry Lee Swint, *The Northern Teacher in the South: 1862–1870* (Nashville, 1941); William Preston Vaughn, *Schools for All: The Blacks and Public Education in the South 1865–1877* (Lexington, 1974).

2. Lester C. Lamon, *Blacks in Tennessee, 1791–1970* (Knoxville, 1981), 29–33; Gilbert E. Govan and James W. Livingood, *The Chattanooga Country: 1540–1976, From Tomahawks to TVA* (Knoxville, 1976), 211–52; idem., "Chattanooga Under Military Occupation, 1863–1865," *Journal of Southern History* XVII (February, 1951), 23–47; John T. Trowbridge, *The South: Its Battlefield, Its People, Its Prospects* (Hartford, 1866), 252–62; "Rules and Regulations for the Government of the 'Freedmen's Village' on the North Side of the Tennessee River, Near Chattanooga, Tennessee, October 11, 1865," Box 52, "Tennessee," RG 105, Records of the Bureau of Refugees, Freedmen, and Abandoned Lands, National Archives, Washington, D.C., hereinafter referred to as "BRFAL."

3. Lyman W. Ayer to M.E. Strieby, 18 February 1865, AMA Archives.

4. 1870 Mss. census schedules, Hamilton County, Tennessee; Tade to Whipple, 27 March 1858, Tade to "Brother Jocelyn," 7 August 1860, Tade to Whiting, 29 December 1864, all in AMA Archives; biographical information on Tade was generously supplied by Harold F. Worthley of the Congregational Christian Historical Society, of Boston, Mass. The *Chattanooga Daily Herald*, 5 May 1872, contains a sketch of Tade and his work.

5. F.E. Ensign to M.E. Strieby, 15 July 1865, Tade to Strieby, 3 January and 23 March 1866, all in AMA Archives. See also Fisk's Report for 1 November 1866, Senate Executive Document #6, 39th Congress, 2nd Session, p. 133.

6. Tade to E.P. Smith, 6 December 1866 and 12 March 1867, AMA Archives; "Report of Howard School for December 1, 1866," Box 53, "Tennessee," BRFAL.

7. Tade to E.P. Smith, 15 May 1867, AMA Archives; Lamon, *Blacks in Tennessee*, 41; James B. Campbell, "East Tennessee During the Federal Occupation, 1863–1865," East Tennessee Historical Society *Publications* XIX (1947), 64–80; Govan and Livingood, *Chattanooga Country*, 253–80. W. B. Caw, General Order Number 36, 29 December 1865, entry 210, pt. 4, RG 393, National Archives, Washington, D.C.

8. Tade to Barnum, 29 November 1867, in John Eaton Papers, University of Tennessee, Knoxville. I am indebted to John Dobson for his assistance with the Eaton Papers. S.A. Gaylor to E.P. Smith, 1 May 1867, AMA Archives; Trotter to Steedman, 6 August 1866, in "Telegrams Received and Sent, Chattanooga, Tennessee, 1866," BRFAL; *Chattanooga Times*, 9 May 1974; See also the Howard High School Collection, Local History Department, Chattanooga Public Library; Alrutheus Ambush Taylor, *The Negro in Tennessee, 1865–1880* (Washington, D.C., 1941), 172; John W. Alvord, *Tenth Semi-Annual Report on Schools for Freedmen, July 1, 1870* (Washington, D.C., 1870), 54–55; Paul D. Phillips, "A History of The Freedmen's Bureau in Tennessee" (PhD Dissertation, Vanderbilt University, 1964), 176–266.

9. Tade to E.P. Smith, 4 October 1867, 12 March, and 16 November 1868, AMA Archives; "Minutes of the Board of Aldermen of the City of Chattanooga, Tennessee, from October 7, 1865, to January 2, 1869," MSS in Local History Department, Chattanooga Public Library, p. 308, entry for 13 December 1867. See also Goodspeed's Hamilton County edition of the *History of Tennessee* (Nashville, 1887), 843; clippings from "The Twenty-Third Annual Report of the American Missionary Association," 45–6, and "The Twenty-Fourth Annual Report of the American Missionary Association," 42, both in the Howard High School Collection, Chattanooga Public Library; "Monthly Report of Education for September 1867, of James M. Johnson," Box 54, "Tennessee," BRFAL; Henry Lee Swint, "Reports From Educational Agents of the Freedmen's Bureau in Tennessee, 1865–1870," *Tennessee Historical Quarterly* I (March 1942), 71–4.

10. N.B. Lucas to Major Cochran, 30 October 1865, in "Telegrams Received and Sent, Chattanooga, Tennessee. 1866," BRFAL: Trowbridge, *The South*, 251.

11. Tade to M.E. Strieby, 1 August 1865, AMA Archives; "Monthly Report of Outrages for May, 1867, by James W. Johnson," Box 54, "Tennessee," BRFAL; Goodspeed's *History of Tennessee*, 854; *Chattanooga Daily Republican*, 17 November 1867; Taylor, *Negro in Tennessee*, 202; "Twenty-Second Annual Report of the American Missionary Association," Clipping in Howard High School Collection, Chattanooga Public Library. 12. Tade to E.P. Smith, 15 February 1867, and 19 February 1870, AMA Archives.

13. 1870 Mss Census Schedules, Hamilton County, Tennessee; Tade to E.P. Smith, 23 July 1869, 1 September 1869, and 7 January 1870, all in AMA Archives; E.M. Cravath to Whiting, 19 June 1867, AMA Archives; Charles D. McGuffey, *Standard History of Chattanooga, Tennessee* (Knoxville, 1911), 204; Carl B. Osthaus, *Freedmen, Philanthropy, and Fraud* (Urbana, Ill., 1976), 230; Louis L. Parham, *Parham's First Annual City Directory for the City of Chattanooga for 1871–2* (Knoxville, 1871). 32.

14. *Chattanooga Daily Republican*, 20 December 1867; 28 January, 22 February, and 28 July 1868 and 1 June and 15 August 1869. LeRoy P. Graf, editor, "Education in East Tennessee, 1867–1869: Selections from the John Eaton, Jr. Papers," East Tennessee Historical Society Papers XXIII (1951), 101; *Annual Report of the Commissioner of Education Made to the Secretary*

*of the Interior for the Year 1870* (Washington, D.C., 1870), 288; John Eaton, *Grant, Lincoln, and the Freedmen: Reminiscences of the Civil War* (New York, 1907), 119–22;

Swint, *Northern Teacher*, 92; John Eaton, Jr., *First Report of the Superintendent of Public Instruction of the State of Tennessee* (Nashville, 1869), cxxiii; *Chattanooga Daily Herald*, 11 November 1872.)

15. Tade to Eaton, 20 January 1869, Eaton Papers; 1870 Mss census schedules, Hamilton County, Tennessee; *Parham's ... City Directory*, 131; Tade to E.P. Smith, 7 December 1867, AMA Archives; See also Robert H. White, *The Development of the Tennessee State Educational Organization. 1796–1920* (Kingsport, Tennessee, 1929), 92; Eaton, *First Report*, 141, cxxiii–cxxiv.

16. Tade to Eaton, 28 November 1868, Eaton Papers; Alvord, Eighth Semi-Annual Report, 61–2; Tade to Cravath, 15 February 1868, 2 October 1871, Tade to E.P. Smith, 12 March 1868, 20 April 1869, all in AMA Archives; Taylor, *The Negro in Tennessee*, 153 ff.; James B. Campbell, "East Tennessee During the Radical Regime, 1865–1869," East Tennessee Historical Society *Publications* XX (1948), 84–102; James W. Livingood, "Chattanooga, Tennessee: Its Economic History in the Years Immediately Following Appomattox," East Tennessee Historical Society *Publications* XV (1943), 28; Eaton to Tade, 18 February 1869, quoted in Eaton, *First Report*, xxxv. See also Eaton's assessment of the Brownlow legislation in *First Report*, 97, 125, passim; Phillips, "Freedmen's Bureau," 209ff.

17. Tade to Eaton, 15 May 1869, 10 February 1870, Eaton Papers; Tade to E.P. Smith, 8 May, 15 May 1867, 3 March 1868, all in AMA Archives.

18. Tade to E.P. Smith, 17 and 18 May 1867, AMA Archives; Tade to Eaton, 28 November 1868, Eaton Papers; Phillips "Freedmen's Bureau" 203–4, 260.

19. Roger L. Hart, *Redeemers, Bourbons & Populists: Tennessee 1870–1896* (Baton Rouge, 1975), 1–28; White, *Tennessee State Educational Organization*, 113; Thomas B. Alexander, *Political Reconstruction in Tennessee* (Nashville, 1950), 199–225.

20. Tade to E.P. Smith, 15 February 1867, 7 January 1870, Henry B. Wolcott to Cravath, 25 November 1872, all in AMA Archives; Tade to Eaton, 10 February 1870, 28 December 1870, Eaton Papers; Alvord, *Tenth Semi-Annual Report*, 41; Taylor, *The Negro in Tennessee*, 176–82.

21. Tade to Eaton, 13 and 23 June 1871, Eaton Papers; Tade to E.P. Smith, 11 October 1869, 7 June 1870, 19 September 1870, T.C. Steward to E.M. Cravath, 7 July 1871, all in AMA Archives; Osthaus, *Freedmen, Philanthropy and Fraud*, 62; Alvord, *Tenth Semi-Annual Report*, 55; Box 53, "Tennessee," BRFAL, contains a steady procession of land titles returned to their original owners.

22. Tade to E.M. Cravath, 12 September 1873, 3 January 1874, Tade to Strieby, 14 September 1875, all in AMA Archives; "Tusculum College Trustees' Minutes, 1874–1876," Mss in Tusculum College Archives, Greenville, Tenn. en tires for June 1874, 23 April 1875, and 21 April 1876. See also *Sixth Annual Catalogue of Greenville and Tusculum College, 1873–4* (Green-

ville, 1874). I am greatly indebted to Wayne W. Dobson, Archivist of Tusculum College, for the preceding manuscripts, photocopies of which are in my possession.

23. Tade to Strieby, 4 August 1876, 14 and 23 May, 13 August 1877, all in AMA Archives.

24. Tade to Whiting, 3 January 1874, AMA Archives; Biographical information from the Congregational Christian Historical Society, Boston, Mass.

25. Petition signed by William Lewis et alia, 3 September 1874, AMA Archives; *Atlanta Constitution*, 7 March 1875; *Annual Report of John M. Fleming, State Superintendent of Public Instruction for Tennessee, For the Scholastic Year ending August 31, 1874* (Nashville, 1875), 64.

26. "Report of the Committee of the Senate upon the Relations Between Labor and Capital and Testimony Taken by the Committee," 4 Volumes, 48th Congress, 1st Session, 1885, Vol. IV, pp. 124–75; Goodspeed's *History of Tennessee*, 847, 886; *Chattanooga Times*, 20 January 1958; Joseph H. Cartwright, *The Triumph of Jim Crow: Tennessee Race Relations in the 1880s* (Knoxville, 1976), 147–8; Jasper T. Duncan, "From Slavery: Negroes' Progress," *Chattanooga Times*, 18 September 1938; Roy D. Coulter, "The Negroes of Chattanooga, Tennessee," B.D. Thesis, Vanderbilt University, 1934; Lester C. Lamon, *Black Tennesseans, 1900–1939* (Knoxville, 1977), vi, 3, 9, 39, 142–3, 219; Howard's inadequacy is painfully exposed in a report of the Southern Regional Council. See Dr. M. J. Jones, editor, *Chattanooga: The Negro and Employment* (Chattanooga, 1962), 4–14.

27. Tade to E.M. Cravath, 29 September 1873, AMA Archives.

# THE NASHVILLE INSTITUTE AND ROGER WILLIAMS UNIVERSITY:

Benevolence, Paternalism, and Black Consciousness, 1867–1910

*Eugene TeSelle*

The campus of Peabody College of Vanderbilt University was the site of a black institution, supported by the American Baptist Home Mission Society, from 1874 to 1905. Almost totally forgotten in Nashville except for an oral tradition in the black community and the work of a few history buffs, the school touched the lives of a number of important black leaders in the Mid-South. From the scattered remains that survive it is possible to reconstruct the course of a typical black educational institution from Reconstruction to the return of Jim Crow, caught in the shifting fields of force among Southern blacks, their Northern benefactors, and the whites of the region.

Daniel W. Phillips (1809–1890) was the principal figure in the growth of the Nashville Institute.[1] Born in Wales in humble circumstances, he learned English after the age of 18. He emigrated first to the Maritime Provinces of Canada, then to Boston. After attending Brown University and the Newton Theological Institution he served several churches in Massachusetts. His thinking paralleled that of other Northerners:

> From the very commencement of the war it was his strong expectation that the hostilities would end in the entire removal of their cause. As the war progressed the conviction took deeper and deeper hold of his mind that when peace would

be established there would be very great work for true patriots—and especially for Christians—to do among the freedmen to fit them for the many responsibilities of freedom. He felt that the Baptists would be under particular obligations, because such a multitude of the colored people professed to be of their faith. Gradually it came over him that he must give himself to their work.[2]

He came to Tennessee in 1864, as he put it, "without means and without a plan." First he preached in Knoxville, and then for several years he was pastor of the white Central Baptist Church in Nashville. But he also taught a class for black ministers, first in his own home, then in the black First Baptist Church.[3] He was aware that he himself had once thirsted for education, with almost no way to get it.[4] A local black Baptist minister recalled his activities during those years:

> We went with him over the city, and he ate at our tables, as poor as we were. He identified himself with us to lift us up, to bring life to us and open up a way by which we might be educated.[5]

Phillips and his colleague, Z.C. Rush, went North in 1866 and raised money with which they were able the next year to buy a lot near Fort Gillem, at the southeast corner of Park Street and Polk Street. Phillips purchased a government-surplus building for $1,000 and had it moved to this location. The building, 120 x 40 feet, had two stories and a partial basement; there was space for classrooms, a chapel, a library, and accommodations for about forty-five men and twelve women.[6] The school opened at the end of August, 1867, with Z.C. Rush as principal and D. W. Phillips as instructor in theology.[7]

This was the year in which Tennessee opened free public schools for blacks, and therefore there was an opportunity to shift the focus from basic education to the training of ministers and teachers. Fisk University, Central Tennessee College, and the Nashville Institute all began operations about the same time. But the 1867 school law was repealed in 1869–70 with the downfall of the Reconstruction government, and about the same time the Freedmen's Bureau withdrew from the scene, leaving education at all levels to the benevolent societies of the Northern churches.[8]

As the school continued to attract students, Phillips thought of expansion. He first hoped to purchase the hilltop site of Fort Gillem, but Fisk University acquired it before him, using the first $20,000 raised by the Jubilee Singers, and in 1874 Phillips had to write, "Jubilee Hall is being erected on the brow of the hill, overlooking our present position."[9] J.B. Simmons, Secretary of the Home Mission Society, spent a month in Nashville seeking a new site. The location chosen was the estate of William H. Gordon on Hillsboro Pike, 1½ miles south of Nashville, between the newly founded Vanderbilt University and Adelicia Acklen's Belmont mansion. At first the board of the Home Mission Society was hesitant to purchase the property, but the $30,000 needed was supplied by Phillips's classmate at Brown, Dr. Nathan Bishop, and his wife.[10] Phillips was aware of rumors "that some of our neighbors were in great alarm fearing that neither honor nor prosperity would be safe;" at first they thought of offering money for them to move, but instead they waited to see what the results would be, and Phillips never heard a complaint.[11]

The campus, covering thirty acres enclosed by a wall, had ample space for orchards, gardens, and pasturage for livestock. The report to the society commented that it was located in the "most popular suburb" of Nashville and had a commanding view of the city. Arrangements had been made by H.G. Scovel, described as the chief white real estate agent in the city, and Abram Smith and Henry Harding, the chief black agents.[12] The two-story Gordon home, which came to be called "Mansion House," had been built in the 1850s on the hilltop where the Social-Religious Building of Peabody College now stands. In 1875 a third story and a mansard roof were added, converting it into a building for teachers and female students, and in 1876 a large three-story building with a frontage of 160 feet was built next to it, connected by hallways. This building, "Centennial Hall," was made possible by an additional gift from Dr. and Mrs. Nathan Bishop of New York.[13]

Phillips was joined in 1870 by Carrie V. Dyer (1838–1921), whose life had been shaped by her childhood experience of seeing slave hunters seeking fugitives in Michigan, then by the zeal of an uncle with whom she lived in Vermont, a Garrisonian abolitionist who ran a station on the Underground Railway and had renounced organized religion because of its weak position on slavery. She dedicated her life to the emancipated slaves, teaching at a school for black children in Providence, Rhode Island, before coming to Nashville.[14]

In 1874 the faculty of the school was strengthened by the coming of Lyman Beecher Tefft (1833–1926), a graduate of Brown University and Rochester Theological Seminary.[15] His daughter, Mary Abby Tefft, was one of the students at the Nashville Institute (Charles Currier Phillips, son of the founder, was another), for the school was open to all, without regard to sex or race, class or denomination.[16] After attending Wellesley College she taught at the black Hartshorn Memorial College in Richmond, where her father was president from 1884 to 1913.[17]

The school began to offer the A.B. degree in 1877. One member of the first class to receive this degree was Charles Spencer Dinkins (1856–1901), who studied at the Nashville Institute from 1870 to 1877. He taught at the school during the following year, then studied at the Newton Theological Institute near Boston. Eventually he became president of Selma University.[18]

Another black Baptist leader who attended the school for a time was Lewis Garnett Jordan, who was born in slavery and acquired trousers and a name at the age of 10 (he later added his middle name in honor of the black leader Henry Highland Garnett). After preaching for some years in Yazoo City, he felt the need for more preparation; in December, 1879, he took the train to Nashville, along with six of the young people from the churches.[19] During the 1880s his parishioners became interested in emigration to Africa because of oppression in America, and in 1885 he went to Liberia to look over the situation. The result was that he became hopeful about the impact that a missionary effort, directed toward a still largely independent Africa, might have upon the future of that continent's people.[20] A number of black Baptist missionaries went to Africa, and in 1896 Jordan was elected Corresponding Secretary of the Foreign Mission Board of the National Baptist Convention. He was also a delegate to the organizing meeting of the Federal Council of Churches in 1905 and to the World Missionary Conference in Edinburgh in 1910.[21]

During the 1870s the catalogues of the school list a Board of Examiners, which included a number of important Baptist leaders, both black and white, in the city and the region. The black members of the board were the Rev. Randle B. Vandavell (1832–1898), minister of the black First Baptist Church of Edgefield, the long-time companion of Phillips[22]; the Rev. Allen Allensworth (1842–1914), who served in the Civil War, was a minister in Kentucky, and then became a leading chaplain in the U.S. Army[23]; the Rev. George Washington Dupee, who had been an active minister in Kentucky even as a slave and continued to be a leader after Emancipation[24]; the Rev. Nelson G. Merry (1824–84), minister of the black First Baptist Church of Nashville[25]; and the Rev. W.P.T. Jones, pastor of the Mulberry Street Colored Baptist Mission. The white members of the board included the Rev. Tiberius Gracchus Jones, minister of the white First Baptist Church from 1871 to 1883; the Rev. William A. Nelson, pastor of the Edgefield Baptist Church; the Rev. A.D. Phillips, minister of the North Nashville Mission of the First Baptist Church, which later became Third Baptist; the Rev. W.D. Mayfield, a Baptist editor; and the Rev. L.B. Fish, who was called to the Third Baptist Church in 1876. He was widely admired as a tenor and for a few years taught vocal music at the institute. Fish was especially appreciated by Phillips, who said, "Bro. Fish is the only pastor that is really not ashamed of us.... the very few that will have anything to do with us are shy."²⁶

But the two most interesting and most active white supporters of the institute were lay people, both physicians. Dr. William Palmer Jones (1819–97) was remembered by Phillips as his first white supporter in Nashville. Phillips and his wife had been left to themselves by the white community, but then, he said, he received a letter from Dr. Jones, saying that he approved his object and method and was ready to help. This, said Phillips, broke the ice.²⁷ Jones was an active Baptist, the only lay person to be elected president of the Tennessee Baptist Convention (indeed, several times). Politically he was linked with Henry Clay's Whigs, and then with the Republican Party. Thus he was a Unionist, but he was tolerated in Nashville and was even elected president of the city council in 1862. In 1873 he was elected to the state senate, with a commitment to free public schools and equal educational advantages for all; but it is also clear from the school laws which he introduced that he favored separate education for the races.

Dr. Jabez Philander Dake (1827–1894) was a homeopathic physician with national stature in that movement. He came to Nashville in 1869 because of his wife's health.²⁸ His ancestry went back to seventeenth-century Rhode Island on both sides (his family name was Hungarian, originally spelled Deak, and it was shared with an honored leader of the Hungarian independence movement in the mid-nineteenth century). All his biographical sketches, which clearly go back to his own statements, mention that his mother "favored moral reforms and denounced shams, and urged independence and vigor of action in all good measures, evincing the spirit of her Roger Williams, Quaker-Baptist ancestry."²⁹ One may suspect that it was Dake who suggested the new name of the school when it was incorporated in 1883.

In 1881 Lyman B. Tefft became principal of the Nashville Institute, and largely at his urging the Executive Board of the American Baptist Home Mission Society decided in 1882 to incorporate the school as a degree-granting university. Phillips, who had continued as professor of theology, deplored the change: "The new name does not convey the truth.... It turns us away from what should be our true aim. We naturally seek to conform to our name."³⁰

His objection was that the mission schools should not assume high-sounding titles, and that in any case secular learning could not take the place of the word of God in transforming lives. Nevertheless Phillips agreed to be one of the incorporators of Roger Williams University. The others named on the document, filed on February 13, 1883, were John M. Gregory of Chicago, Jabez P. Dake, William P. Jones, Nelson G. Merry, and Randle B. Vandavell. Dake probably had a hand in the naming of the school, since the name originally proposed was simply Nashville University.³¹ Thus Roger Williams University became the first of the Home Mission Society schools to offer college-level work, and until it closed in 1905 it led all the schools in number of college students.³²

It had a succession of presidents, appointed by the Executive Board in New York and coming from outside the region, with varied experience in education and in race relations: Williams Stewart (1883–84), Edward D. Mitchell (1884–85), William H. Stifler (1885–87), William R. Morang (1887), Alfred Owen (1887–95), Owen James (1895–98), A. T. Sowerby (1898–99), and Peter B. Guernsey (1899–1905).

In 1883 a new house for the president was begun, and in 1886 a teachers' residence was built.

The faculty of the university usually included six to eight teachers, graduates of Colby, Brown, Colgate, Bucknell, Franklin, Hartshorn—and Roger Williams. Certainly the most widely honored of the people associated with the university was John Hope (1868–1936), born in Augusta, Georgia, of a Scottish father and a free Negro mother. Blond and blue-eyed, he remained associated with the black community, not only in Georgia but at Brown University, from which he graduated in 1894. He chose to return to the South and taught at Roger Williams from 1894 to 1898, declining a better-paid position at Tuskegee because he already sensed his disagreement with Booker T. Washington's views.³³

Those who knew him during these years recalled the setting:

> Beyond the college farm not a house was to be seen for miles. Near the campus was a creek with a bridge across it. Persimmons grew along Hillsboro Road, which led out into the deeper country. On one side of this road lay Roger Williams University, on the other side Vanderbilt. To get to Nashville, Roger Williams students crossed the road, then cut over the Vanderbilt campus to the trolley line.
>
> Relations between the two schools were entirely friendly. Vanderbilt students came over to join in religious meetings at the colored college. Roger Williams boys waited on tables at Vanderbilt. Vanderbilt football coaches coached the Negro team. Roger Williams students went to the games at Vanderbilt and sat with the others on the bleachers—a practice which would not be allowed today. Individual students, white and black, formed friendships that outlasted school days.³⁴

In 1898 Hope was invited to Atlanta Baptist College (later Morehouse), and in 1906 he became president. In 1929 Hope supported the federation of Morehouse, Spelman, and Atlanta University, giving that complex a united strength that the black schools in Nashville had never been able to gain.[35]

The university was the scene of a student protest (they denied that it was a "rebellion") in the winter of 1886–87. The focus of controversy was T.E. Balch, the treasurer and superintendent of industrial work, who came to the school from Wakefield, Massachusetts, at the same time the president, William H. Stifler, came from Davenport, Iowa. Tension grew during two academic years (1885–86 and 1886–87), and the students blamed Balch for a drop in enrollment during this period. George T. Robinson, black editor of the *Nashville Star*, began editorial attacks on Balch late in 1886, and claimed that the local trustees and the faculty, with one exception, sided with his position.[36] The *Star* asserted that in November Balch had insulted a female student, and "It was for this insult that the boys would have used a rope, but for good old Dr. Phillips."[37]

Eventually a committee of students drew up formal charges against Balch, as follows:

> 1. In his unfair and financial dealings with the students.
> 2. Unfair proposal to a lady teacher (white) and to a young lady who is a student.
> 3. Speaking contemptuously of Dr. D.W. Phillips, and even objected to a glass of milk being given him at the University.
> 4. Furnishing nauseous food and accusing all the students of theft, and in many ways exerting a deadening influence on our school.[38]

Stifler refused to hear the charges and threatened to expel the fifty-six students who signed them. He also refused to let them appear before the local trustees (who at that time included D.W. Phillips, president; J.P. Dake, secretary; W.P. Jones; C.H. Strickland, pastor of the First Baptist Church; and R.B. Vandavell), insisting that the local board had no authority since his appointment was from New York. Thereupon the students communicated with the Board of the Home Mission Society and added the following charges against Stifler:

> 1. Non-recognition of the above charges; attempting to smuggle [sic] them by threats to expel those concerned, and did expel one.

2. He is a man in whom we can place no confidence, an upholder of immorality, and has no regard for the truth.

3. Using abusive language and also calumniating students, such as liars, fools, stabbers, mobers and worse than the heathen in Africa. Simply because they presented the above charges.

4. Refusing to let the matter come before the faculty and misrepresenting the local Board of Trustees.

5. Using religion deceptively as a means of carrying out his diabolical schemes.[39]

While the controversy went on, the officials received anonymous notes penciled in two different hands on lined school paper[40]:

old bald red head Stifler

you and your old white headed demercrat are not wanted here and if you dont move out y'll both wish you had. if he does pat some of us on the back we niggers no what it is for. your old red skull lies to us. you think we dont see through yu, but we do you old hipocrite. your long prayrs ude better for the lies you tell us. If you dont give us some milk and some things fit to eat you and old Balch will get more rotten eggs round you than youll want. Spose the old white headed demercrat dont know his daughter makes love to one of us niggers.

Tom Balch—

Sir—You have been making a reputation at our expense long enough and if a stop is not put to it your will suffer for it and that soon. We give you a few days to give us better and more food and be more respectful to we students. You say you have a call from some where else, we will be devilish glad to know that you have accepted it. The teachers pay the same for board that we do but you and your clan of devils slip around and give them tea, milk and extra dishes in order that they may stay shut mouth. We are going to petition the Society to move you and if it does not do it we will move you if we have to do it in the dark. You dirty grand rascal you think that Negroes are blind fools but we will show you how to come here acting a dog and calling us rogues. We know how you said you were going to kick Jody's ass out of the office and other slight talk that you make to these poor boys. This is our home and you dirty pup we will kick your ass out if you do not act better.

The students sent a telegram to New York on January 7: "To decide that Dr. Stifler and Balch remain means students leave. Committee: E.T. Saddler, S.W. Anderson, J.B. Palmer, F.L. Trimble, James Branham."[40] Henry L. Morehouse, the corresponding secretary of the board, penciled a note: "To this telegram I replied: The case will be decided on its merits and not by threats from anybody—!"[41]

On January 10 the executive board in New York adopted a resolution allowing one more month for the settling of grievances and establishing a sequence of appeals from Stifler to the faculty, the local trustees, and the executive board.[42] A copy of the resolution was sent to S. W. Anderson of the student committee on February 1.[43] When the students received no communication about the results of the February 14 meeting of the board, and then learned that on February 21 its education committee had approved a resolution stating that the charges were unfounded, trivial, or susceptible of explanation, they decided to leave the school.[44] On February 28 they presented the faculty a written request by 117 students for honorable dismissal from the school and promised to leave the next Thursday morning, March 3. The faculty, meeting on that same day, granted the request and also voted to ask the board in New York to remove Stifler and Balch. The school was virtually shut down after Saturday, February 28. The faculty members agreed to be in their classrooms as usual, but they did not expect the students to be there. The students repeated their threat to leave unless a demand for the two resignations came by Thursday, March 3. Stifler telegraphed New York that the students were "in rebellion," which they denied. The faculty's own position was "The students are not in rebellion; they have been honorably dismissed."[45]

On March 3, E.C. Hiscox, president of the board, telegraphed to D. W. Phillips, "Hold the student quiet till letter comes, if possible." Dr. J.P. Dake, deputized by the local trustees, took the train to New York. The faculty members went to their classrooms, and the students remained quietly in their rooms with their trunks packed, the women serenading the men.[46] They felt confident that the school would reopen the following Monday without Stifler and Balch. Stifler did not help the situation by putting up a notice encouraging the students to leave saying: "Students entitled to them can get reduced fare permits by calling at the office."[47]

The board, meeting on March 5 in New York with Dake present, decided to seek a new president and appointed William E. Morang, professor at Roger Williams for three years, as acting president. But he filled the office for only a few months, dying on June 30 at the age of 37, and Dake considered the board in New York responsible for his death. The student committee eventually signed their own "explanation and apology," regretting some of their language but stating that it was used "under excitment caused by, what seemed to us, an in-competent, unwise, and injurious state of affairs."[48]

Incredibly the board, and Morehouse in particular, refused to let the matter rest. The education committee prepared its own form of retraction, which was approved by the board on May 9; Morang was "authorized and directed" to secure the signatures of the members of the student committee, and in the event of their refusal "the two young men who are prepared to graduate shall not be permitted to do so, and any others intending to return to the institution shall be denied its privileges hereafter."[49] When this was communicated in a letter from Morehouse, the local trustees rebelled. May 24 was Commencement Day, and the annual meeting of the trustees was held that afternoon. They stated that they held legal authority, under the charter of incorporation, to confer degrees, and that the board could not interfere when students had completed the prescribed course of study and given proper testimonials of scholarship and deportment. They further stated that the students "had good cause for complaints against the administration and personal conduct" of Stifler and Balch, and alluded to Morehouse's "extraordinary efforts" to "belittle" the complaints of the students.[50] It appears from the catalogues of the school that the two students in question, S. W. Anderson and E.I. Saddler, received the A.B. degree in 1887 in defiance of the directive from New York, and Anderson was immediately elected president of the Alumni Association.

The board in New York refused to let Morehouse be the sole target. They reminded the local trustees that they themselves had asked for the retraction of the offensive utterances and had forbidden the graduation of two students, and ended by asserting that the Board "will expect in the future as in the past to have a voice in the management and discipline of all schools whose property it owns, and whose support it assumes."[51] Dake saw in all of this an "arbitrary and threatening" course of action, unparalleled in the history of schools with charters and trustees.[52] In fairness to the New York faction it must be said that the catalogue, in every year from the incorporation of the university in 1883, always listed, in addition to the local trustees, four others: Dr. J.M. Gregory of Washington, D.C., the Rev. E.T. Hiscox of New York, the Rev. H.L. Morehouse of New York, and the Rev. J. B. Thomas of Brooklyn, and the heading always stated that "the following Trustees were chosen under the direction of the Board of the American Baptist Home Mission Society." On the other hand, neither the incorporating document filed with the Secretary of State nor any other document made the university a subsidiary of the board in quite the way claimed in 1887.

The local trustees adopted a resolution on October 25 with strong language. They felt that they must protest in the name of the customary usages in higher education, which recognized the prerogatives of faculties and trustees against "arbitrary dictation" and "extraordinary interference," and they declared their "loss of confidence" as a result of the board's approval of Morehouse's actions.[53] The resignations of Dake, Jones, Strickland, and Vandavell—all the resident trustees except Phillips—were placed in the hands of President Owen, who requested that they not be announced until he could hear from New York. At the end of the year nothing had been done, and at Dake's request the catalogue for the 1887–88 school year came off the press with only Phillips, Gregory, Hiscox, Morehouse, and Thomas named.[54] D.W. Phillips wrote to New York, "I feel mortified;" he expressed the view that the board's "decree" in May, followed by renewed controversy and Branham's enrolling in Fisk University, had exposed the weakness of the school to a wide public.[55]

Morehouse came to Nashville in September, 1888, ironically for a long-planned conference between the Home Mission Society and several black Baptist organizations. The duel between Dake and Morehouse, two proud and articulate men, continued. Dake requested of Morehouse a statement that he had come to Nashville "with pacific intentions, hoping to restore right feelings between the late Trustees and yourself." Morehouse penciled a draft for a reply—noting also that it was never sent—on a Western Union form in his room at the Nicholson House. His tone was sharp, and he ended by saying that his self-respect prevented any further communications with Dake.[56]

At the conference Randle B. Vandavell consented to be named again to the board of trustees. Phillips died in 1890, a disappointed survivor of an earlier generation of black education. The school recovered and filled its role in the education of black leaders, even with some success. But the crisis years of 1886–88 manifested tensions that had been building for two decades, and they were a sign of troubles still to come in the tenuous relationships between black and white, North and South.

The home missions meeting held in Nashville in September, 1888, was the occasion of significant contacts, not only with Northern white leaders, but among blacks themselves, leading to the formation of the National Baptist Convention in 1895.[57] And as the Northern leadership became more conciliatory toward the attitudes of Southern whites, black Baptists became steadily more assertive. A proposal was made to establish a national university for black Baptists,[58] and it appears that at least some leaders were suggesting that it be located at Roger Williams. As a direct result, it seems, there were proposals to sell the campus and move the school elsewhere. A.G. Haygood of the Slater Fund supported the move and expressed the opinion that the property could bring $150,000.[59]

There were objections from the black community. On Sunday, March 29, 1891, all the black churches in the Nashville area held meetings and voted to ask the executive board not to dispose of the campus, made memorable by leaders like D.W. Phillips and Nelson Merry. They had just begun contributing their "mite" to their own education when this news came.[60] In April Alexander Bradford, a real estate agent, offered a six-month option on the property at a price of $150,000 if he could secure an option on other land suited to the school.[61] In June the board named its terms: $225,000, plus a satisfactory replacement site worth not less than $25,000, and all this to be accomplished within ninety days.[62] The terms were not met, and the board had to live with the suspicions that had been aroused in the black community. It was obvious that residential growth was moving around the Roger Williams campus, and efforts were being made to relocate the institution, especially if black participation in its governance were to be increased.

On the night of January 24, 1905, the main building at Roger Williams University, Centennial Hall, was destroyed by a fire that started near the roof and was attributed to a defective flue.[63] In the local press there were expressions of sympathy and of hope that the school would soon be rebuilt, "if not at the present location, at some other, and one possibly more favored for such a college."[64] The school's treasurer said that an offer of $300,000 had been received, and the reporter added, "For a long time people near the University have been trying to buy the property."[65]

Within a few days a telegram came from H.L. Morehouse: "Announce our purpose to have buildings ready for school next fall."[66] But in February the board adopted a report recommending the sale of the property if the offered price of $180,000 could be obtained.[67] The local press reported that a real estate company had offered to buy the property and subdivide it into lots for residences; there were also promises to extend the streetcar line along this portion of Hillsboro Pike.[68]

The question was decided by a second fire on May 22 of the same year, destroying Mansion House, the old Gordon home which had been used as the girls' dormitory. This time there was open speculations about arson; those living in the building had heard noises in the middle of the night, as though furniture were being knocked over.[69] It was impossible to reopen the school in the fall of 1905 and the board offered advanced students the opportunity to attend other schools supported by the Society, subsidizing all travel costs beyond what they would have paid to go to Nashville. It was decided not to rebuild on the existing campus, because of the cost of new construction and the fact that the campus, "in a choice section of the city," had appreciated in value.[70] In June the board decided to purchase quietly the "Rocky Hill tract" of about thirty acres a few blocks east of the campus.[71]

The board first attempted, during the fall of 1905, to offer the entire twenty-eight acres to a single purchaser at a price of $150,000. When this failed they decided to have the tract subdivided and sell residential lots themselves, and this was done in 1906.[72] Their chief local adviser in all of this was Adolphus B. Hill, owner of the Standard Snuff Company and an active Baptist layman.[73] He was given power of attorney to dispose of the property, and under his supervision it was subdivided into building lots, water and gas lines were laid, streets were macadamized, sidewalks were poured, a widening of Hillsboro Pike was agreed upon, and a contract was made to extend the streetcar line past the campus. Many lots were sold, with the standard deed restriction that the property was not to be conveyed "to any person of African blood or descent."

The initiative now shifted to the black Baptists. At Chattanooga in July, 1907, at a meeting of the Baptist Missionary and Educational Convention of Tennessee, it was voted to assume responsibility for the school, with a black faculty and a predominantly black board of trustees. The convention found what it considered a more desirable site of twelve acres on White's Creek Pike, across the river north from Nashville, and the Society gave financial assistance and approved a transfer of the corporation to the new trustees.[74] During the fall of 1907 a dormitory and classroom building were erected in the new location. The school was officially reopened on Emancipation Day, January 1, 1908.

The story of the old campus was not finished. Beginning in 1901 there had been proposals to elevate the all-white State Normal College (renamed Peabody Normal College in 1889) to a college for teachers on the model of that at Columbia University, and in 1903 public funds were committed by the state, the county, and the city.[75] Chancellor James H. Kirkland of Vanderbilt had been making efforts as early as 1903 to locate the George Peabody College for Teachers nearer to Vanderbilt for their mutual strengthening. But there was weighty sentiment for keeping its location on Rutledge Hill, and questions were raised concerning the relationship of Vanderbilt, still a "sectarian" school, to nonsectarian Peabody.

On January 24, 1905 (coincidentally the same day as the fire that destroyed Centennial Hall at Roger Williams University), the Peabody Education Fund was dissolved by its trustees and $1 million was given to Peabody College. When operations were suspended at Roger Williams there was no immediate thought of purchasing that campus. It was only in 1909 that the Peabody College trustees decided to move to a location near Vanderbilt, and they first looked for land to the south and west of the Vanderbilt campus. In 1910 the Peabody trustees began considering the old Roger Williams property, but Chancellor Kirkland opposed it. He wanted the Teachers College to be "within five minutes walk of the main building on our campus."[76] Otherwise, he said, there would be not "one educational system" but independent and rival institutions.[77] And the Peabody trustees actually did purchase a portion of the Vanderbilt campus, north of Garland Avenue, which was later acquired for the Vanderbilt Medical School.[78]

A.B. Hill, as agent for the Home Mission Board, negotiated with the Peabody trustees to sell about twenty-five acres, the major portion of the old Roger Williams campus. A number of lots had already been purchased, but Hill gained assurances from the owners that they would sell these back at a total cost of $92,258.75.[79] The property was eventually transferred on October 18, 1910, for a consideration of $170,462.86.[80] Hill, who had handled matters for the Home Mission Board through these years with no agreement about compensation, "for the reason that no one could foresee how long they would be required, nor how complicated and responsible would be his duties," was given $4,000 in cash and the Rocky Hill tract, valued at about $10,500, for his troubles.[81]

The land purchased for the new Peabody campus was only a part of the old Roger Williams tract, extending only to Capers Avenue. The remaining lots between Capers and Madison Avenue (now Belcourt) were sold by the board over a period of years. The last of the lots, on the east side of Hillsboro Pike, were purchased by the H.G. Hill Company in 1925.[82] A portion of the Hillsboro Village shopping area, from the First American National Bank (Regions Bank in 2013) to the Pancake Pantry at 1796 21st Avenue South, occupies a corner of the old Roger Williams campus. The four-lane Wedgewood-Blakemore thoroughfare crosses Hillsboro Pike where a stream formerly ran, now submerged into a storm sewer trunk line.

Some of the proceeds from the sale to Peabody College were used toward the construction of buildings on the new Roger Williams campus on Whites Creek Pike, and $25,000 went into an endowment designated for teachers' salaries at Roger Williams.[83] But wounds remained unhealed. One of the more sympathetic black leaders wrote,

> Negro Baptists of Tennessee have always felt that they had at least a moral equity in the old Roger Williams property, and that equity should have been recognized by a more liberal share of the proceeds from the sales of that property to be used in buildings and in the operation of the new plant across the Cumberland.[84]

Eventually a theological seminary was established, under the joint control of the National Baptist Convention and the Southern Baptist Convention, on a site adjacent to Roger Williams University. The university, which remained distinct, was moved to Memphis in 1928 and was merged with the Howe Junior College to become Roger Williams College.

The Nashville Institute, renamed Roger Williams University in 1883, was one of the monuments to the personal dedication of the many Northern Baptists who taught in the South, and to the financial generosity of many more who supported their work, in an era in which the freed people had limited resources and white Southerners were both unable and unwilling to accomplish much in their behalf. What is also apparent from the beginning, however, is a failure to achieve free and open communication, to say nothing of mutually agreed cooperation, between three constituencies that remained distinct and separate: the Southern blacks who were striving to exercise their new political rights and to develop their own religious and cultural traditions; the Northern whites whose benevolence, though crucial to the development of the major educational institutions for blacks in the South, was all too often paternalistically motivated and bureaucratically organized; and the Southern whites who, after acquiescing for two decades in an order of legal equality, at least in principle, found themselves permitted to reimpose inequality by any means.

Much that we have discovered here simply confirms and sharpens the picture we already have of those decades. But one of the functions of history may also be to give testimony to past achievements, to refuse to allow them to pass into oblivion. And another function of history may be to enable us to understand our present situation better, so that in seeing where we have come from we may deal more adequately with the obstacles to cooperation that have long since been created for us.

*This article first appeared in the Winter 1982 issue of the* Tennessee Historical Quarterly.

1. See the sketch of Daniel W. Phillips, based on a personal interview, in W.W. Clayton, *History of Davidson County, Tennessee, With Illustrations and Biographical Sketches of Its Prominent Men and Pioneers* (Philadelphia, 1880; reprinted in 1971), facing p. 263; and also the article by his son, Charles Phillips, in *Baptist Missionary Pioneers among Negroes: Sketches Written by Mary C. Reynolds and Others* (n.p., n.d.), 18–21. The only first-hand accounts of the Nashville Institute are by Phillips himself: see D. W. Phillips, "The Nashville Baptist Institute," in G. W. Hubbard, *A History of the Colored Schools of Nashville, Tennessee* (Nashville, 1874), 25–27, and his "Reminiscences," *Baptist Home Mission Monthly*, 10 (November, 1888), 281–84. Pioneering work on the origins of the school was done by Charles Edwin Robert, *Negro Civilization in the South* (Nashville, 1880), 141–43, and Alrutheus Ambush Taylor, *The Negro in Tennessee, 1865–1880* (Washington, D.C., 1941), 189–91.

2. Clayton, *Davidson County*, facing p. 263.

3. *Baptist Missionary Pioneers*, 21; Phillips, "The Nashville Baptist Institute," 25. The First Baptist Church was located, from 1848 to 1873, on "Lick Branch" (later Pearl Street) between Cedar and Gay, west of McLemore.

4. Phillips, "Reminiscences," 281.

5. Randle B. Vandavell, "Reminiscences," *Baptist Home Mission Monthly*, 10 (November, 1888), 294.

6. The deed, registered 21 May 1867, is recorded in Book 38, Page 77 at the Register of Deeds, Davidson County. The lot measured 230 x 160 feet, and was located at what is now the corner of 16th and Ireland. The property was sold on 2 December 1876 to the School Commissioners of the Thirteenth Civil District (Book 156, Page 488); the building came to be known as the Knowles Street School, and then it was replaced by the old Pearl School, which was closed in 1971 and razed in 1979.

7. *Nashville Daily Press and Times*, 31 August 1867,

8. It has been shown by Ronald E. Butchart, *Northern Schools, Southern Blacks, and Reconstruction: Freedmen's Education, 1862–1875* (Westport, Conn., 1980) that not only Southern political pressures but Northern social attitudes led the mission societies to abandon the typical Northern policy of the undenominational "common school" and reintroduce the sectarian spirit into the schools attended by blacks.

9. Phillips, "The Nashville Baptist Institute," 27. The tone of disappointment is stronger in "Reminiscences," 282.

10. Phillips, "Reminiscences," 282.

11. Ibid., 283.

12. American Baptist Home Mission Society, *Annual Report*, 1874, p. 37.

13. For the location of the building, see Walter Stokes, Jr., "Hillsboro Pike and Something Personal," *Tennessee Historical Quarterly*, 24 (Spring 1965), 77. Concerning the additional construction, see *Baptist Home Missions in North America* (New York, 1883), 447.

14. *Baptist Missionary Pioneers among Negroes*, 22–28.

15. *Baptist Missionary Pioneers*, 29–34; *National Cyclopaedia of American Biography*, XX (New York, 1929), 367–68.

16. Roger Williams University, *Catalogue*, 1873–74. A microfilm copy of all the catalogues can be consulted in the Dargan-Carver Library, Historical Commission and Sunday School Board of the Southern Baptist Convention, Nashville; the originals are at the American Baptist Historical Society, Rochester, New York.

17. W.N. Hartshorn, ed., *An Era of Progress and Promise, 1863–1910: The Religious, Moral, and Educational Development of the American Negro since His Emancipation* (Boston, 1910), 121.

18. See the obituary notice in *The Rogerana*, 16 (November, 1901), 8.

19. Lewis G. Jordan, *On Two Hemispheres: Bits from the Life Story of Lewis G. Jordan as Told by Himself*. Introduction by Dr. A. Clayton Powell (Nashville, 1935), 19.

20. Ibid., 36–37.

21. Ibid., 30–31.

22. See William J. Simmons, *Men of Mark: Eminent, Progressive and Rising* (Cleveland, 1887), 847–59, with a portrait on p. 577; A.W. Pegue, *Our Baptist Ministers and Schools* (Springfield, Mass., 1892), 496–99; and his "Reminiscences," *Baptist Home Mission Monthly*, 10 (1888), 293–95.

23. See *Men of Mark*, 843–46; Charles Alexander, *Battles and Victories of Allen Allensworth* (Boston, 1914); and Earl F. Stover, *Up From Handymen: The United States Army Chaplaincy, 1865–1920* (Washington, D.C., 1977), 53–57, 109–10, 127–28, 151–52.

24. *Men of Mark*, 147–59.

25. *The Baptist Encyclopaedia*, ed. by William Cathcart (Philadelphia, 1881), 786.

26. Letter of D.W. Phillips to Ebenezer Thresher, 20 March 1877, American Baptist Historical Society, Rochester, N.Y.

27. Phillips, "Reminiscences," 284. For information on Jones see *The Baptist Encyclopaedia*, 622–23; William S. Speer, *Sketches of Prominent Tennesseans* (Nashville, 1888), 412–14; and *National Cyclopaedia of American Biography* (New York, 1901), XI, 368.

28. For Dake see Clayton, *Davidson County*, 435–36, and the portrait facing p. 287; Speer, *Prominent Tennesseans*, 282–86; R.A. Halley, "Dr. J.P. Dake: A Memoir," *American Historical Magazine and Tennessee Historical Society Quarterly*, 8 (1903), 297–346; and his autobiographical sketch in *The Hanemannian Monthly*, June, 1892, pp. 407–13, which, however, has no information concerning his religious and educational interests.

29. Speer, *Prominent Tennesseans*, 283; cf, Clayton, *Davidson County*, 435, and Halley "Dr. J.P. Drake," 307.

30. Phillips, "Reminiscences," 283.

31. Minutes of the Executive Board, American Baptist Home Mission Society, 13 February 1882, Book 9, page 214. Microfilm copies of these minutes are available at the A.B.H.M.S. offices in Valley Forge, Penn. and at the Dargan-Garver Library in Nashville.

32. George R. Hovey, "Christian Schools for Negroes," *Missions*, 19 (1928), 528.

33. Ridgely Torrence, *The Story of John Hope* (New York, 1948), 106–10, 114–16, 123–26

34. Ibid., 108. The information was probably gained from Prof. John W. Johnson, Dr. A.M. Townsend, and Dr. W.A. Reed, p. 383.

35. The later historian John Hope Franklin (1915–2009), while no relation, was named for John Hope. His parents met at Roger Williams during the period when Hope was teaching there, and his father followed him to Atlanta Baptist College, from which he graduated. They later moved to Oklahoma, where the historian was born (Personal communications from Prof. John Hope Franklin, 30 May 1980).

36. *Nashville Daily American*, 1 March 1887. In addition to the press accounts, there is a packet of materials kept by H. L. Morehouse, labeled, in his handwriting, "Documents relating to

the troubles with students and trustees in 1886." These materials are in the Roger Williams University File, Records of the A.B.H.M.S., American Baptist Historical Society, Rochester, N.Y.

37. *Nashville Star*, ? December 1886, R.W.U. File.

38. *Daily American*, 2 March 1887.

39. Ibid.

40. R.W.U. File, American Baptist Historical Society.

41. Ibid.

42. Minutes of the Executive Board, 10 January 1887, Book 10, pages 600–601; cf. *Nashville Union*, 5 March 1887.

43. The letter is printed in the *Daily American*, 1 March 1887 and the *Nashville Union*, 5 March 1887.

44. The full text of these resolutions of the education committee, approved by the board on 28 February, is contained in the minutes of that meeting, Book 10, pages 628–30.

45. *Daily American*, 1 March 1887.

46. *Daily American* and *Nashville Union*, 3 March 1887.

47. *Nashville Union*, 4 March 1887.

48. Undated document in R.W.U. File, American Baptist Historical Society.

49. Minutes of the Executive Board, 9 May 1887, Book 11, pages 16–17.

50. Resolution of the Roger Williams University Trustees, 24 May 1887, R.W.U. File, American Baptist Historical Society; recorded in the Minutes of the Executive Board, 13 June 1887, Book 11, pages 40–42.

51. Reply of Executive Board to the Roger Williams University Trustees, Minutes of the Executive Board, 13 June 1887, Book 11, pages 42–44.

52. Letter from Dr. J.P. Dake to H.L. Morehouse, 4 July 1887, R.W. U. File, American Baptist Historical Society.

53. Resolution adopted by the Roger Williams University Trustees, 25 October 1887, R.W. U. File, American Baptist Historical Society.

54. Letter from J.P. Dake to Alfred Owen, 7 December 1887, R.W.U. File, American Baptist Historical Society.

55. Letter from D.W. Phillips to H.L. Morehouse, 26 November 1887, R.W.U. File, American Baptist Historical Society.

56. Letter from J.P. Dake to H.L. Morehouse, 25 September 1888, R.W.U. File, American Baptist Historical Society.

57. James Melvin Washington, "The Origins and Emergence of Black Baptist Separatism, 1863–1897" (PhD Dissertation, Yale University, 1979), 167–68, 208.

58. American National Baptist Convention, *Journal*, 1889, p. 17.

59. Letter from A. G. Haygood to H.L. Morehouse, 14 January 1891, R.W.U. File, American Baptist Historical Society.

60. Petition from S.W. Duncan, Wm. Crawford, and S.B. Walker to the Executive Board, 31 March 1891, R.W.U. File, American Baptist Historical Society.

61. Letter from Alex. B. Bradford to the Executive Board, 8 April 1891, R.W.U. File, American Baptist Historical Society.

62. Minutes of the Executive Board, 8 June 1891 (Book 12, page 189).

63. *Nashville American*, 25 January 1905; *Nashville Banner*, 25 January 1905; Baptist Home Mission Monthly, 27 (March, 1905), 115–16.

64. *Nashville American*, 26 January 1905.

65. Ibid., The minutes of the meeting of the executive board for 12 December 1904 disclose that a proposition for the purchase of the property had been received, and that it was referred at that time to a committee for study, Book 16, pages 390–91.

66. Ibid., 28 January 1905.

67. Minutes of the Executive Board, 13 February 1905, Book 16, pages 429–31.

68. *American*, 19 March 1905.

69. *American*, 23 and 24 May 1905.

70. A.B.H.M.S., *Annual Report*, 1906, p. 143.

71. Minutes of the Executive Board, 26 June 1905 (Book 16, pages 521–22). I have not been able to find any transaction recorded in the Davidson County Register of Deeds. What comes closest to the description is a set of contiguous parcels of land on the east side of 12th Avenue South, between what are now Argyle and Acklen, which were purchased by A.B. Hill on 16 and 30 Ocotber 1905 (Book 326, Page 283, and Book 328, Page 263, Davidson County Register of Deeds). It is possible that a private contract was made between him and the board. On 2 May 1908—after an alternative site was chosen—this property was subdivided and recorded as A.B. Hill's Subdivision of the Plant Lands (Plat Book 332, Page 65). If this should be the site, then Rocky Hill would be the rise where Wedgewood Towers now stands, around which 12th Avenue made a slight turn toward the west.

72. The surveyor's plan for University Place is recorded in the Davidson County Register of Deeds, Plat Books 332, Page 12, and 421, Page 47.

73. As early as the spring of 1905 Morehouse had commented on the hospitality of the Hills, at whose home he met most of the white Baptist ministers of the city. Cf. *Baptist Home Mission Monthly*, 27 (April, 1905), 149. Hill and Morehouse together acted as intermediaries in an approach made by Vanderbilt to John D. Rockefeller for a contribution to "Southern education." Cf. Letters from A.B. Hill to Chancellor J.H. Kirkland, 2 and 3 May 1905 (Kirkland Papers, Incoming Correspondence, Folder 67, Special Collections, Vanderbilt University Library).

74. Minutes of the Executive Board, 8 July 1907, Book 17, pages 388–89 and 11 November 1907, Book 17, pages 475–77.

75. All the relevant documents are contained in "George Peabody College for Teachers: Its Evolution and Present Status," *Peabody College Bulletin*, New Series, Volume 1, No. 1 (1912).

See also Alfred Leland Crabb, "The Historical Background of Peabody College," *Bulletin of George Peabody College for Teachers*, New Series, Vol. 30, No. 10 (1941).

76. Vanderbilt University, Minutes of the Board of Trust and of the Executive Committee, meeting of the Board of Trust, 13 June 1910.

77. Ibid., meeting of the Board of Trust, 25 October 1910.

78. Ibid., meeting of the Executive Committee, 29 July 1909; meeting of the Board of Trust, 25 October 1910. See also the original plan for the Peabody campus, which includes this land as well as that later purchased.    79. Letter from A.B. Hill to James C. Bradford, Chairman, 5 March 1910, Subject file "Property," Peabody Education Fund Papers, Library of George Peabody College for Teachers, Nashville.

80. The deed is recorded in Book 401, Page 267, at the Register of Deeds, Davidson County.

81. Letter from H.L. Morehouse to Judge Edward T. Sanford, Chairman of the Board of Trustees, Subject File "Property," Peabody Education Fund Papers, Library of George Peabody College for Teachers.

82. The purchase, made on 19 May 1925, is recorded in Book 674, Page 93, at the Register of Deeds, Davidson County.

83. A.B.H.M.S., *Annual Report*, 1911, p. 38.

84. T.O. Fuller, *History of the Negro Baptists of Tennessee* (Memphis, 1936), 127.

# CONTRIBUTORS

CRYSTAL A. DEGREGORY is a native of Freeport, Bahamas, and a graduate of Fisk University and Vanderbilt University, where she received her PhD in history. Her dissertation, "Raising a Nonviolent Army: Four Nashville Black Colleges and the Century-Long Struggle for Civil Rights, 1830s–1930s," focused on the function of American Baptist College, Fisk University, Meharry Medical College, and Tennessee State University and their students in the struggle for equality, justice, and civil rights in Nashville. Her work has been published in *Tennessee Historical Quarterly*, *The AME Review*, *Freedom Facts and Firsts: 400 Years of the African American Civil Rights Experience*, *National African American Biography*, *Notable Black American Men II*, and the *Encyclopedia of African American Business*. DeGregory is an assistant professor at Tennessee State University.

WALTER J. FRASER, JR., is professor emeritus in the department of history at Georgia Southern University. He received his PhD in history from the University of Tennessee and also taught at the Citadel in Charleston, South Carolina. In addition to his articles in the *Tennessee Historical Quarterly*, Fraser has written several books on Georgia and South Carolina.

JUDY BUSSELL LEFORGE is associate professor of history at Union University in Jackson, Tennessee. She received her PhD in history from the University of Memphis. Her articles have appeared in several journals, including the *Tennessee Historical Quarterly* and *Alabama Review*.

BOBBY L. LOVETT is a retired professor of history and former dean of the College of Arts and Sciences at Tennessee State University. A native of Memphis, he earned the PhD at the University of Arkansas. His dissertation was "The Negro in Tennessee, 1861–1866: A Socio-Military History of the Civil War Era." Author of many journal articles and books, among is recent titles are *The Civil Rights Movement in Tennessee: a Narrative History* (2005) and *America's Historically Black Colleges: A Narrative History, 1837–2009* (2011). Lovett has also served the board of directors for the Tennessee Historical Society and on the editorial board of the *Tennessee Historical Quarterly*.

JAMES S. MCRAE received his BA in history from the University of North Carolina-Pembroke and continued his studies in the PhD program at Auburn University. His primary research interest is the American Civil War, with a special interest in battlefield racial atrocities, and military history.

C. STUART MCGEHEE (1954–2010) was a graduate of the University of Tennessee at Chattanooga and received an MA and PhD from the University of Virginia. Chair of the history department at West Virginia State University, McGehee wrote five books and more than fifty articles, including essays for such publications as the *Tennessee Historical Quarterly*, *West Virginia History*, *Civil War History*, the *Journal of Southern History*, *Goldenseal*, and other regional and national publications.

KENNETH BANCROFT MOORE received his MA in history from Auburn University, where his thesis was "'Upon a New Construction': Innovation and Conservatism in the British Military in the Era of the American Revolution." His research interests include military and social history. He worked at the Alabama Department of Archives and History in Montgomery while writing this article.

BRIAN D. PAGE received an MA in history from the University of Memphis, where his thesis was "Ceasing a Revolution: African American Agency, Voting Coalitions, and the Repeal of the City Charter in Memphis, 1865–1879." He has served as an instructor at Rhodes College and pursued a doctorate at Ohio State University.

JOE M. RICHARDSON is emeritus professor of history, Florida State University, where he also received his PhD in history. He is the author of *A History of Fisk University*, *Christian Reconstruction: The American Missionary Association and Southern Blacks, 1861–1890*, *African American in the Reconstruction of Florida, 1865–1877*, and, with Maxine D. Jones, *Talladega College: The First Century*.

EUGENE TESELLE is emeritus professor in the graduate department of religion at Vanderbilt University. He was educated at the University of Colorado, Princeton Theological Seminary, and Yale University. He has been active in social justice issues in Nashville and is an editor of *Southern Communities*. A minister in the Presbyterian Church, he has been president of the Witherspoon Society, the "progressive caucus." He is also the author of *Augustine's Strategy as an Apologist*, *Christ in Context*, and *Thomas Aquinas: Faith and Reason*.

# INDEX

Agnew, Samuel A., 12, 14.
Alexander, Berber, 39, 118 n.60.
Alexander, H., 100.
Allensworth, Allen, 175.
Alvord, John, 165.
Anderson, Alfred E., 96, 106, 107, 118 n.60.
Anderson, James D., 122.
Anderson, S.W., 180, 181.
Ayer, Lyman W., 159.
Baker, B.F., 35.
Balch, T.E., 178-181.
Barber, George, 128.
Barber, Ode, 131.
Barnum, Joseph H., 148.
Bates, Edward, 12.
Bearss, Edwin C., 17.
Betts, Thomas, 29.
Beaumont, S.B., 69, 74.
Bennett, H.S., 123.
Bishop, Nathan, 174.
Bishop, R.M., 40.
Black, George, 39.
Booth, L.E., 20 n.2.
Bouton, Edward, 12, 13, 16, 17.
Bradford, Alexander, 183.
Bradford, William F., 8, 20 n.2.
Bradshaw, Thomas, 31.
Branham, James, 180.
Brinkley, William, 73-74.
Broughton, Virginia Walker, 133, 136.

Brown, David, 70, 80-81.
Brown, Matt, 105.
Brown, Sterling, 152.
Brownlow, William G., 37, 68, 69, 98, 102, 103, 104, 107, 109-110, 115 n.20, 119 n.74, 144, 165.
Campbell, Wallace, 17-18.
Carroll, William, 130.
Carter, Hannibal C., 67-73, 80.
Catron, John, 125.
Chalmers, James R., 11, 12.
Church, Robert, 27.
Cobb, George, 39.
Conrad, Rufus, 130.
Cooke, David G., vii, 1-6.
Cooke, Elizabeth Lockey, 2.
Cravath, Erasmus Milo, 142, 143, 147, 154, 156 n.22, 166.
Creighton, John C., 39.
Crosby, Mrs. Charles, 147.
Dake, Jabez Philander, 176, 178, 180, 182.
Davis, J.C., 112.
Davis, Jefferson, 16.
deGregory, Crystal A., 192.
Douglass, Frederick, 48.
Doyle, Don, 121.
Dresser, Amos, 126, 130.
Drew, Charles, 129.
DuBois, W.E.B., 144.
Dunn, Henry, 34, 36.

Dupee, George Washington, 175.
Durnin, Thomas J., 35, 36.
Dyer, Carrie V., 174.
Easter, E.A., 147.
Eaton, Alince E. Shirley, 75.
Eaton, John Jr., 24, 32, 39, 67, 69, 71-75, 80, 149, 163.
Eaton, Lucien, 67, 72, 80.
Ensign, F.E., 160.
Fish, L.B., 175.
Fisk, Clinton B., 28, 38, 102, 108, 144, 148.
Fitch, George W., 1, 2.
Forrest, Nathan Bedford, 1, 8-19, 23 n.51, 57.
Franklin, John Hope, 188 n.35.
Fraser, Walter J. Jr., 192.
Frierson, B.P., 100.
Fuller, Buck, 27.
Fulsom, Henry, 35.
Gaylor, S.A., 164.
Gentle, M.J.R., 106.
Gerry, Henry, 27.
Glatthaar, Joseph T., 2, 4.
Gooch, Daniel W., 10, 11.
Goodstein, Anita Shafer, 131, 134.
Gordon, William H., 174.
Grant, Ulysses S., 11, 37, 110.
Greeley, Horace, 10.
Gregory, John M., 176, 181, 182.
Guernsey, Peter B., 177.
Hadley, Benjamin J., 95, 96, 99.
Harding, Henry, 96, 99, 174.
Harding, William G., 135.
Hardison, Sergeant H., 100.
Harris, John, 56, 68, 80.
Harris, Ransom, 95, 97, 98, 100, 103.

Harris, Richard, 100, 116 n.40.
Harst, Lewis, 35.
Hayes, Landon C., 76-77.
Haygood, A.G., 182.
Helm, Joe, 68, 80.
Henderson, Morris, 96, 97.
Henley, Hezkiah, 57.
Heyden, George S., 76.
Hickman, Wade, 9, 96, 99.
Hill, Adolphus B., 184, 185.
Hiscox, E.C., 180, 181, 182.
Holmes, Jack, 40.
Hood, John Bell, 1, 19.
Hope, John, 177.
Hopkins, Moses, 73, 80.
Howard, Oliver Otis, 38, 161.
Hubbard, John, 19.
Hunt, Turner, 27.
Hurd, Henry Ewell, 14.
Hynes, Felix, 99.
Ingraham, J.H., 131.
Jackson, Andrew, 125.
James, Owen, 177.
Johnson, Andrew, 24, 39, 69, 95, 96, 97-99, 115 n.17..
Johnson, M.R., 112.
Jones, J.J., 100.
Jones, William Palmer T., 175, 176, 178, 182.
Jordan, Lewis Garnett, 175.
Keeble, Samuel W., 118 n.60.
Kennedy, William, 68-70, 72-73, 80.
Kilpatrick, Judson, 19.
King, George, 39, 118 n.60.
Kirkland, James H., 184.
Lamon, Lester C., 112.
Langston, John Mercer, 96, 135, 149.

Lawrence, John, 148.
Lee, Robert E., 12.
Lee, Stephen D., 15.
Leforge, Judy Bussell, 192.
Letcher, C.P., 118 n.60.
Levere, G.W., 106.
Lewis, Barbour, 67, 69-72, 74-76, 78-80.
Lewis, Buck, 99.
Lincoln, Abraham, 10, 12.
Livingston, E.D., 118 n.60.
Lockwood, Belva V., 135-136.
Lovett, Bobby L., viii, 18, 103, 123, 128, 129, 192.
Lowery, Peter, 95, 97, 98, 100, 105, 135.
Lowery, Samuel, 95, 100, 107, 119 n.70, 135.
Lynch, James D., 94, 101, 113.
Mallory, W.W., 148.
Manley, Joseph, 128.
Maxwell, Henry J., 26, 100-101.
Maxwell, E., 100.
Mayfield, W.D., 175.
McClellan, George C., 96.
McGehee, C. Stuart, ix, 193.
McKee, Joseph G., 123, 132, 133.
McKinney, C. A., 100.
McRae, James S., 193.
Meriwether, Elizabeth Avery, 25-26, 47.
Merriweather, Edward, 39 118 n.60.
Merry, Nelson G., 100, 132, 175, 176, 183.
Mills, Quincy T., 124.
Mitchell, Edward D, 177.
Mitchell, James, 39.
Moore, Ella Shepherd, 126-127, 128, 134, 136.
Moore, Kenneth Bancroft, 193.

Morang, William R., 177, 180.
Morehouse, Henry L., 180, 181, 182, 183.
Morgan, Thomas J., 18.
Motley, A., 100.
Moultrie, Prince, 31.
Murphy, William, 56.
Napier, James C., 112, 130, 135, 136.
Napier, Nettie Langston, 135
Nelson, Julius, 27.
Nelson, William A., 175.
Nunn, David A., 74.
Ogden, John, 142, 143, 146-148, 153, 164.
Owen, Alfred, 177, 182.
Page, Brian D., 193.
Palmer, J.B., 180.
Parks, John, 31, 35, 36-37, 39, 40.
Patterson, Mariah, 131.
Pendleton, George H., 96.
Phillips, A.D., 175.
Phillips, Charles Currier, 174.
Phillips, Daniel W., x, 172-174, 178, 180, 182, 183.
Pile, William A., 19.
Player, Sarah Porter, 127, 129, 134, 138 n.25.
Polk, Leonidas, 16.
Prosser, Gabriel, 129.
Rankin, H.R., 100.
Rankin, Henry A., 36, 41, 100.
Rankin, Horatio N., 49, 97.
Rapier, James T., 101-10, 136.2.
Rapier, John H. Jr., 136.
Rapier, John P. (Thomas), 101, 136.
Rapier, John T., 100.
Reeve, Arthur T., 14.

Richardson, Isaac, 39.
Richardson, Joe M., ix, 193.
Robinson, Armestead, 49.
Robinson, George T., 178.
Ruhm, John, 148.
Runkles, Benjamin F., 37.
Rush, Z.C., 173.
Ryan, James, 40.
Saddler, E.T., 180, 181.
Schurz, Carl, 48.
Scott, William B., 29, 100.
Scovel, H.G., 174.
Scraggs, Davis, 96.
Sears, Barnas, 149.
Senter, Clinton DeWitt, 110-111, 165.
Seward, William H., 11-12.
Shaw, A.T., 56.
Shaw, Edward, viii, 56, 68-80, 105, 107.
Shelton, J.M., 131.
Sherman, William T., 9, 18.
Simmons, J.B., 174.
Smith, Abram, 96, 97, 98, 100, 174.
Smith, Adolphus, 39, 118 n.60.
Smith, Andrew Jackson, 16-17, 23 n.51.
Smith, E.P., 160.
Smith, Edward P., 142, 143.
Smith, Giles, 72-73, 80.
Smith, John E., 28, 29, 30-31.
Smith, William Jay, 56, 69-72, 74-76, 80.
Smith, William Sooy, 17.
Sowerby, A.T., 177.
Spence, Adam K., 153.
Stanton, Edwin M., 11.
Stewart, Williams, 177.
Stifler, William H., 177, 178-181.
Stoneman, George, 31, 35, 36, 38, 40.

Stothard, Jerry, 95, 100.
Streiby, E.M., 159.
Streight, Abel D., 17.
Strickland, C.H., 178, 182.
Sturgis, Samuel D., 12, 13, 15, 17.
Sumner, Alphonso M., 123-124, 125-128, 130, 131, 136.
Sumner, Charles, 116 n.41.
Sumner, J.H., 112.
Sumner, W. Alex, 95.
Sumner, William, 95, 99, 100.
Tade, Amanda Loise, 160, 163.
Tade, Ewing Ogden, ix, 158-167.
Tade, James A., 160.
Tefft, Lyman Beecher, 174, 176.
Tefft, Mary Abby, 174.
TeSelle, Eugene, 193.
Thomas, A.N., 68.
Thomas, Antionette Rutgers, 136.
Thomas, George H., 1, 20, 28, 102.
Thomas, J.B., 181, 182.
Thomas, James P., 125, 136.
Thomas, Sally, 101, 125.
Tillson, Davis, 28, 29, 31.
Toles, S.H., 68-69, 80.
Tomeny, James M., 69.
Trimble, F.L., 180.
Turner, Nat, 124, 129.
Usher, John Palmer, 12.
Van Pelt, Samuel, 34.
Vandavell, Randle B., 175, 176, 178, 182.
Vaughan, W.W., 74-75.
Vesey, Denmark, 129.
Wade, Benjamin F., 10, 11.
Wadkins (Watkins), Daniel, 99, 103, 105, 106, 118 n.60, 125-129, 131-135.

Walker, Nelson, 95, 100, 102, 103, 118 n.60, 135.
Walker, Selina, 131.
Walker, W.P., 11.
Ware, Martha, 51, 62 n.37.
Washburn, Cadwallader C., 15, 16, 22 n.25.
Washington, Booker T., 145, 177.
Welles, Gideon, 11, 12.
Wilson, Lizzie, 145.
Witherspoon, William, 12, 14.
Yandle, John, 127.
Young, J.B., 112.